DATE DUE

DEMCO 38-296

Saudi Arabia

CSIS Middle East Dynamic Net Assessment

Saudi Arabia

Guarding the Desert Kingdom

Anthony H. Cordesman

WestviewPress

A Division of HarperCollins*Publishers*

Copyright © 1997 by Anthony H. Cordesman

Published in 1997 in the United States of America by Westview Press, 5500 Central Avenue, Boulder, Colorado 80301-2877, and in the United Kingdom by Westview Press, 12 Hid's Copse Road, Cumnor Hill, Oxford OX2 9JJ

This book was typeset by Letra Libre, 1705 Fourteenth Street, Suite 391, Boulder, Colorado 80302.

Library of Congress Cataloging-in-Publication Data
Cordesman, Anthony H.
  Saudi Arabia : guarding the desert kingdom / Anthony H. Cordesman
      p.   cm.
  Includes bibliographical references (p.   ).
  ISBN 0-8133-3241-9. — ISBN 0-8133-3242-7 (pbk.)
    1. Saudi Arabia—Armed Forces.   2. Saudi Arabia—Strategic
aspects. I. Title.
UA853.S33C67   1997
355'.0330538—dc20   96-46048
                                                                          CIP

The paper used in this publication meets the requirements of the American National Standard for Permanence of Paper for Printed Library Materials Z39.48-1984.

10   9   8   7   6   5   4   3   2   1

Contents

Tables and Illustrations

Maps

Preface

This volume is part of an ongoing dynamic net assessment of the Gulf. The project was conceived by David Abshire and Richard Fairbanks of the Center for Strategic and International Studies and focuses on the foreign policy, military forces, politics, economics, energy sector, and internal security of each Gulf state, and US strategy and power projection capabilities in the Gulf. Separate volumes are available on Kuwait, Iran, Iraq, Saudi Arabia, and US forces. Bahrain, Oman, Qatar, and the UAE are combined into a single volume.

Each of these volumes is interlinked to provide comparable data on the current situation and trends in each country, and to portray the overall trends in key areas like economy and the military balance. The volume on Iran provides a detailed graphic overview of the military trends in the region, but each volume shows how the key economy and military developments in each country relate to the developments in other Gulf countries.

At the same time, this series deliberately emphasizes nation-by-nation analysis. Iran and Iraq clearly deserve separate treatment. The Southern Gulf states are largely independent actors and are driven by separate strategic, political, economic, and military interests. In spite of the creation of the Arab Gulf Cooperation Council (GCC), there is little practical progress in strategic, economic, or military cooperation, and there are serious rivalries and differences of strategic interest between Bahrain, Kuwait, Oman, Qatar, Saudi Arabia, and the UAE. The Southern Gulf cannot be understood in terms of the rhetoric of the Arab Gulf Cooperation Council or by assuming that developments in Bahrain, Kuwait, Oman, Qatar, Saudi Arabia, and the UAE are similar and these states have an identity of interest.

These Gulf studies are also part of a broader dynamic net assessment of the Middle East, and a separate study is available of the trends in the Arab-Israeli military balance and the peace process. See Anthony H. Cordesman, *Perilous Prospects*, Boulder, Westview, 1996.

Anthony H. Cordesman

Acknowledgments

This volume is part of a six volume series reporting on a dynamic net assessment of the Gulf. The project was conceived by David Abshire and Richard Fairbanks of the Center for Strategic and International Studies, and is part of a broader dynamic net assessment of the entire Middle East.

The author would like to thank Kimberly Goddes and Kiyalan Batmanglidj for their research and editing help in writing this series, and Thomas Seidenstein and David Hayward for helping to edit each volume.

Many US and international analysts and agencies played a role in commenting on drafts of the manuscript. So did experts in each Southern Gulf country. The author cannot acknowledge these contributions by name or agency but he is deeply grateful. The author would also like to thank his colleagues at the CSIS who reviewed various manuscripts and commented on the analysis. These colleagues include Richard Fairbanks and Arnaud de Borchgrave, and his Co-Director of the Middle East Program, Judith Kipper.

A.H.C.

1

Introduction

During the last century, Saudi Arabia has become the largest and most powerful state in the Southern Gulf. Saudi Arabia contains 259 billion barrels of proven oil reserves, or one-quarter of the world's total. The country is also the world's largest oil producer with output of over 8 million barrels of oil per day, and is the world's largest "swing" producer. Saudi Arabia plays a critical role in ensuring moderate and stable oil prices. It is the only Southern Gulf power strong enough to serve as a strategic counterbalance to Iran and Iraq, and is a critical partner in US collective security efforts in the region.[1]

Like its neighbors, however, Saudi Arabia faces many challenges. It cannot deter or defend itself from Iran and Iraq without US military aid, and it must develop a stable basis for a lasting strategic partnership with the US and other Western states. It has not been able to catalyze effective collective security efforts within the Gulf Cooperation Council (GCC) and it still faces problems in eliminating its historical rivalries with other Southern Gulf states. It must modernize its society without losing its Islamic and Arab character, and it must restructure its economy to deal with declining per capita oil wealth and the need to rely on native, rather than foreign labor.

Saudi Arabia should be able to meet these challenges, but the task will be anything but easy. Saudi Arabia faces very real external threats from Iran and Iraq. Although Saudi Arabia has made a serious effort to improve its relations with Kuwait, Oman, and Yemen, change comes slowly in the Gulf. Restructuring Saudi society and the Saudi economy presents the most serious challenge of all, and change must come at a time when Islamic extremism is a serious concern and Saudi Arabia's oil income is not sufficient to meet its social and economic needs. Saudi Arabia's strategic partnership with the West involves inevitable differences in national interest and culture, and its partnership with the US presents at least short term problems in burden-sharing, counter-terrorism, and prepositioning, and longer term problems in defining a stable and equitable division of effort. All of these challenges will require constant attention during the coming decade.

Historical Origins

Saudi Arabia traces its origins to both the ancient culture of Dilmun, a major trading link between Mesopotamia and the Indus River valley, and Arabia Felix, a confederation of states in southern Arabia that formed a network of trade routes between India and Africa. Modern Saudi Arabia, however, has its roots in the rise of Islam. The caravan routes between Arabia Felix and Egypt created trading cities in the Hejaz region, of which the most prominent were Mecca and Medina.

In 570 AD, the Prophet Mohammed was born in Mecca. By the time of the Prophet's death in 632, most of the Arabian Peninsula had become united under Arab rule. This combination of Arabian culture and Islam has shaped the character of the region ever since.

Although the Arabian Peninsula came under the nominal suzerainty of the Ottoman sultans in Istanbul in the 16th century, it remained largely under the rule of various tribes and families, and religion was more important than politics. The importance of religion was evident in the 18th century when a major religious reformer—Mohammed ibn Abd al-Wahhab—began to preach a return to the strict, puritanical practices of Islam at the time of Mohammed. Wahhab formed an alliance with the Saud clan, which then dominated much of the Najd. Strengthened by the military and political leadership of the Sauds, the Wahhabi movement quickly grew in strength and expanded far beyond its base in Najd to Mecca and Medina and parts of Iraq and Syria.

In response to the expansion of the Wahhabi movement, the Ottoman Empire sent an army—under Mohammed Ali Pasha of Egypt—to Arabia. While Ali Pasha was able to defeat the Arab forces in two campaigns (1811–18 and 1838), he did not defeat Arab nationalism. The Saud family continued to rule the interior until 1890, when the Rashids, a rival Turkish-backed family, seized control of Riyadh.

In 1902, Abd Al-Aziz Al-Saud (also known as Ibn Saud) attacked Riyadh and regained power over the region. He expelled the Rashids, revived the Arab and Wahhabi cause, and became the ruler of the Najd. At the start of World War I, he controlled central Arabia and the Al Hasa coast, although the Hejaz and western Arabia still acknowledged Ottoman rule.

In 1916, a broader Arab revolt began against the Turks. Hussein ibn Ali, the Hashemite Asheriff of Mecca, proclaimed independence, declared war on the Ottoman Empire, and claimed the title of King of the Hejaz. In the battles that followed, Hussein liberated much of southern Arabia, while Abd Al-Aziz subdued Al-Hasa, the rest of Najd, and the borders of the Hejaz.

The resulting division of much of Arabia between Saud and Hashemite rule led to a growing rivalry between Abd Al-Aziz and Hussein after

World War I. This rivalry turned into a war when Hussein proclaimed himself the caliph of Islam in 1924. Abd Al-Aziz invaded the Hejaz and conquered Mecca and Jeddah in 1926. Abd Al-Aziz then steadily expanded his rule to include much of western and south eastern Arabia. In 1932, Abd Al-Aziz Al-Saud created the modern Kingdom of Saudi Arabia.

Strategic Background

Today, Saudi Arabia contains nearly 60% of the population of the Southern Gulf states. It is the richest single prize in the Middle East, and possesses the largest oil reserves of any country in the world. This oil wealth makes Saudi Arabia a natural target of radical political movements and ambitious states throughout the Middle East, as well as the natural target of other oil exporting states that seek to restrict the volume of world oil exports and raise world oil prices.

Unlike Middle Eastern states with large populations and declining oil reserves, Saudi Arabia's economic interests often coincide with those of the West. It benefits most from moderate, stable long-term prices and relatively high production levels. In contrast, states like Iran and Iraq benefit from limited world oil production, high prices, and quotas that favor them at the expense of Saudi Arabia.

These threats from the Northern Gulf are real, not theoretical. During the Iran-Iraq War, Iranian fighters attempted to invade Saudi air space and Iran's naval and Revolutionary Guards forces attacked tanker and maritime traffic in the Gulf. Iraqi forces massed on the Saudi border immediately after Iraq's conquest of Kuwait, and Saudi Arabia was a key member of the UN Coalition that defeated Iraq in the Gulf War.

Territory, Strategic Depth, and Vulnerabilities

Saudi Arabia must defend a total of 2,510 kilometers of coastline on the Gulf and Red Sea. The Saudi Gulf coast is within five minutes flying time of Iran by jet fighter, and a causeway connects Saudi Arabia with Bahrain—a small island state that Iran has claimed in the past. Saudi Arabia's ports on the Red Sea make Saudi Arabia a major Red Sea power and link its politics and security position with that of Egypt, the Sudan, Ethiopia, and Djibouti. Saudi Arabia must guard against threats to maritime traffic through the Red Sea, and against any spillover of the continuing political upheavals and conflicts in the Horn.[2]

Saudi Arabia's large territory does provide strategic depth, but its critical oil fields and many of its key ports, facilities, and cities are clustered along the upper Gulf coast—opposite Iran and Iraq. Saudi Arabia's size also prevents strategic concentration. Saudi Arabia must cope with the fact that its population is dispersed into cities that are separated by long distances and vulnerable to attacks on their infrastructure. Saudi Arabia offers many high value targets in terms of oil and gas facilities, and central power grids. It is heavily dependent on secure maritime and air traffic for imports and exports.

Saudi Arabia's forces must defend the territory of a nation with a total area of 2,150,000 square kilometers, roughly one-fourth the size of the US. Saudi forces must either help defend Kuwait or defend a 222 kilometer border with Kuwait, and defend a 448 kilometer boundary with Iraq. Saudi Arabia also has a 742 kilometer border with Jordan, a 676 kilometer border with Oman, a 586 kilometer border with the UAE, a 40 kilometer border with Qatar, and a 1,458 kilometer border with Yemen.[3]

Strategic Concerns

Saudi Arabia's mix of oil wealth, geography, boundaries, coastlines, and vulnerabilities explains both its strategic importance, and many of its problems in developing and expanding its military forces. Unlike the other Southern Gulf states, Saudi Arabia cannot shape its strategy only around potential threats in the Northern Gulf. Saudi Arabia faces a radical Sudan across the Red Sea, and the prospect of continuing instability in the other Red Sea states. While Saudi Arabia has consistently tried to distance itself from military involvement between Israel and the Arab states, it can never be certain that it will not be threatened by the escalation of an Arab-Israeli conflict or pressure from one of the Arab confrontation states.

Saudi Arabia's strategic position forces it to disperse its limited military resources to forward bases throughout the country, leaving it with limited forces on any given front. For the last quarter century, Saudi Arabia has made a "brute force" effort to build up its military forces. It has transformed its army from a small and lightly mechanized force—concentrated near urban areas—to heavy armored forces, deployed in new military cities near its strategic borders. Saudi Arabia has built up the nucleus of a two fleet navy out of what was a small coast guard, and has transformed a small showpiece air force into one of the most effective air forces in the developing world.

This modernization effort has cost Saudi Arabia at least $290 billion in military expenditures in constant 1993 dollars over the last decade, of which nearly $71 billion was spent on arms transfers.[4] The modernization of Saudi forces, however, is still very much in process. The Saudi army is in the process of developing the capability to fight independent maneuver and armored warfare against potential foes like Iraq, and the Saudi

MAP ONE   Saudi Arabia

Navy is far from being ready to directly challenge the Iranian Navy or deal with a serious submarine and mine warfare threat.

Air power is Saudi Arabia's only means of compensating for the weakness and dispersal of its land and naval forces. Saudi Arabia can only use air power decisively if (a) its limited first line fighter strength has the range and refueling capability to mass quickly, (b) its air units can maintain a decisive technical and performance edge over threat forces, (c) it can provide sufficient air defense capability to provide air cover for Saudi ground forces, naval forces, and key targets, (d) it can provide sufficient dual capability in the attack mission to offset its limited ground strength and give it time to reinforce its army units, and (e) its air units are cumulatively strong enough to provide at least limited coverage of the Northern Gulf or Red Sea front while facing an active threat on the other front.

Even with air power, Saudi Arabia must cooperate closely with the West and the United States. Saudi Arabia is vital to the West in terms of its oil resources, its geographic position, and its ability to provide facilities and forces that allow the West to deploy and operate in strength without a massive and time consuming build-up. At the same time, the West is vital to Saudi Arabia. As a conservative monarchy that lacks the population and skills to create military forces large enough to defend its territory or regional position, Saudi Arabia is dependent on Western power projection capabilities to check Iran and Iraq, and contain any spillover of an Arab-Israeli conflict. This dependence, however, confronts Saudi Arabia with the dilemma of maintaining close ties to the US—a secular democracy and Israel's greatest ally—as the ultimate guarantor of its security.

2

External Security Issues

Saudi Arabia demonstrated during the Gulf War both that it could play a major role in its own defense, and that it could be an important strategic partner of the West. Saudi Arabia played a major role in organizing the Arab side of the UN Coalition and commanded both of its Arab task forces—Joint Forces Command (East) and Joint Forces Command (North).[5] These forces were organized under the command of Lt. General Prince Khalid Bin Sultan al-Saud.[6] By the time the Air/Land phase of the war began, the Saudi ground forces in the theater totaled nearly 50,000 men, with about 270 main battle tanks, 930 other armored fighting vehicles, 115 artillery weapons, and over 400 anti-tank weapons.[7] The Saudi Air Force flew a total of 6,852 sorties between January 17, 1991 and February 28—or about 6% of all sorties flown—ranking it second after the US in total air activity.[8]

Saudi Arabia, however, could not have defended itself against Iraq without mass Western aid. It also continues to face many strategic, military, and economic challenges. Its primary threats are Iran and Iraq, but Saudi Arabia also faces a potential threat from Yemen. Its long coast along the Red Sea also means that it cannot ignore the constant turmoil in the Horn of Africa. Its western border with Jordan, and its close proximity to Egypt, Israel, and Syria means that it must pay close attention to the resolution of the Arab-Israeli conflict. At the same time, Saudi Arabia must deal with its southern Gulf neighbors and has often had tense relations with Oman and Qatar.

Iran and Iraq: The Primary Threats

Iran has been actively hostile to Saudi Arabia ever since the Iranian Revolution in 1979. It is a natural rival in terms of power and influence in the Gulf, and in many aspects of oil policy. Iran has often violently attacked both the character and religious legitimacy of the Saudi regime. It has continued to sponsor riots and unrest during the Haj, and has provided at least limited support to Shi'ite extremists in Saudi Arabia's Eastern Province.

Saudi Arabia has not cut off communication with Iran, but senior Saudi officials treat Iran as a hostile power committed to trying to dominate the Gulf and exporting its own brand of revolutionary extremism. They fear Iranian efforts to acquire weapons of mass destruction and modern weapons, as well as Iranian attempts to build-up the capability to threaten tanker and other shipping through the Gulf. They feel Iran is provoking unrest within the Saudi Shi'ite community, deliberately causing unrest among Shi'ite and other pilgrims during the Haj, and supporting Saudi Sunni Islamic extremists who attack the legitimacy the Saudi royal family and its interpretation of Islamic law and religious practices.

Senior Saudi officials see little prospect that this situation will change. Even if a more pragmatic regime should emerge in Iran, they feel that Saudi Arabia is still likely to compete with Iran for political influence in the region and over oil prices and quotas. Saudi Arabia will continue to have to deal with an Iranian search for hegemony in the Gulf, and Iranian efforts to intimidate Saudi Arabia or its neighbors. It must plan to meet military threats from Iran's conventional forces, unconventional forces, and weapons of mass destruction until a new regime in Iran has proven its moderation over a period of years.

Saudi Arabian officials feel they face an even more serious threat from a revanchist Iraq. They note that Saudi Arabia has obtained little benefit from its long efforts to develop friendly relations with Iraq. These efforts date back to at least the late 1970s. Saudi Arabia reached a tentative agreement with Iraq on the partition of their neutral zone in 1981, and a full border settlement 1983. Saudi Arabia was one of Iraq's strongest backers during the Iran-Iraq War, and provided it with massive aid.

These efforts had little impact on Iraq's behavior when it invaded Kuwait in 1990. Iraqi forces massed on the border and posed a major threat to Saudi Arabia. The end result was the Gulf War, and the creation of a legacy of Iraqi hostility that may long outlive Saddam Hussein. It is hardly surprising, therefore, that Saudi Arabia has been a strong supporter of the UN sanctions against Saddam Hussein's regime. Saudi officials oppose any sudden lifting of sanctions, or forgiveness of Iraqi loans and reparations payments. They feel Saudi Arabia must plan to deal with a revanchist Iraq which eventually will be able to rebuild its conventional forces and resume its efforts to acquire weapons of mass destruction.

As is the case with Iran, Saudi officials see few prospects for long-term accommodation. Most Saudi officials seem to feel there will be no way to trust a new regime in Iraq, even if it does appear to be moderate. They fear that such a regime will still seek to re-acquire weapons of mass destruction and pursue Iraqi hegemony. Most indicate that it will take years of proven moderation by a new Iraqi regime before Saudi Arabia can relax its guard.

Further, Saudi officials feel that Saudi Arabia cannot deal with the Iranian and Iraqi threat simply in terms of the defense of Saudi territory. They feel that Saudi Arabia must plan to provide for the security of smaller and more vulnerable neighbors like Bahrain and Kuwait, and for the waters of the Gulf and Gulf of Oman.

Border Disputes and Tensions

At the same time, though, there are many sources of tension between Saudi Arabia and its Southern Gulf neighbors. Saudi Arabia is a relatively new state, formed by the conquests of Abd al-Aziz. Saudi Arabia's boundaries with Jordan, Iraq, and Kuwait were established in the 1920s and 1930s as a result of British intervention when Saudi conquests threatened to overrun areas of British interest. Britain negotiated a series of treaties with Abd al-Aziz, which created two "neutral zones"—one with Iraq and the other with Kuwait. There were many ambiguities in these agreements, which did not involve the rest of the Trucial states and Yemen. This has left a legacy of border disputes that has affected Saudi relations with virtually all of its neighbors.

Relations with Yemen

Saudi Arabia has long seen Yemen as a potential threat, in part because Yemen is an extraordinarily poor state with a population that has equaled or exceeded that of Saudi Arabia and which now totals well over 14.7 million compared to 18.7 million for Saudi Arabia.[9] Yemen and Saudi Arabia fought a war for control of their border area in the early 1930s, and have had conflicting border claims ever since. Although the Imam of Yemen invaded Saudi Arabia, Saudi Arabia won the war. The Taif Agreement of 1934 resolved the war in Saudi Arabia's favor and gave Saudi Arabia additional territory in the Jizan, Asir, and Najran. Ever since, various Yemeni leaders and nationalists have indicated that they would like to reverse the Taif Agreement.

New tensions arose between the two countries in 1962, when civil war broke out between Yemeni royalists and republicans. Egyptian forces entered North Yemen to support the new republican government, while Saudi Arabia backed the royalists. These tensions only subsided after 1967, when Egypt was forced to withdraw its troops from North Yemen because of its defeat in its 1967 war with Israel. The republicans won the civil war in North Yemen in spite of Egypt's withdrawal of its troops and support. Further, Britain left Aden and South Yemen came under the rule of Marxist extremists. This led to continuing Saudi tension with the government of North Yemen. Although Saudi Arabia provided North Yemen with aid, and allowed nearly a million Yemenis to work in Saudi Arabia, it also continued to interfere in North Yemeni affairs and constantly attempted to divide North Yemen's tribes and prevent a strong central government from emerging. Saudi Arabia saw South Yemen as a major threat, backed by the Soviet Union, and substantially increased its military presence in the border region.

During the 1970s and 1980s, Saudi Arabia fought repeated clashes with Yemen over control of the potential oil reserves in the 1,458 kilometer long border area. This hostility increased after the unification of North and South Yemen in 1992. Yemen sided with Iraq in 1990, leading to a virtual severing of relations between the two states and the expulsion of tens of thousands of Yemeni expatriate workers from Saudi Arabia. Saudi Arabia then backed South Yemen against the central government in the Yemeni civil war of 1994, only to see South Yemen defeated. A new series of border clashes also took place in the Najran region in areas with potential oil reserves.

In late 1994, however, both sides began to mediate their border disputes. In spite of a January, 1995 incident in which Yemen opened fire on Saudi aircraft believed to be violating Yemeni airspace, this mediation resulted in the signing of an 11 point agreement in Mecca on February 26, 1995. The agreement was negotiated by Prince Sultan, Saudi Arabia's Second Deputy Prime Minister and Minister of Defense and Aviation, and Sheik Abdullah Al-Ahmar, the Speaker of the Yemeni House of Representatives, and approved by King Fahd and President Ali Abdullah Saleh of Yemen.

The agreement recognized the validity of the borders set forth in the Taif agreement of 1934. It also set up a joint committee to use "modern technology" to establish border markers in the area from Raseef Al-Bahr (Ral Al-Mewaaj Shami) to Radeef Qrad (between Meedi and Al-Mosem) and then to a point near Al-Thar mountain, and to then demarcate the remaining borders. Additional joint committees were established to demarcate marine borders along the Red Sea Coast, guarantee non-military movements or establishments in the border area, and promote economic and cultural ties. A higher committee was set up to oversee and facilitate the work of the other committees. Both countries also agreed to prohibit the use of their territory for hostile acts against the other; to refrain from hostile propaganda; and to report all actions in official minutes of meetings signed by officials of both countries.

King Fahd and President Saleh reinforced this agreement with a meeting on June 6, 1995, and Saudi Arabia agreed to allow more Yemeni workers into the Kingdom and provide some aid.[10] Although it is far too early to talk about smooth relations between the two countries, Saudi Arabia perceives Yemen to be less of a threat today than in the past.

This improvement in Saudi-Yemeni relations is particularly important because Yemen has few prospects for stable economic development unless significant numbers of Yemenis can work in Saudi Arabia, and the border is peaceful enough to allow Yemen to develop its oil resources. The World Bank projects that Yemen's per capita income only totaled $540 in 1991, the last year for which data are available. It also estimates that Saudi Arabia's expulsion of Yemeni workers during the Gulf War led to a sudden 8% increase in the population, while a cut off in aid and worker remittances cost Yemen over $1 billion a year. These developments produced a more than 15% cut in Yemen's GDP during 1990–1992, and Yemen still has not demonstrated that it can sustain real economic growth equal to its population growth. An impoverished Yemen could lead to critical regional instability, and the World Bank projects that Yemen's population will increase to 17 million by the year 2000, 20 million by the year 2005, and nearly 24 million by the year 2010.[11]

Relations with Oman

Saudi Arabia also has a history of tension and conflict with Oman. Skirmishes occurred over control of the Buramai Oasis and Western Oman during the time the Trucial States were still under British protection. More recently, Saudi Arabia attempted to seize part of Western Oman during the 1960s. Since that time relations have often been tense. There has been a continuing low-level rivalry between Oman and Saudi Arabia over collective security arrangements in the GCC. Oman has claimed that Saudi Arabia is attempting to dominate the GCC, and Saudi Arabia has claimed that Oman is trying to use GCC aid to become a major Gulf military power.

In 1990, Saudi and Omani negotiators reached an agreement that demarcated 657 kilometers of their border and agreed to negotiate the rest. On July 9, 1995, these negotiations resulted in both nations signing an agreement in Riyadh that demarcated the entire border.[12] This agreement may not end the rivalry between the two states, but it has reduced the tensions between them and seems to have eliminated an important potential source of conflict.

The rivalry between Oman and Saudi Arabia now seems to focus on the leadership of the Southern Gulf and the future role of the GCC. Sultan Qabus of Oman has played a growing role in mediating between the smaller Gulf states—a role which proved to be critical during the tensions between Qatar and the other Gulf states in 1995 and 1996. Oman has also had close relations with Qatar and taken the lead in normalizing relations with Israel in ways which Saudi Arabia opposes. The difference is not so much one of substance, but one over the independence of Oman's actions and the rate at which it has improved its relations with Israel. Saudi Arabia also takes a much harder line towards Iraq than Oman, and feels Oman has been too aggressive in its efforts to create a constructive dialogue with Iran.

Saudi Arabia and Oman have disagreed over Sultan Qabus's call for the creation of an integrated 100,000 man GCC force and efforts to strengthen the military integration of the GCC. Saudi Arabia feels that such efforts would result in making Omani military manpower a major force within the GCC while forcing the other GCC states to provide Oman with significant military aid. Saudi Arabia has also tacitly opposed Oman's efforts to develop a GCC-wide approach to funding gas and oil pipelines to Omani ports on the Indian Ocean to reduce dependence on tanker traffic through the Gulf. These tensions are the products of significant differences in the strategic interests of the two states and are likely to lead to a lasting rivalry for influence in the region.

Relations with Qatar

Saudi Arabia has long standing territorial disputes with Qatar. These disputes initially centered around the control of Khaur al-Udaid, a long winding inlet at the base of the eastern side of the Qatari peninsula, and control over the territory behind it. The Al Thani family of Qatar and the Al Nihayan family of Abu Dhabi had long disputed control of the Khaur al-Udaid. This dispute broadened in 1935, however, when Saudi Arabia asserted its own claims to the area, along with claims to much of Abu Dhabi.[13]

The disputes between Saudi Arabia and Qatar seemed to have been resolved in 1965 when Qatar gave up its claims to the Khaur al-Udaid in return for territorial concessions at the base of the Peninsula. Qatar also signed a bilateral security agreement with Saudi Arabia in 1982, although the border was never fully demarcated.[14]

In the early 1990s, Qatar felt that Saudi Arabia was infringing on its territory by building roads and facilities in the border area. A confrontation between roving Bedouins caused a minor clash between Saudi Arabia and Qatar on September 30, 1992. This clash took place at a small outpost at al-Khofuous, about 80 miles southeast of Doha. Two Qataris were killed and a third taken prisoner. Qatar reacted by canceling its participation in the GCC's Peninsular Shield exercises, which practice the defense of Kuwait and the Saudi border against Iraq.

The clash led to new talks between King Fahd and the then Emir of Qatar, Sheik Khalifa bin Hamad Al Thani in December 1992, which supposedly resolved the issue. However, tensions continued. A brief incident in October 1993 resulted in several more deaths. Five Qatari-Saudi border skirmishes occurred during 1994 as well as a diplomatic row in which Qatar boycotted the November 1994 GCC summit conference. As of December 1994, Qatar and Saudi Arabia were considering the formation of a joint committee to investigate the conflicts but no real progress took place. The ruling elites of both countries remain divided over the issue and show considerable private distrust of the other's position. The Qataris tended to see such disputes as a symbol of Saudi pressure to dominate the smaller Gulf states, while their Saudi counterparts tended to see them as a result of Qatari provocation.[15]

These territorial disputes kept Qatar from tying its security closely to Saudi Arabia and the tensions between Qatar and Saudi Arabia grew notably worse when Sheik Hamad bin Khalifa al-Thani deposed his father in the spring of 1995, and became Qatar's new Emir. Saudi Arabia was quick to recognize Sheik Hamad as Emir, but members of the Saudi royal family had long felt that Sheik Hamad was deliberately challenging Saudi leadership in the Gulf, and provoking differences between Saudi Arabia and the other Southern Gulf states. One senior Saudi prince privately described the new Emir and his new foreign minister, Sheik Hamad bin Jassim Bin Jabr al-Thani, as a "dangerous and disruptive influence."

These tensions reached the crisis point when the two nations clashed over the appointment of a new Secretary General to the Gulf Cooperation Council in December, 1995. Qatar accused Saudi Arabia of forcing a Saudi Secretary General—Ambassador Jamil Al-Hujailan—on the GCC. Although the GCC had no formal rules regarding the nationality of the Secretary General, Qatar felt that custom dictated that the Secretary General should be chosen through alphabetical rotation. The previous Secretary Generals had been Kuwaiti and Omani, and this would have meant that the new Secretary General should be a Qatari candidate. The situation was made worse when the Emir and Foreign Minister of Qatar walked out of the GCC meeting. Saudi Arabia, Bahrain, and the UAE felt that Qatar had failed to observe the normal courtesies between GCC states in handling the dispute and that Qatar had insulted Sheik Zayed bin Sultan Al Nuhayyan of the UAE when he attempted to mediate.

Saudi Arabia retaliated for the Qatari walkout by joining Bahrain and the UAE in receiving the Emir's deposed father—Sheik Khalifa bin Hamad—who made it clear during his visits that he was actively seeking to regain power. The UAE received Sheik Khalifa bin Hamad on December 21, 1995. Sheik Khalifa then announced that he would set up "temporary quarters" in Abu Dhabi until he returned to power in Doha and pledged that he would improve relations between Qatar and its neighbors if he resumed power.[16] Sheik Khalifa then went on to visit Cairo and Damascus, and again announced he was seeking to resume the throne.

Qatar's new Emir, Hamad bin Khalifa al-Thani, responded by visiting Cairo, Jordan, and Oman to demonstrate that he had influence in other Arab states, and gave an interview indicating that he hoped to solve Qatar's border disputes with Saudi Arabia in a "brotherly way." He clarified his position on the selection of a new Secretary General of the GCC by stating that, "If people thought what happened in Muscat was a result of the border (dispute with Saudi Arabia), that is not right at all . . . We don't mind the Secretary General being a Saudi . . . (But) all six countries have to agree on this issue. We don't mind Saudi Arabia coming in with its candidate. (But) the way they . . . did it was not a way we can accept. It was a way that did not happen before in the GCC." [17]

What happened next is hotly debated by the Gulf states. Qatar's leadership feels that Bahrain, Saudi Arabia, and the UAE allowed Sheik Khalifa bin Hamad to prepare a coup attempt. They claim the coup was planned to combine Qataris loyal to the deposed Emir with a force of up to 2,000 Yemeni and other Arab mercenaries which was to assemble on the Saudi side of the border. They claim that this force was under the leadership of a French officer who had commanded Sheik Khalifa bin Hamad's personal guard and had previously been one of the leaders of the French special forces that suppressed the uprising in the Grand Mosque in Mecca. They accuse Bahrain, Saudi Arabia, and the UAE of allowing the deposed Emir to prepare the force in their countries, of allowing the plotters to stage two Transall transports to move the forces involved, and even of plans to provide air cover for the coup.

It is clear that Qatar took events seriously enough to mobilize the Emiri Guard on February 17, 1996, and carry out several hundred arrests. Beyond this, the details of what happened remain unclear. Bahrain, Saudi Arabia, and the UAE deny that a coup attempt ever reached the point where Sheik Khalifa bin Hamad assembled any significant forces on their soil and that a major recruiting effort ever took place. They accuse Qatar of making false charges to deliberately embarrass them and provide an excuse for its arrests.

The views of other states are ambiguous. Oman denounced the coup attempt, but Kuwait was silent. No build-up prior to the coup attempt was detected by US intelligence, but several senior US officials in the Gulf feel that a coup attempt was being mobilized. The US also encouraged the Southern Gulf states to resolve their differences peacefully, and supported Qatar in a call for a special summit meeting to deal with the issue. Both France and the US also carried out exercises with Qatar to help show their support.[18]

The situation improved in March and April, 1996, and Qatar and its neighbors reached a compromise over the GCC. In March, 1996, Qatar agreed with the other GCC states that the Secretary General of the GCC would now be selected from each Gulf state in alphabetical order and that a Secretary General could only serve for a maximum of two three year terms. This compromise seemed to support Qatar's original position, but the fact that the GCC had just selected a Saudi meant that Qatar would now only receive its turn after a Secretary General had served from every other Gulf state. The de facto result was a Saudi victory over the GCC.

Bahrain, Saudi Arabia, and the UAE did, however, seem to endorse the rule of Emir Hamad. Bahrain also agreed to accept the International Court's jurisdiction over the Hawar Islands dispute while Qatar ceased to allow the Bahraini opposition to make statements attacking the Bahraini government from Qatari soil.

These compromises restored an image of unity, but it was clear that the royal families of Qatar and Saudi Arabia remained at odds. The Saudis saw the Qatari Emir and Foreign ministers as young, brash, inexperienced, and as a source of division within the Gulf. The Qatari royal family saw the Saudis as bullies, attempting to dominate the GCC, and as forces of reaction led by a generation too old to adapt to the changes in the Gulf. Although both states adhere to the Wahhabi sect of Islam, the Saudis saw the Qataris as slack and as deviating from the dictates of Wahhabi beliefs, while the Qataris saw the Saudis as accommodating Islamic extremists by adopting exaggerated and overly rigid religious practices. There seems to be little prospect that this rivalry for power and influence will cease or stop undermining the GCC's efforts to build collective security.

Relations with Kuwait

Saudi Arabia has better relations with its other Southern Gulf neighbors. This is particularly important in the case of Kuwait and Bahrain because the defense of the Saudi border with Iraq, and the key Saudi oil fields and facilities in the Upper Gulf, is dependent on close cooperation between the three states.

The Saudi-Kuwaiti neutral zone was partitioned for administrative purposes in 1971. Each state continued to share the petroleum resources of the former zone, now called the "divided zone" equally. Saudi Arabia and Kuwait continued to dispute ownership of Qaruh and Umm al Maradim Islands and offshore areas, but both states entered into new negotiations after the Gulf War, and demarcated the rest of their borders in July, 1995.[19]

Since the Gulf War, Saudi Arabia and Kuwait have cooperated with the US in developing a common defense against Iraq. While the Gulf Cooperation Council's (GCC) Peninsula Shield force is little more than an exercise in hollow symbolism, Saudi Arabia and Kuwait have begun to conduct air and land exercises that are far more realistic than in the past. The

Saudi and Kuwaiti air forces have cooperated closely with US air units, and can now cooperate in mission planning and battle management using advanced command and control systems like the AWACS and JSTARS. Further, the Saudi and Kuwaiti armies began common brigade-level combined arms command post exercises in 1995, supported by battalion-level field exercises.

There are, however, tensions between the two countries on political and social grounds. Saudi Arabia sees Kuwait's National Assembly as a symbol of a destabilizing tolerance for political dissent. It opposes Kuwait's relatively free media, and tolerant social customs at a time when Saudi Arabia is attempting to use the strengthening of Wahhabi orthodoxy to counter Saudi Islamic extremists. Saudis also often see Kuwaitis as arrogant and as refusing to cooperate in many areas.

Kuwait sees Saudi Arabia as attempting to preserve outdated political and social customs, as defending an interpretation of Islamic law and custom that is too conservative to function in the modern world, and as attempting to interfere in Kuwaiti domestic matters. If Saudi Arabia sometimes sees Kuwait as slow to cooperate, Kuwait sees Saudi Arabia as a power that sometimes attempts to intimidate its neighbors and is careless of their sensitivities. These tensions do not block cooperation between the two states, but they cannot be disregarded.

Relations with Bahrain and the UAE

Saudi Arabia has good relations with Bahrain and the UAE. It provides Bahrain with the oil it needs to operate its refinery and cooperates closely in internal security matters and defense. There is, however, some tension between the governments of the two countries.

Saudi Arabia is concerned with the Shi'ite unrest in Bahrain and has recommended that Bahrain's government take a strong, if not repressive, approach to dealing with dissent. Saudi Arabia is also ambivalent about Bahrain's social tolerance of secular customs, including tourism and the ability to buy alcohol, and sometimes attempts to push Bahrain towards more "Islamic" behavior.

Some Bahrainis, including several senior officials, feel that Saudi Arabia is blocking necessary reforms and making it difficult for the Bahraini government to reach a settlement with Bahrain's Shi'ites. They feel Saudi Arabia has failed to provide the economic aid and support Bahrain needs and has concentrated on repression to the exclusion of peaceful solutions to the problem. At the same time, they note that many Saudis use Bahrain as a social outlet for relief from the increasingly strict interpretation of Wahhabi Islam adhered to by Saudi Arabia and does so with the tacit acceptance of the Saudi government.

Similarly, some Saudi officials feel that the UAE has become equally liberal in dealing with foreigners and Islamic customs. They admire Sheik Zayed, but feel the UAE has done little to support Gulf security and help integrate the oil policies of the Southern Gulf states. There is still lingering tension over the past border disputes between Saudi Arabia and the UAE, and Saudi officials express some concern that the UAE may not remain united once Sheik Zayed gives up power.

Relations with Israel and
Policy Toward the Arab-Israeli Conflict

Saudi Arabia's attitudes towards Israel have shifted with time. During the reign of King Faisal, Saudi Arabia was one of Israel's strongest opponents. Since that time, Saudi Arabia has become progressively more concerned with its own security and has adopted a policy of trying to decouple Saudi foreign policy from the Arab-Israeli conflict by supporting the Arab-Israeli peace process.

Relations with Israel

Saudi Arabia did not support the Camp David accords, but King Fahd did put forth a peace plan designed to encourage peace without committing Saudi Arabia to taking a stand that might lead to sharp criticism from other Arab states. Beginning in the late 1980s, a number of Saudi princes and officials began to play a more active behind-the-scenes role in the peace process, and Saudi relations with Israel eased significantly after the Gulf War. Saudi Arabia effectively ended support of the secondary Arab boycott of Israel. Prince Saud, the Saudi Foreign Minister attended some of the ceremonies relating to Israel's peace settlement with the Palestinians, and Saudi Arabia has advocated a comprehensive peace settlement.

At the same time, Saudi Arabia has kept a low public profile in dealing with Israel and the peace process, and has lagged behind Gulf states like Oman and Qatar in improving relations with Israel. Saudi policy is one of caution, emphasizing efforts to minimize Arab criticism of Saudi Arabia. This represents a basic theme of Saudi foreign policy: a cautious emphasis on Saudi security where other considerations are always secondary.

Relations with Egypt

Saudi attitudes towards Egypt, Jordan, and Syria vary with time and the reality has little to do with the Pan-Arab rhetoric that is normally used by all four countries. Egypt and Saudi Arabia now cooperate in many areas, but a rich, ultra-conservative Saudi monarchy and a poor, secular Egypt differ in many ways and scarcely have identical interests. Saudi Arabia also perceives Egypt as a natural rival for power and influence in the Arab world.

Saudi Arabia and Egypt were de facto enemies during most of Nasser's rule, and fought a proxy war in Yemen. Saudi Arabia improved its relations with Egypt when Sadat came to power and then distanced itself from Egypt after Camp David. It never supported the efforts of some Arab leaders to isolate Egypt, however, and Saudi Arabia gradually improved relations once Mubarak came to power. Saudi Arabia and Egypt cooperated closely during the Gulf War, but Saudi Arabia did not support Egypt's efforts to create a common military command and obtain Saudi subsidies for an Egyptian power projection force to defend the Gulf after the war.

Senior Saudi officials strongly deny that they ever indicated to Egypt or Syria that the Damascus Accords signed after the Gulf War would lead to anything other than the creation of a small headquarters in the Gulf, and the stationing of a limited number of Egyptian and Syrian officers at that headquarters. They make it clear that Saudi Arabia does not want a significant Egyptian or other Arab military presence from outside the Gulf on its soil during peacetime, and sees any such relationship with Egypt as creating problems in terms of constant Egyptian requests for financial aid and interference in Saudi affairs.

Senior Saudi military officers also severely criticized Egypt's performance during the Gulf War. They note that Egypt was slow to deploy, showed few skills in power projection, required massive aid in terms of support, and did not organize well for the offensive in Desert Storm. They claim that the Egyptian air force lacked the training and technical capability to operate in the complex and demanding air combat environment over the Kuwaiti Theater of Operations. They also feel that Egyptian land forces panicked during the crossing of the Iraqi forward line, when Egyptian intelligence detected non-existent Iraqi counterattacks. They feel Egypt showed little aggressiveness and only limited proficiency and only met its military objectives because other Coalition forces had driven virtually all Iraqi forces out of the Egyptian line of advance. They see little prospect that Egypt can develop the military effectiveness to match or replace Western forces in the defense of the upper Gulf.[20]

Relations with Syria

Saudi Arabia has long sought friendly relations with Syria and has provided Syria with substantial aid. This Saudi effort initially stemmed from its opposition to Israel and fear that Syria might support radical movements within Saudi Arabia. Over time, however, Prince Abdullah developed close relations with President Asad of Syria, and Saudi Arabia began to see Syria as a strategic counterweight to Iraq.

Saudi Arabia actively sought Syrian support during the Gulf War, and provided both aid and political support for Syrian intervention in Lebanon. Syria's military deployments to the Gulf, however, exhibited much less power projection capability than Egypt, and Syria sent second-rate forces that played a largely passive role. As a result, Syria's military performance did little to impress either members of the Royal Family or Saudi military officers with Syria's ability to support Saudi Arabia in the defense of the upper Gulf.

Saudi Arabia continues to maintain good relations with Syria, but has not provided significant military or economic aid since 1992. It currently sees little prospect that Syria can play a major role in supporting any of the radical groups that threaten Saudi and Gulf internal security, and no longer supports Syria in its efforts to obtain military parity with Israel.

Relations with Jordan

The Saud dynasty was the rival of the Hashemite dynasty in seeking control over the territory that has become modern Saudi Arabia, and there still are lingering aspects of that rivalry in the relations between Saudi Arabia and Hashemite-ruled Jordan. Saudi Arabia did provide aid to Jordan as part of the Arab-Israeli conflict, and allowed many Jordanians and Jordanian Palestinians to work in Saudi Arabia, but relations between the two regimes were never close.

Saudi Arabia abruptly halted all aid and expelled most workers with Jordanian passports in 1990, when King Hussein of Jordan tilted to the side of Iraq. Saudi Arabian intelligence also concluded that Jordan provided Iraq with significant arms shipments and support during the period before Desert Storm—a perception that worsened relations as time went on.

The two nations slowly improved relations after 1992, and Saudi Arabia began to provide token amounts of aid. Relations improved still further in 1995, after King Hussein broke more openly with Saddam Hussein. Saudi officials did, however, raise the issue of whether King Hussein had ambitions to restore Hashemite influence in Iraq. They also show little current interest in military cooperation with Jordan, or trust in a stable, long-term relationship. Some question how long the Hashemite dynasty will be in power once King Hussein is gone, and fear they may have to deal with a more radical Jordanian-Palestinian entity.

The Greater Arab World

Saudi Arabia is scarcely unique in focusing on its own national and strategic interests. It is hardly surprising that a state as conservative and inward-looking as Saudi Arabia has tensions with many of its neighbors. It is also scarcely surprising that Saudi Arabia has grown more cautious about any relationship that might lead to new demands for foreign aid when its economy is experiencing severe structural problems and it has major budget deficit.

At the same time, it is important to understand that it is these realities that govern Saudi relations with the greater Arab world and not the Kingdom's Pan-Arab rhetoric. Saudi Arabia continues to seek prestige and influence throughout the Arab world, and to define its legitimacy as the Arab custodian of Mecca and Medina and the site of the pilgrimage. It does not, however, define its security or trade relations in terms of ties to Arab states outside the Gulf. This is likely to be an enduring reality. It may not endear itself to Arabists, but it must be treated as such.

3

Internal Change
and Internal Security

The primary threats to Saudi security come from its hostile or radical neighbors, principally Iran and Iraq. Saudi Arabia does, however, face problems in dealing with its internal security, and challenges to the political and religious legitimacy of its royal family and ruling elite. Saudi Arabia faces challenges in dealing with both the near-term economic problems caused by the cost of the Gulf War and low oil prices, and with the socio-economic impact of the radical process of modernization and social change that has affected every aspect of Saudi society for a quarter of a century.

The Monarchy, the Majlis al-Shura, and the Royal Family

The Saud family seems to be in secure control of the country, and relies more on coopting opposition than on repressing it. The monarchy remains the key source of power in the Saudi Arabian government. There is no formal constitution and there are no political parties or elections. The king's power is, however, limited by religion, custom, and the need for consensus. The king must observe Islamic law (Shari'a) and other Saudi traditions. He must maintain the support of senior members of the Saudi royal family, and the support of religious leaders (ulema) and other important elements in Saudi society. Like the other Southern Gulf countries, Saudi Arabia also has a long tradition of public access to high officials (usually at a majlis, or public audience) and the right to petition such officials directly.

Since 1953, a Council of Ministers has been appointed by to the king, and has advised on the formulation of general policy and helps direct the activities of the growing bureaucracy. This Council consists of a prime minister, the first and second deputy prime ministers, 20 ministers (of whom the minister of defense is also the second deputy prime minister), two ministers of state, and a small number of advisers and heads of major autonomous organizations.

Saudi laws are promulgated by a resolution of the Council of Ministers. This must be ratified by royal decree, and be compatible with the Shari'a. The Saudi legal system is administered according to the Shari'a by a system of religious courts. The judges in these courts are appointed by the king on the recommendation of the Supreme Judicial Council, and composed of 12 senior jurists. The independence of the judiciary is protected by law, although the king acts as the highest court of appeal and has the power to pardon. Saudi Arabia is divided into 13 provinces, governed by princes or close relatives of the royal family. These governors are appointed by the king.

Rumors and a History of Stability

The stability of the Saudi royal family is critical to the security of the Saudi government, and this has led to constant speculation over divisions within the royal family and possible conflicts over the succession. This speculation is not simply Western. Rumor mongering regarding the royal family is a Saudi national sport—although a discrete one—and few educated Saudis seem to feel they lack inside information on the detailed political maneuverings of the major princes. The fact that there appears to be nearly as many authoritative rumors as there are Saudis does little to discourage such speculation, and Saudis from the Hejaz take a particular delight in reporting possible divisions between princes and conflicts over the succession.

The long series of reports of imminent conflict that have emerged out of Saudi "royal watching" have rarely proved reliable. There have been few divisions within the royal family that have threatened the government's cohesion since the death of King Abd Al-Aziz in 1953. The only major conflict between the senior members of the royal family that has threatened to lead to open struggles over the succession occurred in 1958–1962.

Abd al Aziz was succeeded by his eldest son, Saud, who reigned for 11 years. King Saud proved unable to manage the nation's finances, however, and created serious problems in the kingdom's foreign affairs. In 1958, this led to a meeting of a powerful and secretive body of senior princes known as the *ahl-aqd wal hal*, or "those who tie and untie," which forced King Saud to delegate direct conduct of Saudi government affairs to Prince Faisal and make him Prime Minister.[21] King Saud fought back against this arrangement, however, and regained control of the government in 1960–62. This led to a struggle with Faisal and other members of the royal family, a struggle which Saud lost decisively in October, 1962.

Faisal regained power as prime minister, and began to implement a broad reform program that stressed economic development. Faisal was proclaimed King by senior royal family members and religious leaders in 1964. He continued to serve as Prime Minister, however, and this practice has been followed by subsequent kings. King Faisal proved to be an extremely competent ruler, and dealt effectively with problems arising from the Six-Day (Arab-Israeli) War of June, 1967, the 1973 Arab-Israeli war, the subsequent Arab oil boycott, the sudden massive increase in Saudi oil wealth, and the resulting rise in Saudi political influence.

After King Faisal was assassinated by a mentally ill nephew in 1975, the royal family dealt with the succession smoothly, quickly appointing Faisal's half-brother Khalid as King and prime minister. The appointment of the next Crown Prince, however, was somewhat more contentious. Prince Fahd, Khalid's half-brother, was in line for appointment as Crown Prince, but his "Western" lifestyle as a young adult prompted opposition from the traditionalists in the family. The result was a series of deliberations within the royal family which produced a compromise between the Western-oriented family members, who favored Prince Fahd, and the traditionalists. Fahd was appointed as Crown Prince and First Deputy Prime Minister, with the understanding that the next in line for this position would be Prince Abdullah, one of Prince Fahd's half-brothers and a traditionalist.[22]

During his reign, King Khalid empowered Prince Fahd to oversee many aspects of the government's international and domestic affairs. This period saw the continuation of rapid economic development within Saudi Arabia, and the Kingdom assumed a more influential role in both regional political and international economic and financial matters. Prince Fahd's growing prominence allowed his seven full brothers, known as the Sudairi Seven because of their clan affiliation, to begin consolidating their power within the government.[23]

The Rise of King Fahd

With the death of King Khalid in June, 1982, Fahd became King and Prime Minister. Prince Abdullah, the commander of the National Guard, was subsequently named Crown Prince and First Deputy Prime Minister. One of King Fahd's full-brothers, Prince Sultan, the Minister of Defense and Aviation, became Second Deputy Prime Minister. Fahd's reign allowed for a further consolidation of power among the Sudairi Seven. This posed a potential problem for the next succession, since the Sudairis were from the Western-oriented wing of the family, while the Crown Prince was a traditionalist.[24] In 1992, King Fahd addressed the issue of succession by decreeing that, "Rule passes to the sons of the founding king . . . and to their children's children. The most upright among them is to receive allegiance in accordance with [the principles] of the Holy Qu'ran and the tradition of the Venerable Prophet."[25]

Fahd's decree attempted to alleviate concerns over the creation of a perpetual gerentocracy in Saudi Arabia by opening the succession to the grandsons of Abd Al-Aziz. However, Saudi officials qualified the statement by indicating that succession would still be according to seniority for the foreseeable future.[26]

Current Prospects for the Succession

The ruling elite within the royal family is divided between the Sudairi family and other sons of Abdel Aziz. The Sudairi leaders of the royal family include the King, Minister of Defense Prince Sultan, and Prince Naif. The Sudairis are balanced by Crown Prince and Deputy Prime Minister Abdullah, the head of the General Intelligence Directorate Prince Turki, Prince Saud al-Faisal, the Foreign Minister and son of King Faisal, and a number of other senior princes. The relations among these princes, and any friction between them, make up most of the political life of Saudi Arabia.

The issue of succession has become more pertinent since 1995 because of the ill health of King Fahd, who is well over 70 years old. On November 30, 1995, Fahd was rushed to a hospital emergency room suffering from what most experts believe was a stroke. One month later, he temporarily turned control of the government over to Crown Prince Abdullah (age 71), who proceeded to attend the summit of GCC leaders in Oman in place of the King.

Prince Abdullah ruled in his absence without incident until King Fahd formally reassumed his position as head of the government on February 21, 1996. He also continued to be the effective ruler of Saudi Arabia because King Fahd was incapable of exercising power for more than brief, sporadic incidents.

Nevertheless, King Fahd's reassumption of his position prompted intense speculation as to who would ultimately be Fahd's successor. The most likely report was that Prince Abdullah would act as effective regent until King Fahd was willing to formally relinquish power or died. Another possibility was that King Fahd would formally give up ruling because of his health, and retire to a foreign country where he could obtain continuing medical treatment. This would allow while Prince Abdullah to formally become king or regent without leaving any uncertainty as to who was in charge of Saudi Arabia's government.

However, there were rumors of possible challenges to Abdullah's succession. The most popular of these rumors involved the possibility that Prince Sultan (age 68), a Sudairi and the Minister of Defense might seek the throne.[27] Other scenarios speculated that Prince Saud al-Faisal might be promoted to Crown Prince in place of an aging Abdullah. This might be accomplished through an alliance with Prince Salman, the governor of Riyadh and one of King Fahd's younger brothers. Another scenario indicates that King Fahd might make Prince Salman the Crown Prince, with the succession bypassing both Prince Abdullah and Prince Sultan. A third scenario indicated that Sultan would become the next king, followed by Prince Mohammed ben Fahd, the son of King Fahd.[28]

It is impossible to dismiss such speculation, but Prince Abdullah is a formidable figure. He may be less visible in the West than the Sudairi, but he seems to be in good health and a highly effective leader within Saudi Arabia. He commands the National Guard, and maintains strong support among the large Bedouin tribes of the Najd, from which the Guard is drawn. Abdullah is also a member of the Bani Shammar, a powerful tribe which drove the Saud family into exile in the 19th century before being co-opted by King Abd Al-Aziz who brought them into the royal family through inter-tribal marriage.

Abdullah is a strong Arab nationalist who has criticized the West's close association with Israel in the past—criticism which has gained him support among traditionalist and conservative Saudis. Abdullah also maintains close personal ties to Syria's President Hafez al-Asad. However, there are good reasons to challenge reports that Abdullah would weaken Saudi Arabia's ties to the West.

The consensus among most experts is that Abdullah fully recognizes both Saudi Arabia's vulnerability and its need for close ties to the US. He has long relied on the US and other Western states to train and equip the National Guard, and is credited with playing a major role in Saudi Arabia's decision to allow the US to base forces in Saudi Arabia after the Iraqi invasion of Kuwait. If anything, Abdullah might be able to do a better job of balancing the conflicting needs of military ties to the West, Saudi military development, the Saudi economy, and the need to deal with Islamic extremism than either King Fahd or Prince Sultan.

Prince Abdullah is widely viewed as a more traditional leader and one who gives more weight to religion and Arab causes than other leading princes. He is viewed as having a high degree of integrity and as opposing the kind of massive showpiece purchases and projects that waste government funds and the kind of fees and corruption that affect many government purchases and contracts. At the same time, his ties to traditional elites and his "conservatism" do not seem to prevent him from understanding Saudi Arabia's needs for economic reform and from having good relations with many of the younger and more progressive princes. As a result, Abdullah's succession seems more likely to change the personal style of the monarchy than lead to major changes in Saudi Arabia's relations with the West and the United States.[29]

In any event, there is little concrete evidence that current rivalries will lead to any conflict between the top members of the royal family. Quiet competition over the succession and senior appointments has been a factor in Saudi politics since King Ibn Saud (Abd Al-Aziz) first met President Franklin Roosevelt. However, the Saud family has managed to resolve each succession both peacefully and privately, and deal with far more serious problems than exist today. The evidence suggests that the succession is likely to continue to be determined by internal consultation among the *ahl-aqd wal hal*, or other senior members of the royal family—at least until Prince Abdullah and Prince Sultan are dead.

The Need for Change in the Next Generation

What is far more uncertain is what will happen once there is a basic generational change within the Saudi royal family, and the choice of the King and senior ministers must be made from the large number of junior princes that will compete for power once the sons of King Saud are gone. There is no consensus over how many such "princes" there now are, and how many have the status to compete for power. It is almost certain, however, that there are over 5,000 males who can make some claim to ties to the Saudi royal family and well over 80 princes that have significant status as ranking members of the "next generation" and have some claim to power.

More is involved than control of the government. Some 2,000 princes play an active role in the economy. Many have a normal role in business, but some demand special privileges and/or use their influence corruptly or to violate Saudi law.[30] This mix of royal political and economic power has caused a substantial amount of jealousy and political friction within Saudi society. Saudi Arabia's economy and political stability has suffered from a failure to demarcate clearly the powers and rights of members of the royal family. The corrupt minority has sometimes abused its political power to dominate major military and civil deals and developments.

These problems extend to the military command level, where the divisions between members of the royal family sometimes prevent the full operation of objective criteria in the selection of commanders or effective unity of command. Senior Saudi officers, unrelated to the royal family have been denied promotion for internal political reasons—although the politics of the ruling elite has limited the careers of other princes as well as those outside the royal family. For example, Prince Fahd Abdullah, widely recognized as one of the most outstanding officers in the RSAF, was not promoted to a top command position. Prince Khalid bin Sultan, who successfully led the Arab forces in the Gulf War, was also not promoted to the post of military chief of staff and resigned in September, 1991.[31]

Further, the high birth rate within the royal family means the number of "princes" now doubles every 22–26 years and that there are about 70% more "royal" males under the age of 18 than there are above it. This trend also extends to the Wahhab and other leading families. At some point in the near to mid-term, Saudi Arabia simply will not be able to afford subsidizing either its expanding royal family or the descendants of other leading families.

The exponential growth of the size and potential cost of the Saudi royal family is scarcely a unique problem in the Southern Gulf, but Saudi Arabia would already benefit from putting an end to most of the subsidies and large numbers of special accounts and commissions given various princes. While many members of the royal family do provide active public service or engage in legitimate business, there are many that are little more than parasites and whose abuse of public funds, threatening Saudi Arabia's political cohesion and popular support for the members of the royal family who actually rule.

These problems do not mean that it is impossible for Saudi Arabia to maintain its stability as a monarchy. Many princes are highly respected and play a major role in public service. There is a need, however, to find a stable answer to the problem of who will rule once the direct sons of Ibn Saud no longer participate in the succession, and to define the role of the royal family to reduce state subsidies as well as the abuse of royal status. The royal family must ensure that commoners can count on promotion for merit, and that the Saudi people do not believe members of the royal family abuse the courts and legal system. Democracy may not be a critical aspect of Saudi Arabia's political and social development, but the rule of law is essential. In short, difficult decisions will have to be made about the reallocation of power at some point in the near future or the growth and cost of the Saud family will become a serious destabilizing factor in Saudi politics.

The Creation of the Majlis al-Shura

This does not mean that other political changes are not taking place, or that the Saudi government does not need to broaden its base of power in other ways. The complex mix of social and economic pressures that arose during the Gulf War led King Fahd to reorganize his cabinet on August 5, 1990, and announce a series of reforms on March 17, 1991. These reforms included the formation of a Council of Saudi Citizens or Majlis al-Shura, the introduction of a basic body of governing laws, and increased autonomy for the provinces.[32]

King Fahd's announcement of his intent to form a Majlis al-Shura was a reaction to the demands of both fundamentalists and secular reformers for greater participation in the government. His announcement was followed by further speeches by the king; by senior religious figures like Sheik Ibn Baz, who denounced religious extremism; and by senior political figures like Prince Turki Faisal, who gave a rare speech in a Mosque condemning those who used Islamic extremism to attack Saudi society.

The King announced on March 2, 1992, that the Majlis would have 61 members, and would include the speaker of the consultative council who would act as prime minister. The Majlis would have a four year term of office, and the right to examine plans for economic and social development, question cabinet members, examine annual plans submitted by each ministry, and propose new laws or amendments. He announced that similar 10 man councils would be set up in each of the 14 provinces, and that the provincial governors would have added power and autonomy.

The King issued a long written list of laws setting forth the basic rules of the government, the first codification of these laws since the founding of Saudi Arabia 60 years earlier. The code included the following provisions: making the king the commander-in-chief of the armed forces, calling for the succession to pass to the most qualified member of the royal family, rather than according to the order of succession, establishing an independent judiciary, guaranteeing the privacy of the home, mail, and phone; and prohibiting arbitrary arrest.

On September 23, 1992, the sixtieth anniversary of the founding of the monarchy, King Fahd appointed Mohammed bin Ibrahim bin Jubair as speaker. At the same time, the King delayed appointing the council, stating that, "The democratic systems prevailing in the world are systems which, in their structure, do not suit this region and our people . . . The system of free elections is not part of Islamic theology."[33]

On August 21, 1993, the King appointed all 60 of the members of the Majlis al-Shura—including one Shi'ite—for a four year term. In doing so, King Fahd read a decree over state television that again made it clear that the role of the Majlis was purely advisory. He also stated that he was retaining the power of the monarchy, and that Saudi Arabia would remain an Islamic state and would not become a Western democracy.[34]

The Council began to meet in 1994. Its initial meetings focused on procedures and regulations, and the establishment of various technical and administrative committees, such as those on foreign affairs and defense. The Council met 29 times in 1994, discussed 45 issues, and presented 25 recommendations. The Council's General Authority held 21 meetings and reached 23 decisions, and the various committees of the Council held more than 260 meetings, and submitted more than 50 studies and reports. On January 8, 1995, the Consultative Council begun the second year of its first session, and King Fahd presented a national budget to the Council for the first time. The Council dealt with a wide range of social and policy issues during the course of the 1995 session.[35]

The Majlis al-Shura may not mark a shift towards a Western-style representative democracy, but it does mark significant change towards broadening the base of power in Saudi Arabia. Members of the Majlis take their role very seriously and members of the royal family indicate that it is King's Fahd's intention to make the Majlis and the Council of Ministers equal branches of government.

Any analysis of the royal family's effort to broaden and restructure its political base must also take account of the fact that Saudi Arabia is caught up in a constant struggle between efforts to preserve the nation's character as an Islamic state and the need to adapt religious and social custom to modern social and economic needs. The creation of a purely advisory Majlis, a written code of law, and other limited reforms may well mark the present limits of how far the Saudi government can go without increasing internal instability, rather than reducing it.

Western concepts of democracy may or may not suit Saudi Arabia in the long term, but in the near term it needs stability to evolve, and avoid civil conflict. A slow and steady process of change and compromise is far more likely to serve Saudi interests, and protect the human rights of all Saudis. It is far from clear that a sudden effort to make broader and more sweeping reforms would do more than lead to open confrontation between Saudi Arabia's advocates of secular reform, Islamic fundamentalists, and Islamic extremists.

Changes in the Saudi Cabinet

The Saudi cabinet is also of major importance and reflects the distribution of power within the senior ranks of the royal family and Saudi Arabia's technocrats. The Cabinet is a large body headed by the king, with 23 members, including six ministers of state. There are 22 separate ministries, with the king acting as prime minister. Prince Abdullah is First Deputy Prime Minister and head of the National Guard. Prince Sultan is Second Deputy Prime Minister and Minister of Defense and Aviation. Prince Saud al Faisal is Foreign Minister, Prince Naif is Minister of the Interior, and Prince Mutib is Minister of Public Works and Housing.[36] These appointments give the senior members of the royal family control over the government, defense and internal security, and other key areas of patronage.

At the same time, the cabinet includes a wide range of technocrats, heading well organized and relatively modern ministries. This point is often ignored in discussions of Saudi Arabia's government. Much of the planning and management of the Kingdom is conducted by Western-educated experts, who are supported by a total of roughly 250 other senior appointments and a network of some 700 senior civil servants. Only about one-third of these appointments come from traditional leading families. The rest are "new men," a few of which are one generation away from nomadic tribesmen.

In the past, these technocrats and senior officials have usually served for most of their professional life. Many appointments have lasted 15–25 years. As a result, Saudi technocrats have often been slow to adapt to changing circumstances and many ministries have developed an institutional resistance to change. This problem became clear during the Gulf War, when many civil ministries had severe difficulties in meeting the sudden, new requirements necessary to support the Saudi military and foreign troops. As a result, King Fahd issued a decree in 1992, declaring that cabinet ministers could not remain in their posts for more than five years without a special royal decree. This decree, however, did not lead to rapid turnover within the cabinet and senior ranks.

Between 1993–1995 Saudi Arabia experienced a growing economic crisis. It again became apparent that many ministries were slow to adapt to Saudi Arabia's growing debt, income, and cash flow problems. Many ministries were slow to control expenses. They continued to advocate very large and grandiose projects, and failed to give priority to social and political needs. At the same time, Saudi Arabia began to experience growing problems with Islamic extremists.

By the spring of 1995, these problems had reached the point where King Fahd and the Saudi royal family began to take dramatic action. Significant shifts took place in appointments within the Saudi bureaucracy affecting around 160 of 250 top posts. At the same time, changes were made in appointments to senior religious and educational positions. These changes reached a scale close to a "generational change" in the senior ranks of the Saudi government.[37]

In late July, King Fahd replaced 157 of Saudi Arabia's senior officials. On August 2, 1995, he made the first sweeping changes in the Saudi cabinet in twenty years and replaced six members of the Majlis as-Shura. While the role of senior members of the royal family did not change, 16 of 28 cabinet members were replaced and two ministers swapped jobs.

These changes in the Cabinet affected high profile ministries like the Minister of Petroleum and Mineral Resources and the Ministry of Information. Hisham M. Nazer, the Minister of Petroleum and Mineral Resources, was replaced by Ali al-Naimi, a "new man," who was chairman of Aramco. Mohammed A. Aba al-Khayl, who had been Minister of Finance for 25 years, was replaced by Sulayman al-Sulayman, the Minister of Commerce. Other key ministries relating to the economy and social welfare services were replaced, including the ministers of Telecommunications and Electricity. These changes resulted in a cabinet which included 15 members with postgraduate degrees from Western universities.[38]

It is impossible for an outsider to determine the purpose or exact scale of these changes, many of which went far beyond the cabinet. It seems clear, however, that they reflected growing concern with the problems of dealing with Islamic extremism and finding jobs for Saudi Arabia's young population. They reflected a concern over the age and lack of flexibility of many Ministers and other officials, and their failure to control costs and expenditures, scale back projects, be far more demanding in planning its investments, and emphasize privatization.

One factor that almost certainly influenced the King's action was Saudi Arabia's 1995 budget deficit, which was rising well above the planned $4 billion—although oil revenues were nearly $2.3 billion higher than forecast during the first five months of the year, and King Fahd had asked ministers to propose new cost cutting measures on July 9, 1995.[39]

Demographics and Population Pressures

Saudi Arabia faces other internal problems that may ultimately be more important than the politics of its royal family. What was once a rural and isolated Saudi society, divided into regional and tribal groups, has become a society that is largely urbanized, exposed to a wide range of electronic media, and dependent on a modern petroleum driven economy. Virtually all children now receive education through the secondary school level. The CIA estimates that the once largely illiterate population has reached an overall literacy rate of 62% (73% for males), although the World Bank puts the literacy rate at only 52% for males and 38% for women.[40]

At the same time, Saudi Arabia is in the process of rapid demographic change. It has a population growth rate of 3.68%, and a fertility rate of 6.48 children per woman. Roughly 43% of Saudi Arabia's population is 14 years of age or younger, and more than 58% of the Kingdom's population is under the age of 17. As a result, approximately 164,000 native male citizens reach the military age of 17 each year.[41] Chart One shows how these trends have affected the Saudi population in recent years and the fact that population growth has already interacted with a decline in oil revenue to produce a serious cut in per capita income.

There is no way to estimate how quickly Saudi Arabia's population will grow. If Saudi Arabia's current growth rate continues, its population

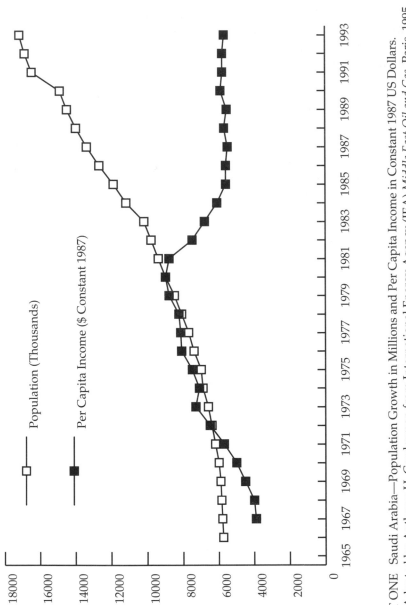

CHART ONE Saudi Arabia—Population Growth in Millions and Per Capita Income in Constant 1987 US Dollars.
Source: Adapted by Anthony H. Cordesman from International Energy Agency (IEA) *Middle East Oil and Gas,* Paris, 1995, pp. 305–309.

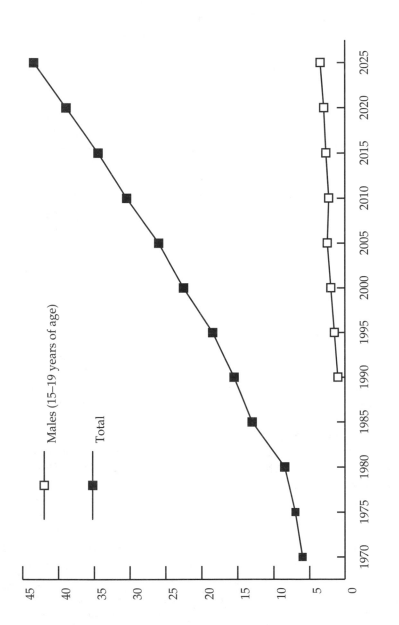

CHART TWO Estimated Trends in the Saudi Population During 1990–2035. *Source:* Adapted by Anthony H. Cordesman from World Bank, *World Population Projections, 1994–1995,* Washington, World Bank, 1994 and material provided by the CIA.

will reach 22 million in 2000, 26 million in 2005, 30 million in 2010, and 42 million in 2020. Even if Saudi Arabia's population growth rate can be cut back to a much more moderate 2%, its total population will reach 20 million in 2000, 22 million in 2005, 25 million in 2010, and 30 million in 2020.

Chart Two shows that a conservative World Bank estimate projects that Saudi Arabia's population will grow from 15.8 million in 1990, and 16.6 million in 1995, to 22.0 million by the year 2000, 25.8 million by 2005, 30.0 million by 2010, and 38.7 million by 2020.[42] There are few prospects that Saudi Arabia can prevent such growth. The "demographic momentum" of its existing youth will produce at least a generation of major future growth even if the birth rate drops. This population growth is also having a major impact on the Saudi budget. For example, the 1996 budget allocates 18% of its resources to education.[43]

Further, the fact that Saudi Arabia has such a young population means that the work force will grow at an especially high rate. The World Bank and ILO estimate that the annual growth rate of the working age population will rise from 3.06% per year in 1960–1975, and 3.51% in 1975–1990, to 3.91% during 1990–2010. This is the highest growth rate for the working-age population of any nation in the Middle East.[44] The World Bank also estimates that the total number of young Saudi men reaching job age (15–19 years) will rise from 789,000 in 1990 and 1.0 million in 1995 to 1.3 million in 2000, 1.5 million in 2010, 1.8 million in 2015, and 2.1 million in 2020.[45]

Saudi Arabia will only be able to cope with even the low estimates of population growth by instituting strong family-planning measures, privatizing and diversifying its economy far more rapidly than in the past, expanding oil production capacity to levels of 12 to 13 million barrels per day; developing far more comprehensive water planning, and eliminating virtually all foreign labor.

A combination of lower oil prices and population growth has already made major cuts in Saudi Arabia's per capita oil wealth. Studies by the World Bank estimate that the Saudi GDP dropped by an average of 3.3% per year during 1980–1992, almost solely as a result of cuts in oil prices. This, combined with population growth, reduced petroleum wealth per capita to a little over one-third of the peak level of the 1970s, and major reductions took place in the 1980s. According to US estimates, the Saudi GDP per capita in constant 1993 US dollars dropped from $13,060 in 1983 to $7,359 in 1993.[46]

Current projections indicate that petroleum wealth per capita will drop by another 50% by the year 2010 and possibly as soon as 2005. Although Saudi per capita income rose back to $9,510 in 1994, there is little prospect that oil prices will rise to the point where oil wealth alone will allow Saudi Arabia to meet the economic expectations of much of its youth, or to sustain the present living standards of many families.[47] Saudi Arabia will only be able to maintain current living standards if it achieves substantial growth in the productive sectors of the Saudi economy, and is able to change from reliance on a largely foreign labor force to one that is largely Saudi.

Islam and Secularism

Islamic extremism and secularism pose additional problems for Saudi Arabia. Saudi Arabia is an Islamic fundamentalist country, led by a conservative royal family and the descendants of Mohammed ibn Abdul Wahhab—a conservative and fundamentalist reformer who reshaped the worship and social practices of virtually all elements of Sunni society in the mid-1700s. This sometimes makes it difficult to distinguish between fundamentalism and extremism because the mainstream Wahhabi sect is so fundamentalist and conservative.

Many Saudi supporters of the current Islamic revival simply support a strict interpretation of Wahhabi doctrine and pose no threat to the regime. The same is true of most of the ulema, the senior scholars and interpreters of Islam. Both groups may oppose or challenge some aspects of secular changes and Western behavior, but they neither foment violence nor are in opposition to the Saudi government.

In contrast, most Islamic extremists are radicals or "Neo-Wahhabis," who oppose virtually all secular authority. They are strongly anti-Shi'ite and fear Judeo-Christian conspiracies against Islam. Such extremists had little organizational unity at first, but have gradually gathered substantial support in cities such as Buraida, and among the younger generation of Saudis. This support has proved to be particularly strong among Saudis who had only recently become urbanized, who lived in the Najd, and who lived outside the mainstream economy. Some extremists, however, are descendants of established families and are well-educated.

There is opposition from the opposite end of the political spectrum. The social and economic stresses in Saudi society have led to very different demands from some of Saudi Arabia's technocrats and businessmen. This class does not support a strict or extreme interpretation of Wahhabi doctrine. Its members have strongly supported the creation of a broad majlis and some support the creation of a national assembly. Some have also complained about nepotism and the abuse of power and legal rights by members of the royal family.

Many of Saudi Arabia's technocrats and businessmen support the liberalization of Wahhabi restraints on subjects such as commerce, the role of women, and social custom. Secular reformers have petitioned the King, and Saudi women made a brief protest for women's rights at the time of the Gulf War by driving their own cars. A few businessmen and secularly educated professionals have been arrested, or have had difficulties with the authorities, but such incidents are relatively rare and are considered only a minor problem for the government. As a result, the government has increasingly chosen to meet the demands of those who advocate Islamic extremism over those who advocate modernization.

Trying to Co-opt Islamic Extremism

Islamic extremism was a significant internal security problem long before the Gulf War, and caused a major uprising at the Grand Mosque in Mecca in 1979. Extremism has become far more serious, however, since the Gulf conflict. The presence of Western forces in Saudi Arabia gave new Islamic extremists reason to attack the "corrupt" Western influence over the Saudi government. Since that time, other factors have also fed the extremist cause.

Low oil prices and payments for the cost of the Gulf War have reduced both government welfare payments and the Saudi economy's ability to create new jobs while broadening the base of education and population growth has meant that younger Saudis have had to accept progressively less prestigious and well paid positions. Further, the conflict between secularism and religion has been fueled by the spread of over 300,000 satellite TV receivers in Saudi Arabia, and some 8 million VCRs. Western media is widely available, and many Saudis seem to see no contradiction between simultaneously watching such media and denouncing its influence.

These forces have led Islamic extremists to heighten their demands that Saudi Arabia conform to their particular definition of Islam. The Saudi royal family and Wahhabi leaders have increasingly become a target for those who wish to use Islam to serve their own ambitions. The Saudi government has responded by trying to defuse Islamic extremism by increasing official and popular adherence to strict religious law and custom, and by strengthening the role of the religious police. These efforts have sometimes helped win popular support—but each new accommodation of extremist demands has both strengthened the hands of extremists and caused resentment among the many Saudis who favor modernization.

In the process, the Saudi government has become linked to abuses of personal freedom which have little to do with orthodox Islam. It is turning a blind eye to the increasingly violent and rigid actions of the religious police or Mutawwa'in and related actions by the civil police. The Mutawwa'in have always been an artifact of Saudi Arabia's past—often going beyond religious custom to enforce arbitrary interpretations of religious law. Since the Gulf War, they have increasingly been allowed to abuse women and foreigners, and detain and sometimes beat and torture Saudi men. There have been many sudden raids of private homes on the basis of suspicion alone, and use has been made of "fallaqa," or beating the soles of the feet, and systematic beating of the body.

The Mutawwa'in have increasingly been allowed to detain suspects for more that the legal maximum of 24 hours for violations of behavior standards and there have been growing reports of sleep deprivation and torture. Although current procedures require a police officer to accompany the Mutawwa'in before the latter makes an arrest, this requirement is often ignored. A number of long-term foreign residents have attested that the Mutawwa'in are much more active in harassing individuals than a decade ago, and have become increasingly active since the Gulf War. The Saudi government has also increasingly tolerated civil interpretations of Shari'a—or Islamic law—that seem far more designed to appease religious extremists than to enforce the traditions of Islam.

More important, the government's efforts to co-opt Islamic extremism are compounding Saudi Arabia's demographic, modernization, and economic problems. Saudi Arabia's forms of Islamic extremism—like most forms of such extremism in the Moslem world—have the practical impact of encouraging students to pursue patterns of education for which there are no real jobs. They create the illusion that faith can substitute for economic realities and create serious problems in terms of investment and the modernization of the economy. They also present problems in terms of efforts to reduce the Saudi birth rate, make productive use of female labor, reduce dependence on foreign labor, encourage labor mobility among the natives of the GCC, and integrate the economy of the Southern Gulf. Like most forms of extremism, regression neither serves the purposes of religion or of realism.

The government has also tolerated a sharp decline in educational standards. The ulema have been allowed to increase their influence over the curriculum, and more and more students are encouraged to pursue Islamic studies which do not offer any career opportunities and increase the disaffection of Saudi youth. The futility of such education is exemplified by a glut of Ph.D.s in Islamic studies whose degrees are not taken seriously by Islamic scholars in other Arab countries and who have often become the opponent of the government that has educated them.[48]

Mixing Co-option with Repression

At the same time, no action the government takes within the limits imposed by orthodox Islam can hope to meet the demands of the more radical Islamic extremists. Religious fundamentalists like Sheik Safr al-Hawali illustrate this point. They have rejected King Fahd's reforms in a manner that poses a far more serious challenge to Saudi internal stability than any of the efforts of Saudi moderates. Even more mainstream religious leaders like Sheik Abdul Aziz ibn Baz—a venerated blind leader who has also publicly condemned the circulation of cassettes with Islamic fundamentalist messages—have opposed some of the government's efforts to suppress political opposition by the clergy.

This criticism reached the point in 1992, where 107 leading clerics signed a petition—or "Memorandum of Advice"—which called for the strict enforcement of Islamic law, severing relations with all non-Islamic countries and the West, and the punishment of all who gained wealth through illegal means, "whoever they are and without any exception of rank." This memorandum called for a majlis al-shura that was certain to be dominated by religious figures, a separate review body of ulema to review every state regulation and edict to ensure compliance with the Shari'a, the creation of a religious supreme court with the power to invalidate any law or treaty found to be in conflict with the Shari'a, and making the ulema a separate and co-equal branch of government with its own budget and sources of revenue.

The Saudi government responded to the memorandum by forcing other senior members of the ulema to condemn it, and by stepping up surveillance of the ulema by the security forces. Since that time, the government has steadily been forced to take more active measures to control Islamic extremists as well as attempt to coopt religious fundamentalism by supporting a far more rigid and conservative interpretation of Wahhabi law and custom.

In December, 1992, King Fahd dismissed seven elderly religious leaders from the Supreme Authority of Senior Scholars, the most senior clerical body in the country. This was in reaction to the fact that they would not join the other 10 members of the council in denouncing the "Memorandum of Advice." King Fahd also gave a speech in December, 1992 that attacked the use of mosques for political proselytizing. He stated that, "The pulpit was only made for certain limited things." He attacked the role of Iran and Islamic fundamentalists from other countries in supporting Islamic extremism:[49]

> Two years ago, we started seeing things unfamiliar to us that were non-existent here . . . Do we accept that somebody comes to us from outside our country and directs us? No. . . . Has it come to the point where we depend on criticism and cassette tapes that do us no good? . . . We should not follow the path of foreign currents, foreign to our country.

The Saudi government has since engaged in various actions designed to handicap extremist organizations. The first of these involved the imposition of limits on the funding of Islamic extremist movements overseas. Private and public Saudi money played a key role in supporting the Afghan freedom fighters in their struggle with the Soviet Union, and has recently aided the Muslims in Bosnia. At the same time, it has contributed to hard-line Islamic movements in Algeria, Egypt, Jordan, Tunisia and the Sudan—largely because the government made no effort to control the flow of private funds to charities and Islamic movements until late 1992. In April, 1993, the Interior Ministry required Islamic civic and religious groups to obtain government authorization before soliciting funds. The Ministry actively started to prevent the flow of funds to groups that may have used Islam as their rationale, but who sought political power— sometimes with Iranian and Sudanese support.[50]

It has proven virtually impossible, however, to control the flow of private spending outside Saudi Arabia. Many of the Saudis involved have large foreign investments, or handle large flows of transfers as part of their business. The government also cannot clearly identify which movements are legitimate religious efforts, and which are cover organizations for extremist movements. As a result, large cash transfers have continued. At least some Saudi religious extremists see funding movements outside the country as the best way of supporting opposition to the Saudi regime.[51]

In addition, the Saudi government has engaged in the systematic arrest of individuals suspected of supporting terrorists and extremists. In some cases, such as that involving Osama Bin Laden—the leader of the anti-American Advice and Reformation Committee—citizenship was revoked.[52] The government also arrested Sheik Salman al-Audah and Safr al-Hawali, two radical clerics, in 1994. Their detention incited a rare instance of open civil unrest in the northern city of Buraida which resulted in a large number of additional arrests.

These actions may have done more to drive the government's Islamic opposition underground than to suppress it. They have also led some extremists to change their tactics, and seek foreign support. The Committee for the Defense of Legitimate Rights (CDLR) is a good case in point. The CDLR was established in 1993 by six Saudi citizens. It is headed by Mohammed al-Mas'ari, a former physics professor whose interviews and writings indicate support for both fundamentalism and the far left, with little demonstrated regard for human rights or democracy except as a rhetorical device to achieve his goal of overthrowing the Saudi government.[53]

The CDLR claims in the West that it was formed for the purpose of supporting human rights and democracy in Saudi Arabia.[54] In fact, it supports an extreme interpretation of the Shari'a and Islamic custom, opposes most modern rights for women, has made strong anti-Shi'ite statements, opposes the Arab-Israeli peace process and denies Israel's right to exist. It does not advocate internationally recognized human rights but takes a rigidly Islamic fundamentalist approach.

The CDLR began to be treated as an extremist group after it openly criticized the Saudi government in the international press in 1993. The security forces detained 38 of its members, including Al-Mas'ari, confiscated their passports, and forbade them to travel or speak publicly. Al-Mas'ari was released in November 1993, but only after spending 6 months in detention. The security forces subsequently released the rest of the detainees, but only after they signed statements promising not to discuss the Government's policies or communicate with anyone outside the country by telephone or facsimile machine. The authorities also dismissed several founding members of the CDLR from their government jobs.[55]

In 1994, Al-Mas'ari secretly fled to the United Kingdom, where he sought political asylum and established an overseas branch of the CDLR. He then continued to disseminate tracts critical of the Saudi government from the UK. He was particularly critical of King Fahd, the Interior Minister Prince Naif, and the governor of Riyadh, Prince Salman. He continued to express opposition to peace with Israel and to Saudi support for the peace process. He also expressed the CDLR's "understanding" of the National Guard headquarters bombing in 1995.

After Al-Mas'ari fled to England, the Saudi security forces arrested 15 to 20 of his relatives and supporters. The Saudi government released several of these detainees in late 1994, including Dr. Fouad Dahlawi, Al-Mas'ari's brother, Lu'ay Al-Mas'ari, and Al-Mas'ari's brothers-in-law, Rashad and Nabil Al-Mudarris. However, the government did not publicly acknowledge any such detention of CDLR supporters until 1995.

The government announced in August 1995, that it had executed Abdullah Bin Abd Al-Rahman Al-Hidaif for assaulting a security official with acid. It also sentenced one Saudi man to five years in prison in part for possessing leaflets and posters mentioning the CDLR, and another to three years in prison for attending meetings in support of the group and its exiled spokesman, Mohammad Al-Mas'ari. Both were associates of Abdullah Bin Abd Al-Rahman Al-Hidaif.[56] The Saudi government also began to put intense pressure on the British government to expel Al-Mas'ari and the CDLR from England, threatening it with trade restrictions and cutbacks on arms purchases. This effort ultimately failure, however, after Al-Mas'ari appealed to the British courts.[57]

The CDLR has made repeated claims that more than 300 clerics are currently detained for political reasons, but such detentions are impossible to confirm. The US State Department indicates that Saudi authorities continue to detain Salman Al-Awdah and Safar Al-Hawali, the Muslim clerics arrested in September, 1994 for criticizing the Government. At the end of 1994, the government also still detained 27 men pending investigations out of the 157 persons arrested for antigovernment activities in October, 1994. The Saudi government did not announce the release of any of those detainees during the year, and thousands of prisoners and detainees released in February 1995 under the annual Ramadan amnesty did not include any political dissidents.[58]

Islamic Extremists Turn to Violence

Islamic extremist groups have begun to respond to the government with violence. On November 13, 1995, a 150–225 pound bomb placed in a pickup truck exploded outside the building housing the headquarters of the US Army Materiel Command's Office of the Program Manager for the Saudi National Guard. OPM is a program which provides training support to the National Guard. The blast killed seven people, including five Americans, and wounded 60 others, of which 37 were American. The timing of the bomb indicated that it might have been directed primarily at Americans. It was detonated at 11:30 A.M. when most Saudis would be at prayer and off the streets and none of the 67 casualties were Saudi citizens.[59]

An extremist group called Movement for Islamic Change in the Arabian Peninsula-Jihad Wing claimed responsibility, as did two previously unknown groups calling themselves the Tigers of the Gulf and the Combatant Partisans of God. All demanded the immediate withdrawal of US troops from Saudi Arabia. The Combatant Partisans of God also demanded the release of Sheik Omar Abdel-Rahman and Mousa Abu Marzouk from US custody. The CDLR, which indicated it had never heard of these groups, officially condemned the attack, but al-Mas'ari's equivocation in commenting on the bombing prompted the British government to order his expulsion.[60]

While Western and Saudi sources had no information on two of the groups claiming responsibility, the third group, the Movement for Islamic Change, had sent two previous warnings to the US Embassy in Riyadh in April and June, 1995, via fax. The statements demanded a withdrawal of all US forces from the Kingdom by July, 1995. Receipt of the faxes was admitted after the bombing by US Ambassador Raymond E. Mabus, who indicated that they were not taken seriously enough because, "of all the places in the world, [Saudi Arabia] was deemed one of the safest."[61] A review of the faxes also revealed phrases which suggested that the group adhered to mainstream Sunni beliefs and was likely to be indigenous to Saudi Arabia.

The bombing was the first such attack on Western military forces in Saudi Arabia since 1991, when two Americans were wounded in an attack on a shuttle bus in Jeddah, and it clearly stunned both American and Saudi officials.[62] The Saudi government also was initially unwilling to publicly acknowledge the possible involvement of indigenous opposition groups. In a letter-to-the-editor in 1995, the Saudi ambassador to the US, Bandar Bin Sultan Bin Abdulaziz, declared that "dissidents did not cause the car bombing."[63] These public denials were partly the result of a Saudi belief that acts this violent had to be the acts of foreign groups and partly the result of an effort to discourage indigenous groups from copy cat incidents. They also were affected by US intelligence reports of increased surveillance of US installations by Iranian agents prior to the attack.[64]

Nevertheless, the investigation by the Ministry of the Interior focused on both foreign and indigenous opponents of the regime, and Saudis inside and outside the country. The Saudi authorities sorted through the files of some 15,000 known Saudi "Afghanis" and Islamic extremists. Shortly after the blast, the Saudis released a sketch of one suspect and the Saudi and US governments offered a $3 million reward for information regarding those responsible. The US assisted by providing technical expertise, and dispatched 19 FBI investigators and two State Department security officials to the site of the bombing within days after it occurred.

The first arrests indicated that Saudis outside Saudi Arabia might be involved. On February 1, 1995, Pakistan extradited an individual believed to match the sketch, a Saudi national named Hassan Sarai, at the request of the Saudi government. Sarai was known to have fought with Islamic groups in Afghanistan in the early 1990s and to have supported Islamic militants in India's Kashmir region.

However, Sarai was not charged with the attack. Instead, the Saudi government arrested four Saudis living in Saudi Arabia, and broadcast their confessions on April 22, 1996. The four men were Abdulaziz Fah Nasser, Riyadh Harji, Muslih Shamrani, and Khalid Ahmed Said. The Interior Ministry announced that three of the four men were Saudi Islamic extremists that had joined the mujahideen forces fighting in Afghanistan in the late 1980s, and the fourth had fought in Bosnia. They had smuggled in the explosives from Yemen, and had at least some ties to the Islamic Group in Egypt.

The four men had planned a much more extensive series of kidnappings and assassinations, but had given up their plans because they feared they would be caught as a result of the massive step up in security measures following the bombing. The Interior Ministry did issue press releases that vaguely linked the four men to a foreign power or foreign group, but US experts indicated they had only vague ties to the CDLR, and were influenced by Mas'ari and Osama ibn Laden, rather than any foreign movement.[65]

These arrests do not seem likely to halt further violence, and the consequences good be serious for the US as well as Saudi Arabia. The success of the bombing demonstrated the vulnerability of targets within the Kingdom to terrorist acts and there currently are some 30,000 Americans living in Saudi Arabia, many of whom are easy targets for terrorists.

In December, 1995, the US Embassy released a statement in which it said it had "unconfirmed information that additional bombings may be planned against Western interests in Saudi Arabia, including facilities and commercial centers occupied and/or frequented by Americans."[66] A similar statement was released by the State Department on January 31, 1995, a week prior to a scheduled visit by Secretary of State Warren Christopher to Saudi Arabia. The visit was subsequently canceled, ostensibly due to scheduling conflicts, but possibly because of the terrorist threats.[67] On March 29, 1996, Saudi border guards intercepted a new shipment of explosives at the Jordanian border. The possibility of additional attacks has also prompted concern by corporate contractors in Saudi Arabia as to the safety of their employees and dependents.[68] New anonymous threats were made against Americans in May, 1996, and the US Embassy asked Americans living in Saudi Arabia to keep a "low profile."[69]

At the same time, there is a very real danger that the Saudi government may overreact in its treatment of legitimate critics who do not support the extremists, but who want a more participatory form of government with a greater emphasis on human rights. The arrests of religious figures, academics and staff members at King Saud University prior to the bombing illustrated a lack of discrimination by the government regarding peaceful, legitimate critics, and extremists.[70]

Ethnic, Sectarian, and Regional Frictions

Ethnic, sectarian and regional frictions present still further problems. There are ethnic and religious tensions between some Sunni and Shi'ites in the Eastern Province. There is regional friction between secular moderates in the coastal cities and conservative Wahhabis in the Najd, and between the Shafii and Shi'ite immigrants in the Hejaz. In addition, there is a heritage of tension between the followers of Ibn Saud in the Najd and the north and the citizens of the Hejaz around Mecca and Medina, which date back to the time the Sauds drove the Hashemites into exile.[71] These tensions are compounded by the different application of Sunni law in different parts of Saudi Arabia, and by a variety of tribal resentments and feuds which date back to the rise of Ibn Saud.

The divisions between Sunni and Shi'ite are particularly important in terms of their impact on Saudi internal security. Although Shi'ites make up only about 5–6% (500,000) of Saudi Arabia's total population, a substantial part of the native population of the oil-rich Eastern Province is Arab Shi'ite—possibly as much as 40%.[72] Since the late 1970s, the Saudi government has tried to deal with the Shi'ite problem by improving economic and educational opportunities, and by coopting Shi'ite leaders rather than repressing them. The regime has done reasonably well in providing a mix of personal incentives and internal security controls. It has limited its past use of police power, particularly the sudden search of Shi'ite homes, and has appointed one Shi'ite as a member of the Majlis as Shura. However, Sunni Islamic fundamentalism has acted as a counterbalancing force to the government's efforts that has increased Shi'ite resentment, and the government has increasingly restricted the jobs open to Shi'ites in an effort to reduce any Shi'ite threat to key petroleum and economic facilities.

Although the Shi'ite population is too small to succeed in any kind of uprising or separatism, it is large enough to present a significant source of social tension in the world's most important oil producing area. There have been recurrent, minor incidents of sabotage of oil facilities. There are cells of radical Shi'ites in the Eastern Province that have obtained some support from Iran. There have also been occasional incidents between Shi'ite groups and the government. It is clear that constant, targeted efforts will be required to improve the status of Shi'ites in the Eastern province if the Saudi government is to avoid more serious moves towards separatism.[73]

Reform in Saudi Politics

It is easy to demand that Saudi Arabia deal with the problems in Saudi politics and society by copying the West. In practice, however, any effort at instant reform would be destabilizing and impractical, and any effort at rapid democratization would be more likely to result in "one man, one vote, one time" than progressive social change. Saudi Arabia's complex mixture of ultra-conservative Islam, population and sectarian problems, regional divisions, and a centralized monarchy supported by a modern technocracy is anything but easy to change and peaceful change requires the evolution of a uniquely Saudi form of government.

At the same time, the Saudi government's present approach to change is often more regressive than evolutionary. The Saudi royal family often seems to be in a state of denial in dealing with critical problems or moves so slowly that the growth problem outpaces the impact of the chosen solution. To be specific, there are several areas where reform is needed to cope with current trends:

- The leadership of the royal family needs to set clear limits to the future benefits members of the royal family receive from the state and to phase out special privileges and commissions. It needs to transfer all revenues from oil and gas to the state budget, and to ensure that princes obey the rule of law and are not seen as "corrupt" or abusing the powers of the state. The royal family already has the wealth to do this, and it does not take much vision to see that the Saudi monarchy cannot give 15,000 princes the same rights and privileges it once gave several thousand.
- The Majlis al-Shura needs to be steadily expanded in power, and in regional and sectarian representation, to provide a more representative form of government. The Majlis has made a good beginning, but it needs younger members, members that are moderate critics of the royal family, and some Shi'ites that are permitted to speak for this ethnic group. It needs to play a more direct role in reviewing the Saudi budget, and its debates need to be more open and reported in the media. It may be some years before Saudi Arabia is ready for an elected Majlis or National Assembly, but the Saudi government needs to be more open and some body other than the royal family needs to be seen as playing a major role in decision-making. The present closed, over-centralized process of government breeds extremist opposition.
- The Saudi royal family and government needs to face the fact that Saudi oil wealth is limited and that Saudi Arabia faces a potential demographic crisis. Strong leadership is needed to persuade the Wahhabi ulema that voluntary population control is needed and Saudi families that they should limit their number of children. There needs to be a firm understanding that even the best economic development plan cannot maintain the present standard of real per capita wealth in Saudi Arabia without a sharper decline in the birth rate and that population growth is a major factor affecting political stability.
- The Saudi royal family and government, as well as all educated Saudis, need to start asking existential questions about the future of Saudi society and the role of young Saudis in that society. Even today, most educated Saudi women face a dead end at the end of their education and most Saudi young men graduate into purposeless jobs that offer little real future or productive value to the economy. The impact of Saudi demographics on Saudi society and the Saudi job market is disguised by the fact that half of the population is still under 18 and living with an extended family. With the next half decade, however, something like 20% of the present native population will leave home and will have no where to go. Only radical

efforts to stimulate the private sector and remove foreign labor can begin to deal with this problem.

- At the same time, these same demographic pressures illustrate why the government cannot succeed in dealing with Islamic extremism by a combination of accommodating the most fundamental and regressive Wahhabi practices while forcibly repressing Islamic extremists who actively criticize the government. These policies are dragging Saudi Arabia back into a past that cannot be viable in the future and which makes the problems young Saudis face in finding rewarding careers and a valid place in society even more difficult. The Saudi royal family and government need to face the problem of social alienation and religion much more directly, and push for slow but steady reform. They need to face the fact that the present cost of such efforts at change is likely to be much lower than waiting and relying on the present policy.

- It is unrealistic and impractical for Saudi Arabia to attempt to adopt Western standards of human rights, and the West needs to be careful not to be trapped into supporting the efforts of Islamic extremists who claim to advocate human rights and democracy as a way of attacking the Saudi regime. At the same time, Saudi Arabia does need to accept the need to give Saudi Shi'ites a special religious status and proper economic rights, emphasize the protections of the individual already granted under Saudi law, and sharply rein in the growing abuses of the religious police. The government must reestablish public faith in the Saudi legal process and the rule of law.

Saudis often quite correctly criticize Western analysts for demanding that Saudi Arabia become a mirror image of the West. At the same time, it seems valid to criticize the Saudi royal family and government for being far too slow to react to the seriousness of some of Saudi Arabia's problems and for ignoring the lessons of the past. The Saudi monarchy may not want to adopt Western democracy, but it should pay close attention to the mistakes that helped cause the fall of many Western monarchies as well as those of other Arab states.

4

Economic and Social Issues

Saudi Arabia faces important challenges in funding a level of social services and economic development which will ensure that all regional groups receive a share of the nation's oil wealth and operate within a "safety net" that defuses or reduces social protest. Even "oil wealth" is relative, and must be measured in terms of per capita income, national imports, and government spending—not simply total export earnings or the size of a nation's total oil reserves.

In recent years, Saudi Arabia has maintained much higher levels of public spending than its revenues justify. Until recently, it has kept up its spending on domestic and public services, and military forces, at the cost of growing budget deficits. The rapid increase in Saudi Arabia's population has also meant a steady reduction in its per capita GDP and oil exports, and is imposing growing limits on what Saudi Arabia can afford to spend per person on subsidies and its social "safety net." Like the other Southern Gulf states, Saudi Arabia has tended to minimize deep structural problems in its economy that are not "temporary" or a function of short-term oil prices.

There are many different estimates of the trends in the Saudi economy, although most agree in terms of broad trends. Table One provides a short term picture of the Saudi economy, as estimated by the Economist Intelligence Unit. It shows the importance of oil exports to the Saudi economy, the dependence of the Saudi GDP on oil revenues, and one estimate of Saudi Arabia's budget deficits.

The CIA estimates that the Saudi Arabia's GDP had a purchasing power equivalent of $173.1 billion in 1994. Industrial production, including oil and gas, accounted for 35% of the GDP and had an annual sectoral growth rate of 20% in 1994 because of a rise in oil prices. Saudi Arabia's exports were worth $39.4 billion. Roughly 92% of these earnings came from exports of crude oil, gas and petroleum products. In contrast, Saudi Arabia had roughly $28.9 billion worth of civil imports, with 21% coming from the US, 14% from Japan, 11% from the UK, 8% from Germany, 6%

TABLE ONE Key Economic Indicators in Saudi Arabia

	1990	1991	1992	1993	1994	1995
Production (1,000s of barrels per day)	6413	8118	8332	8048	8049	8010
Oil Exports (millions of barrels per year)	1947	2668	2883	2699	2647	—
Average Oil Export Price (per barrel)	20.61	16.73	16.75	14.30	14.09	—
Oil Export Receipts ($US current billions)	40.1	43.7	46.5	38.6	37.4	—
GDP ($US current billions)	102.8	116.2	120.7	116.0	120.1	125.2
Per Capita GDP ($US current)	6330	7074	7146	6666	6558	—
Annual Change in Per Capita GDP (%)	-2.8	8.7	-0.2	-0.7	-3.1	—
Total Government Revenue ($US current billions)	—	84.0*	45.29	37.75	34.44	—
Total Government Expenditures ($US current billions)	—	122.6*	56.42	50.17	45.69	—
Budget Balance ($US current billions)	—	-37.6	-11.1	-12.4	-11.2	—
Budget Deficit as a Percentage of GDP	—	-17.2	-9.2	-10.7	-7.0	—

*Saudi Arabia combines data for 1991 and 1992 because of the special circumstances of the Gulf War.
Source: Adapted by Wayne A. Larsen, NSSP, Georgetown University, from the EIU, Country Profile, Saudi Arabia, 1995–1996, pp. 54, 55–56, 62, and Middle East Economic Digest, April 5, 1996, p. 30.

from the US, 14% from Japan, 11% from the UK, 8% from Germany, 6% from Italy, and 5% from France.

Chart Three shows a US estimate of the longer term trends in the Saudi GDP, central government spending, and Saudi military spending. The trend data in Chart Three are measured in constant 1993 dollars, and reflect the same dip in the real value of the Saudi GDP that occurred in the GDP of virtually all oil exporting states. They also reflect the fact that Saudi economic growth virtually stagnated after a decline in oil prices and production in 1991. Real GDP growth dropped from 10.8% in 1990 and 9.8% in 1991, to 5.0% in 1992, 1.0% in 1993, and 0.6% in 1994—although Saudi Arabia claimed a growth in GDP of 4% in 1994.[74]

These trends scarcely mean that Saudi Arabia is poor. Chart Three has a positive side as well as a negative one. It shows that Saudi Arabia was able to make major increases in oil export revenues as a result of the Gulf War—which increased both prices and Saudi Arabia's share of the market. It also shows that Saudi Arabia has sharply cut central government expenditures as a share of total GDP since the mid-1980s—although this has not prevented sustained budget deficits.

Saudi Arabia is seeking to improve its rate of growth. Its Sixth Five Year Plan seeks to increase the Saudi GDP from 380.8 billion Saudi Rials in 1995 to 458.6 billion Rials in 2000, and to maintain an average annual growth rate of 3.8%. If the plan is successful, the non-oil sector will grow from 235.9 billion Saudi Rials in 1995 to 285.1 billion Rials in 2000, and to maintain an average annual growth rate of 3.9%. The government services portion of the non-oil sector will grow from 66.4 billion Saudi Rials to 75.8 billion, an average annual growth rate of 2.7%. The private sector portion of the non-oil sector will grow from 169.5 billion Saudi Rials to 209.3 billion, an average annual growth rate of 4.3%. The oil sector will grow from 142.8 billion Saudi Rials to 172.5 billion, and by an average annual growth rate of 3.8%. These targets are ambitious, and heavily dependent on the kind of higher oil revenues that Saudi Arabia received in 1994 and 1995, but they are possible.[75]

Even if Saudi Arabia does achieve these goals, however, it will not change the fact that Saudi Arabia is experiencing growing financial and social strains. The 1991 Persian Gulf War left the country with an estimated $55 billion debt. Saudi Arabia will require as much as $30 billion in foreign loans over the next three years to cover the short-term portion of this debt. Saudi Arabia sustained large current account deficits in the early 1990s, and official reserves fell from $23 billion in 1987 to only $7.4 billion in December, 1994. In spite of increases in oil prices and export revenues in 1995, Saudi Arabia still had a $450 million deficit on current account in 1995, and an estimated deficit of $350 million for 1996.[76]

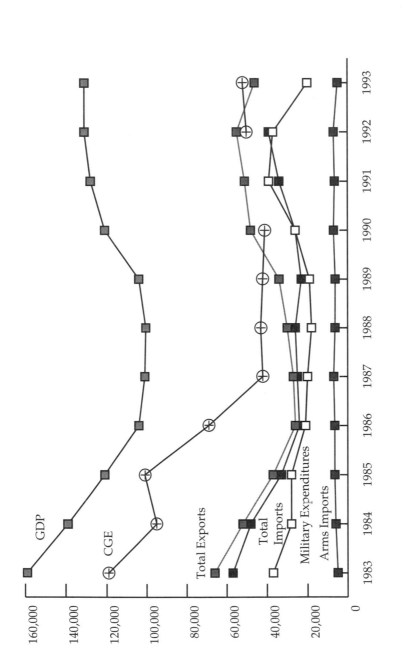

CHART THREE Saudi Gross Domestic Product, Central Government Expenditures, Military Expenditures, Total Exports, Total Imports, and Arms Import Deliveries—1983–1993 (Constant $93 Millions). *Source:* Adapted by Anthony H. Cordesman from ACDA, *World Military Expenditures and Arms Transfers, 1993–1994,* ACDA/GPO, Washington, 1995.

At the same time, a combination of population increases and low oil prices has reduced Saudi Arabia's GDP per capita. Studies by the World Bank indicate that Saudi Arabia's GDP per capita dropped by an average of 3.3% per year during 1980–1992.[77]

Saudi Arabia has experienced budget deficits in each of the last twelve years. Deficit levels grew from 6.4 percent of gross domestic product (GDP) in 1990 to nine percent of GDP in 1993, forcing the government to make cuts in expenditures. This resulted in a 1994 budget plan calling for a 19 percent cut in government spending, from $52.5 billion in 1993 to $42.7 billion in 1994. This was followed by the 1995 budget plan which, based on an underlying oil price assumption of $14.00-$14.50 per barrel, called for an additional cut of 6.25% in spending.

A unexpected rise in average oil prices to $15.50 per barrel made these cuts in the deficit earlier in 1995. A combination of austerity measures and higher oil revenues reduced Saudi Arabia's deficit to 4.1% of GDP in 1995 and this level is projected to remain unchanged for 1996. The budget deficit itself, however, is expected to grow by 19% from the 1995 level, to $4.9 billion. The budget plan for 1996 also maintains the 1995 level and does not call for additional cuts in expenditures.[78]

In the past, Saudi Arabia has done a better job of distributing oil wealth, modernizing education and infrastructure, encouraging the private sector, and providing new job opportunities than most developing nations. Its persistent budget deficits and dependency on volatile oil prices, however, are warnings of growing structural problems in the Saudi economy. They are also a warning that its past policy of using a large portion of the nation's oil wealth to minimize internal tensions and religious friction cannot continue indefinitely.

Over-Dependence on Oil Wealth

The Saudi government has made efforts to reduce Saudi Arabia's dependence on oil wealth, but the petroleum sector still accounts for about 90% of all Saudi export revenues, 75–85% of all budget revenues and 53% of the Saudi GDP. Other activity accounts for 35% of GDP, but virtually all of this percentage is petroleum oriented and more than 55% of Saudi capital investment still goes to oil and petrochemicals. While agriculture accounts for up to 10% of the GDP, it only does so because of vast government subsidies and the waste of irreplaceable "fossil" well water.[79] The new Saudi Sixth Five Year plan, which covers the period from 1996–2000, seems unlikely to achieve a significant change in this situation.[80]

Chart Four shows the distribution of economic activity with Saudi Arabia's GDP, and it is important to note that the decline in the share of

52

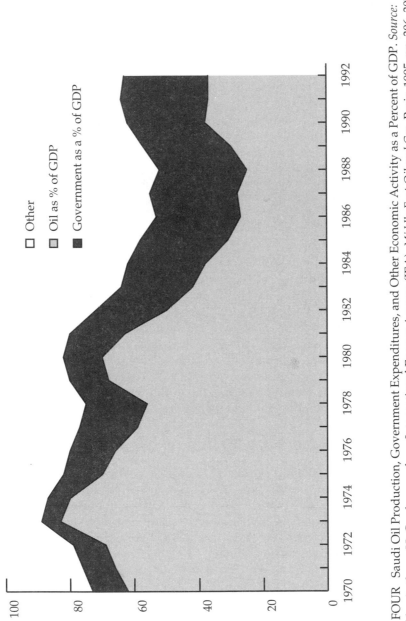

CHART FOUR Saudi Oil Production, Government Expenditures, and Other Economic Activity as a Percent of GDP. *Source:* Adapted by Anthony H. Cordesman from International Energy Agency (IEA), *Middle East Oil and Gas*, Paris, 1995, pp. 306–307, based on SAMA, *Annual Reports.*

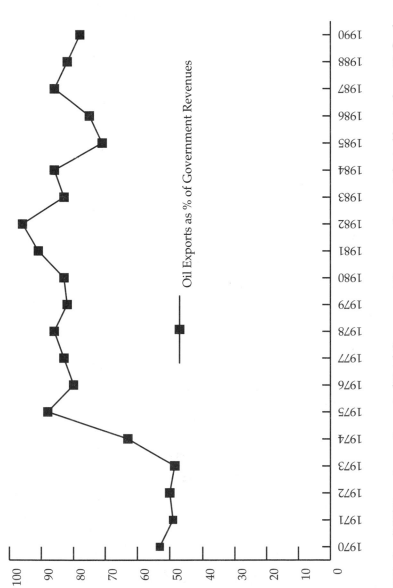

CHART FIVE Saudi Oil Exports as a Percent of Total Government Revenues. *Source:* Adapted by Anthony H. Cordesman from International Energy Agency (IEA), *Middle East Oil and Gas*, Paris, 1995, pp. 320–321, based on SAMA, *Annual Reports.*

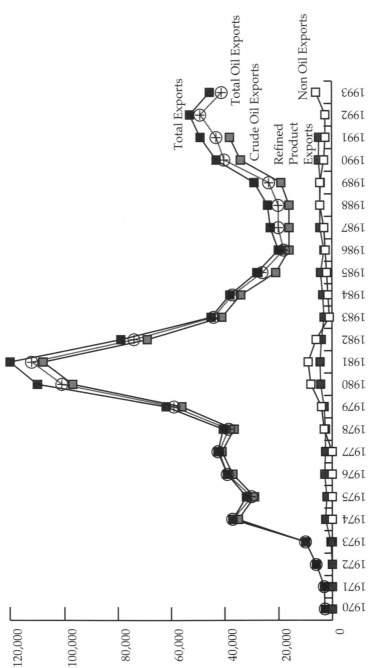

CHART SIX Saudi Oil Exports Relative to Total Exports in $Current Millions. *Source:* Adapted by Anthony H. Cordesman from International Energy Agency (IEA), *Middle East Oil and Gas,* Paris, 1995, pp. 316–318, based on SAMA, *Annual Reports* and OPEC, *Annual Statistical Bulletin.*

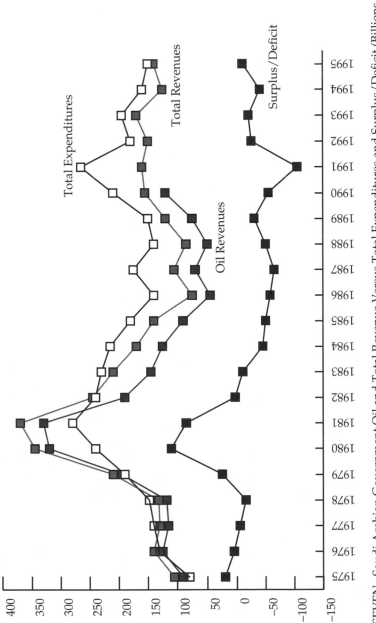

CHART SEVEN Saudi Arabian Government Oil and Total Revenue Versus Total Expenditures and Surplus/Deficit (Billions of Current Rials). *Source:* Adapted by Anthony H. Cordesman from International Energy Agency (IEA), *Middle East Oil and Gas,* Paris, 1995, pp. 256–257, based on data from SAMA, *Annual Report* and *Statistical Summary* and *Middle East Economic Survey,* January 9, 1995.

the oil sector in this chart is largely artificial. It occurs because of the rising share of government activity relating to subsidies, welfare, and defense spending, which simply represents the internal recycling of oil revenues. Similarly, other activity has not only included highly subsidized agriculture but a wide range of non-competitive, offset activity subsidized by government expenditures or out-of-oil export income, and service activity which consists largely of businesses that sell imports and services funded through oil exports. In other words, the apparent growing diversity of the Saudi economy is often more a function of how Saudi Arabia reports its statistics than substance.

Chart Five reinforces this point. It shows that Saudi government expenditures are still financed largely by oil exports and that the Saudi government share of the GDP is funded largely by oil. Similarly, Chart Six shows that virtually all of Saudi Arabia's exports are petroleum related and that Saudi Arabia is only making moderate progress in moving into downstream operations. This is particularly important because Saudi Arabia has few natural resources other than oil. Finally, Chart Seven shows that the Saudi economy became overly dependent on oil-funded imports during the oil boom of the late 1970s and early 1980s, and that this problem became even more serious when Saudi Arabia had to pay for much of the Gulf War.

These charts also show that Saudi oil revenues are highly market-dependent and this can lead to major fluctuations in the Saudi economy. While estimates differ in terms of specific numbers, there is little disagreement over the broad trends involved. According to a typical source, Saudi oil revenues reached a peak of $133 billion a year in 1981, and dropped to $46 billion in 1983. These swings in oil revenues were particularly acute at the end of the 1980s. Saudi oil revenues only averaged around $19 billion to $25 billion from 1984–1988, about one fifth of their 1981 level, and Saudi financial reserves dropped to as little as one-third of their 1981 level of $190 billion.[81] Oil revenues rose to $28.3 billion in 1989, or about 85%–90% of all exports. Sharper rises occurred in 1990 and 1991 because of the Gulf War, but this new burst of oil wealth was more than consumed by the cost of the war and aid to the US and other Saudi allies.

Oil prices and oil revenues then dropped sharply in 1992 and 1993, and remained low in 1994. Saudi Arabia's estimated oil revenues totaled about $33-$35.3 billion in 1995. The higher side of this estimate reflects the fact that oil revenues were 20% higher in the first six months of 1995 than Saudi Arabia originally projected. Even the revised total, however, compares unfavorably with about $111 billion in 1981 from exports of 9 MMBD and $73 billion in 1992 from exports of 5.6 MMBD.[82] Further, oil price projections by OPEC, IEA, and EIA all agree that Saudi Arabia's real oil revenues are highly unlikely to rise back to their past levels in the fore-seeable future.

Chart Seven shows that the cut in oil revenues and Saudi expenditures for the Gulf War have also had a significant impact on Saudi Arabia's trade balance. During the late 1980s the Kingdom's current account deficits ranged from $4.1 billion to $9.8 billion. This figure increased dramatically from $4.2 billion in 1990 to $27.6 billion in 1991. Since that time, the deficit has slowly dropped to $17.8 billion in 1992, $17.3 billion in 1993, $9.1 billion in 1994, and $6.7 billion in 1995. Saudi Arabia has issued forecasts for 1996 that project the value of non-oil exports to be 42% higher than in 1994, and major further reductions in, or near elimination of, Saudi Arabia's current account deficit. It now seems more likely, however, that such projections are unrealistic, and involve an impractical austerity in Saudi imports. Other sources project at least a $5.5 billion deficit for 1996.[83]

As has been discussed earlier, Saudi Arabia is seeking to change this situation and achieve more stable growth during the Sixth Five Year plan period of 1996–2000. The plan, however, only calls for the oil and gas sector to increase from 27% of the GDP in 1990, and 32.9% in 1995, to 33.8% in 2000.[84] This is scarcely a high degree of diversification and the five year plan already seems certain to fall short of most of its goals for 1996.

The plan calls for an average level of 4.2% growth in the producing sectors and 4.4% growth in the service sectors. Meeting these goals requires a 3.4% annual increase in private sector investment, and a 5.5% annual growth in government investment. Annual private investment must rise from 176.9 billion Saudi Rials in 1995 to 126.5 billion in 2000, and government investment must rise from 273.5 billion Saudi Rials in 1995 to 335.5 billion in 2000.[85] The government services share of total investment must rise from 18.1% in 1995 to 25.0% in 2000, and much of the producing sector investment in manufacturing must go to government-run petroleum refining and petrochemical activity. This shift in investment scarcely represents rapid "privatization" and it is highly dependent on improved oil revenues. It scarcely seems to meet the plan's goal of increasing the role of the private non-oil sector, which remains at almost exactly the same 10% share of the economy today as it had in 1990.[86]

There are a number of other reasons to be cautious about whether the new plan can really meet Saudi needs. The Sixth Five Year plan calls for reductions in the past level of subsidies to water-intensive agriculture, but still calls for a 3.1% increase in output and for agriculture to increase from 36.9% of the non-oil GDP in 1990, and 38.3% in 1995, to 40.2% in 2000. It is difficult to see how this growth can be economical. The growth in the service sector is highly dependent on import-related income and leaves the share of government services in 2000 (24.0%) at a level very close to that in 1990 (25.8%).

These problems help explain why the IMF Article IV report for Saudi Arabia, issued in September 1995, paints a very different picture of the Saudi economy. This reports indicates that Saudi Arabia may run a net deficit on current account of $8 billion to $10 billion through the year 2000, that its domestic debt will rise from 77% of GDP in 1994 to 110% in the year 2000, and its annual budget deficit will rise from 23 billion Saudi Rials in 1995 to 52 billion Rials in 2000.[87]

Growing Pressure on the Saudi Budget

Oil revenue problems began to put pressure on the Saudi budget even before the Gulf War. Saudi Arabia's FY1988 budget was projected at 141.2 billion Rials ($37.7 billion), down 17% from the 1987 level of 170 billion Rials. Oil revenues were unofficially projected at 65.2 billion Rials. The 1988 deficit was projected at 35.9 billion Rials ($9.57 billion) versus deficits of about 50 billion Rials in each of the previous four years.

Saudi Arabia sought to reduce this deficit through 12–20% import duties, and local borrowing in the form of some $8 billion in bonds.[88] If it had not been for Iraq's invasion of Kuwait, these measures might have reduced Saudi Arabia's budget deficits, but the cost of the Gulf War made the situation much worse. Although Saudi oil revenues rose, Saudi Arabia had to spend nearly $65 billion on the costs of the crisis, ranging from payments to members of the UN Coalition to expenses for the Saudi military and refugee housing. Estimates of these costs differ, but the IMF puts them at around $65 billion, of which $12.8 billion was paid to the United States.[89]

The resulting impact on the Saudi budget is shown in Table Two and Chart Eight, although these figures omit a portion of Saudi Arabia's extraordinary expenditures on the Gulf War. If these additional expenditures were included, the Saudi fiscal deficit might have reached $37 billion during 1990–1991, and $10 billion during 1992. The war made Saudi financial management so uncertain that Saudi Arabia was forced to adopt a working budget for 1991 because it could not keep track of its expenditures. It then had to raise its estimated 1992 expenditures by 27% over the 1990 budget to allow for unanticipated costs.[90]

Chart Nine shows that Saudi Arabia also experienced a drastic drop in liquidity because of both the cut in its oil revenues and its expenditures for the Gulf War. It had to borrow some $7 billion, $4.5 billion from internationally syndicated loans and $2.5 billion from local banks. This need to borrow while paying interest created new tensions with Saudi Arabia's Islamic fundamentalists—who believe that interest is forbidden by the

TABLE TWO   Saudi Arabia's Annual Budgets

Fiscal Year	Revenues		Expenditures		Deficit	
	B Rials	*B $US*	*B Rials*	*B $US*	*B Rials*	*B $US*
Actual						
1990	118	31.5	143	38.1	−25	−6.7
1991*	118	31.5	143	38.1	−25	−6.7
1992	151	40.3	181	48.3	−30	−8.0
1993	169	45.1	197	52.5	−27.8	−7.4
1994	120	32.0	160	42.7	−40	−10.7
1995	135	36.0	150	40.0	−15	−4.0
Estimated						
1996	131.5	35.07	150	40	−18.5	−4.9
1997	159	42.4	182	48.5	−24	−6.4
1998	165	44.0	189	50.4	−24	−6.4

Note: 3.75 Saudi Rials = $1.

*Major off-budget expenditures to finance Gulf War.

Source: Data for 1990–1995 are adapted from data provided in the monthly newsletter of the Information Office, Royal Embassy of Saudi Arabia, Volume 12, Number 2, February, 1995, p. 3. Data for 1996–1998 has been adapted from IMF Article IV report 1994, *Middle East Economic Digest,* "Special Report: Saudi Arabia," March 10, 1995, pp. 25–48 and *Middle East Economic Digest,* January 12, 1996, pp. 15–16.

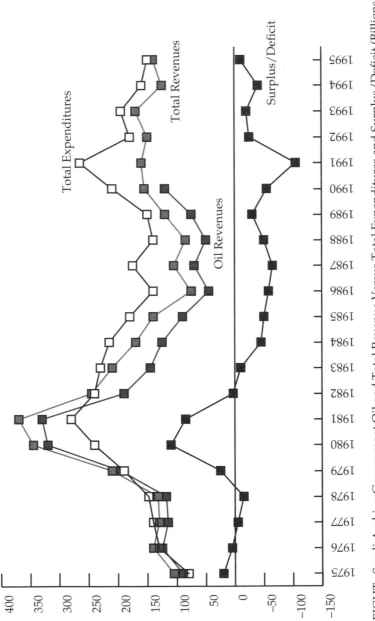

CHART EIGHT Saudi Arabian Government Oil and Total Revenue Versus Total Expenditures and Surplus/Deficit (Billions of Current Rials). *Source:* Adapted by Anthony H. Cordesman from International Energy Agency (IEA), *Middle East Oil and Gas,* Paris, 1995, pp. 256–257, based on data from SAMA, *Annual Report and Statistical Summary and Middle East Economic Survey,* January 9, 1995.

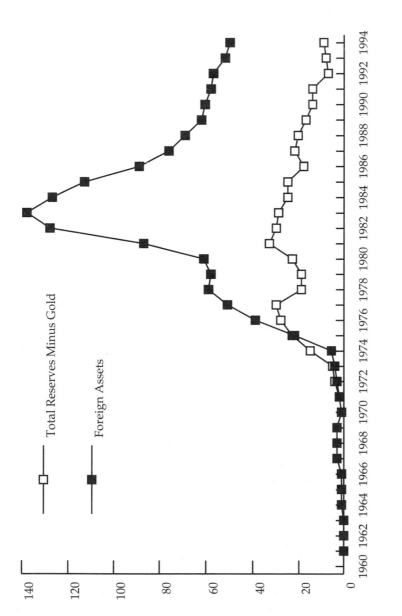

CHART NINE   Saudi Liquidity in Billions of US Dollars—1960–1994. *Source:* Adapted by Anthony H. Cordesman from International Energy Agency (IEA), *Middle East Oil and Gas,* Paris, 1995, pp. 305–309, and based on IMF, *International Financial Statistics.*

Koran.[91] Central bank reserves also dropped from more than $100 billion to around $35–40 billion, and Saudi Arabia had to cut some defense expenditures, including the delay and cancellation of certain arms purchases.[92] Saudi Arabia made the last payment on its $4.5 billion debt in June, 1995, but continued to run a budget deficit. This deficit reached $7.4 billion in 1993 and rose to $10.7 billion in 1994—a rise that finally triggered more decisive action by the Saudi government.

Table Two shows a considerable reduction in the estimated deficit for 1995. The Saudi budget still, however, reflects the government's unwillingness to pursue the additional spending cuts and revenue increases required to offset lower oil prices forecast for 1996. The 1996 budget is projected to make a 19% increase in the deficit over 1995. These 1996 projections also depend on total government expenditures accounting for 33% of the GDP—the lowest percentage since 1988. They require adherence to a policy predicated on low imports, subsidies, and a limit on the growth of military spending. The Saudi budget for 1996 does not specifically identify military spending, but rather lumps it together with various programs into an "other spending" category. This "other spending" accounts for 54% of the 1996 budget.[93]

Saudi Arabia has attempted to limit government expenditures in its sixth Five Year Plan which covers the years 1996–2000. This plan seeks to eliminate all deficits by the year 2000. According to the IMF's Article IV report for 1995, however, the budget deficit could return to a level of 10% of GDP by the year 2000 in the absence of further cuts in expenditures and increases in non-oil revenues.[94]

There are good reasons to be cautious about these Saudi plans. They call for financial austerity without reform, and the IMF has indicated that it would take massive reform for Saudi Arabia to really come to grips with its problems. The IMF has called for:[95]

- Freezing total government expenditures at their 1995 level;
- A consumption tax of 5%; an excise duty of 10% on goods like jewelry, clothes, and vehicles; a 2% turnover tax for local and foreign companies;
- A 20% increase in gasoline and diesel fuel prices in 1996 and subsequent price rises to match inflation;
- An annual wage cut of 1% in government wages in 1996–1997 and a 2% cut in 1998–2000; and
- Further reductions in all subsidies to the minimal level necessary to preserve the social safety net.

It is possible that these IMF warnings may be exaggerated. At the time the Saudi budget for 1995 was issued, some IMF experts believed that the Saudi government might not be able to reduce its annual deficits in 1995 and 1996 to less than 4% of its GDP. In fact, some IMF experts estimated that the Saudi deficit would be closer to $5.5 billion instead of $4.0 billion.[96]

This IMF analysis, however, failed to account for the reduction of imports and subsidies by the Saudi government, a rise in oil prices, and record profits by Saudi Arabia's downstream and industrial operations— like those of the Saudi Basic Industries Corporation (SABIC). These developments led the Saudi government to project a deficit of just under $4 billion for 1995, or 4.1% of GDP. Saudi deficit predictions for 1996 are somewhat higher and total $4.9 billion in current dollars, but the Saudi government also projects oil revenues as high as $29 billion, and government revenues as high as 150 billion Saudi Rials. Given a budget of roughly 165 billion Saudi Rials, this would create a deficit of around 15 billion Saudi Rials or 3% to 4.1% of the Saudi GDP.[97]

Regardless of the exact trends that emerge, there will still be growing limits to Saudi Arabia's ability to pay for its past levels of "guns and butter." A combination of Saudi Arabia's economic problems, budget deficit, and growing population have already steadily increased the burden of military spending per capita relative to GDP per capita. These trends are shown in Chart Ten, although it should be noted that the rate of military spending per capita shown in this Chart peaked in the early 1990s because of the Gulf War. As a result, the recent level of military spending per capita is significantly lower, but still imposes a strain on the Saudi budget and on Saudi capability to meet domestic economic and social needs.

The Problem of Debt

Saudi Arabia has been forced to liquidate a substantial amount of its foreign investment to pay for the Gulf War and its budget deficits. Estimates indicate Saudi investments dropped to as little as $7–30 billion in the early 1990s.[98] Foreign debt rose from practically zero to 2% of GDP in 1990–1991 and then to 4% in 1992–1993, although the debt dropped to 1% in 1994.[99]

Since that time, Saudi Arabia dealt with these foreign debt problems by (a) paying off foreign debt at the cost of increasing domestic borrowing and (b) by delaying payments to foreign contractors. These measures have had some negative impact; increased public borrowing has created a substantial government public debt and has affected Saudi banking and investment capabilities. It has also created a backlog in payments to foreign companies that some sources estimate reached several billion dollars in 1995.[100]

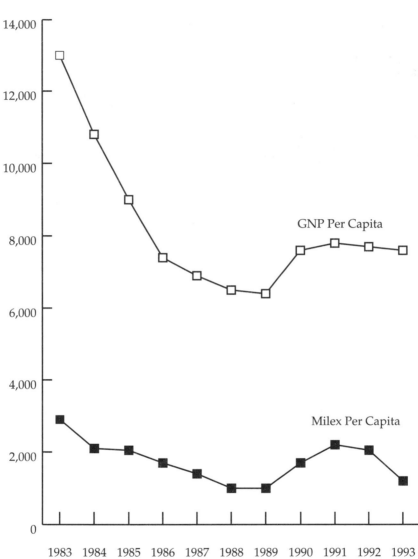

CHART TEN   Saudi GNP Per Capita Versus Military Expenditures Per Capita (Constant $93). *Source:* Adapted by Anthony H. Cordesman from ACDA, *World Military Expenditures and Arms Transfers, 1993–1994,* Washington, ACDA-GPO, 1995, Table I.

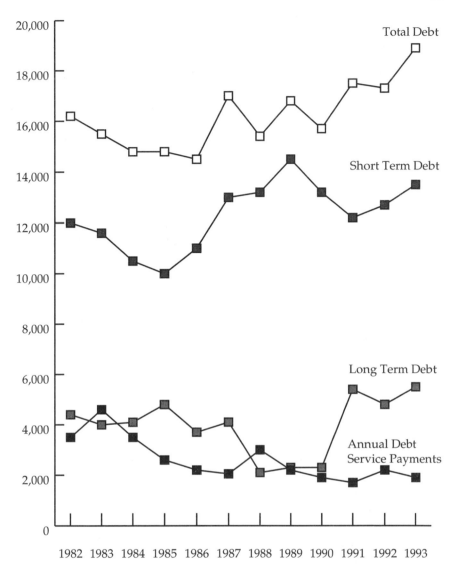

CHART ELEVEN   Saudi Short- and Long-Term Debt Relative to Total Service
Payments (in Current $US Millions). *Source:* Adapted by Anthony H. Cordesman
from International Energy Agency (IEA), *Middle East Oil and Gas,* Paris, 1995, pp.
324–325.

Net outstanding domestic debt increased from about 23–24% of GDP in 1989–1991 to 53% in 1992, and from 63% in 1993 to 70% in 1994. The domestic debt is projected to rise to between 73–81% of the GDP in 1995 and to remain above 75% during 1996–1998. Domestic borrowing equal to, or greater than, 55% of GDP is normally an indication of serious economic problems, but the linkage between these borrowing requirements and the payment of wartime costs, and the fact that Saudi Arabia does not raise revenue from income tax, makes it difficult to apply such indicators to Saudi Arabia.[101]

This public borrowing allowed Saudi Arabia to finance major foreign purchases like the purchase of some $6 billion worth of Boeing and McDonnell-Douglas air liners, but it also raised the Saudi domestic debt to creditors to $94 billion by March, 1995, or about 75% of the GDP. By the end of 1995, government debt consisted of about 30% of the consolidated balance sheet of Saudi banks.[102]

These Saudi policies led to a reluctance on the part of some international banks to approve loans for certain projects. In January, 1996, Saudi Consolidated Electric Company for the Eastern Province (Sceco-East) sought a $500 million loan as part of a $1.4 billion project to boost capacity at its Ghazlan power-generating plant. The uncertain political climate, the distortion of cash-flow assumptions by Saudi subsidies and Sceco's debt to another government entity, Saudi ARAMCO, all raised doubts in the minds of international financial institutions as to the Saudi government's future repayment ability. Some banks were unwilling to invest in a venture with government subsidized companies, such as Sceco, believing them not to be commercially viable risks. This reaction from financial institutions underscores the need for faster privatization.[103]

Further, the Saudi government only avoided further massive increases in domestic borrowing by delaying or defaulting on countless domestic contracts. Saudi Arabia owed its farmers nearly $3 billion in subsidy payments in early 1996. While it has since "paid" them much of the money, nearly $2.5 billion of the the payment consists of non-interest bearing certificates that are little more than IOUs which defer actual cash transfers.[104]

The government provided interest-bearing bonds worth more than 5,200 million Saudi Rials ($1.387 billion) to pay off its overdue debts more than 120 major contractors, and asked other contractors to forgive the government's debt because of past profits.[105] While the government repeatedly denied that it was delaying and defaulting, virtually every Saudi businessman and foreign businessman operating in Saudi Arabia had practical evidence that these denials are false.[106] These delays and defaults raised still further questions about how long the Kingdom can continue its present rate of domestic borrowing, and how much such borrowing will conflict with its efforts to privatize and diversify its economy.

The government was more successful with its military debt. By 1994, its arms purchases during and after the Gulf War had raised its total Foreign Military Sales (FMS) debt to the US to $23 billion. Saudi Arabia had additional military debts to Europe and to US firms that hold sold to Saudi Arabia through commercial sales. This military debt interacted with Saudi civil debts, and forced Saudi Arabia to reschedule its FMS debt. This rescheduling took place in November 1994, and did more than create an extended payment schedule. Saudi Arabia reduced the number of end items it bought, and reduced spending on munitions, military construction, and sustainment. It also eliminated orders to deal with worst case contingencies. King Fahd also issued four major guidelines: No new programs, reduce the total FMS debt to $10 billion, stretch out all military program payments where possible, pay all bills on time, and avoid new starts.

These guidelines had a significant impact. Saudi Arabia's total FMS debt dropped from $23 billion in FY1994, to $18 billion in FY1995, $14 billion in FY1996, and an estimated $10 billion in FY1997. However, Saudi Arabia did not halt all program starts, and did not make all of its military payments to other countries and US contractors on time. The rise in oil prices and revenues in 1995 and 1996 also led Saudi Arabia to slowly increase orders, as part of what one senior advisor called an "insatiable appetite for new hardware."

Water, Economics, and Vulnerability

Water is both an economic problem and a strategic vulnerability. Saudi Arabia's annual rainfall is less than 100 millimeters in most areas. It has only about 2.33 million cubic kilometers of internal renewable water resources. This total is very low, and amounts to about 156 cubic meters per person—less than one-seventh the total for a citizen of the US. It depends heavily on an extensive system of desalinization plants, producing over 300,000 cubic meters a day. These plants are lucrative military targets whose importance will increase with time. Some 75% of the water in the central and eastern regions comes from non-renewable underground lakes, and these reserves will be exhausted within 80 years at present rates.[107]

Saudi Arabia plans to expand its desalination plants to a capacity of over 2 billion cubic meters a year by 2000, and recycles 217 cubic meters of waste water a year.[108] Desalination, however, is too expensive to be a solution to meeting anything other than civil and urgent industrial needs and Saudi Arabia currently wastes nearly 91% of its natural water on agriculture because of government subsidies versus 6% for domestic needs and 2% for industry. Further, Saudi Arabia's rapid increase in population is causing its natural water resources per capita to drop sharply. The World Resources Institute and the World Bank estimate that Saudi natural per capita water resources dropped from 537 cubic meters in 1960 to 156 cubic meters in 1990 and will drop to 49 cubic meters in 2025. Saudi water policy represents a major problem that urgently needs far greater government attention.[109]

Subsidies, Foreign Labor,
and Structural Economic Problems

Saudi Arabia's present and structural economic problems must be kept in careful perspective. None of its near to mid-term financial problems are critical, and Saudi Arabia has ample time in which to take decisive action. Saudi Arabia's budget deficit problem has already been reduced by a combination of higher oil prices and austerity measures. Saudi Arabia has been able to repay its foreign debt and has already financed much of the infrastructure needed to modernize the country. It is unlikely that Saudi Arabia will have to pay for another Gulf War, and many Saudi arms purchases have been "front loaded" so that arms imports in the late 1990s and early 2000s will cost substantially less than in the aftermath of the Gulf War.

In addition, Saudi Arabia is making a massive investment in increasing oil production to reach a sustainable level of 10 million barrels a day. In spite of some cutbacks in foreign investment, Saudi Arabia seems to retain up to $50 billion in SAMA and government entity foreign investments, and $20 billion in foreign assets, controlled by public bodies.[110] Even though real Saudi GDP growth in constant dollars has been low, the US government estimates that the value of the Saudi GDP in constant 1993 dollars grew from a recent low of $100.8 billion in 1988 to $103.8 billion in 1989, $121.3 billion in 1990, $126.6 billion in 1991, $129.6 billion in 1992, and $126.6 billion in 1993.

Many of the government's expenditures on civil domestic debt have gone into investment, rather than services, and these will eventually be repaid in the form of added future revenues. Foreign debt has been reduced to low levels, and domestic debt is still well below 55% of the GDP—a threshold often used to indicate a debt burden that may seriously affect the economy. The domestic bond holdings of Saudi banks are less than $10 billion, and only about 16% of their total deposits. Major private capital inflows and asset repatriation have taken place since the end of Desert Storm. Bank profits, liquidity ratios, and capital to risk weighted assets are all at acceptable-to-good levels.[111]

Yet, Saudi Arabia's current problems do have serious mid- to long-term implications for its internal security. Since 1974, Saudi Arabia has created a welfare-oriented economy which is now dominated by the petroleum and service industries and is largely composed of state sector industrial and service activity.[112]

Saudi Arabia also needs to make major adjustments in its agricultural sector. Agriculture still accounted for 10% of Saudi Arabia's GDP, and 16% of its labor force, in 1995. It only did so, however, because of government subsidies and because the government allowed farmers to draw down fossil water and use other water supplies at a fraction of their market value. These actions allowed Saudi Arabia to be nearly self-sufficient in many grain crops, lamb, chicken, eggs, and milk, but only because the government subsidized at least 65% to 75% of the cost of total agricultural production.[113] The cost of grain subsidies alone, which have greatly accelerated the waste of the Kingdom's fossil water, reached nearly $3 billion in 1992.

The Threat of Subsidies

There are many other subsidies which affect the Saudi budget. Saudi Arabia has no meaningful direct taxation. At the same time, it has long used subsidies to provide nearly-free utilities, low-cost fuel, telecommunications, and air fares, and highly subsidized or free housing, education, and medical services. It has also created subsidies for many forms of Saudi businesses, through offsets, tariffs, and investment and partnership arrangements. Subsidies for electricity, fuel and petroleum products cost an estimated $2.7 billion, relative to world market prices. Diesel fuel, for example, sold for 8.59 cents per gallon, although it costs 12 cents per gallon to produce.[114]

The Saudi government is trying to deal with these problems by raising the cost of some services—like utilities—to market prices. It raised fuel prices two to four times in January, 1995. The price of premium gasoline went up by 82%, kerosene went up by 150%, diesel fuel went up by 250%, gas oil went up 353%. The price of fuel oil and natural gas, however, remained at a small fraction of the normal market price.[115]

Saudi Arabia is also raising service fees, cutting other subsidies, and considering privatizing some state sector firms, such as SABIC. It is also capping some government expenditures and reducing others. It has introduced a massive rise in the visa fees for foreign labor and is attempting to enforce foreign labor restrictions more seriously.[116] Saudi Arabia is also attempting to increase revenues by reducing state-subsidies on gasoline, diesel fuel, water, electricity, and air travel. In January, 1995, the Saudi government doubled gasoline prices to 50 cents per gallon. This rise may generate another $2 billion in revenues a year.[117]

Saudi Arabia's government may take other cost-cutting measures, including the institution of a three-tiered system for public utility billing.

Ostensibly, this will allow the electricity and water generation sectors to break even by charging high-end users substantially higher rates. Also, loans by government development agencies to agricultural, industrial, and real estate projects were cut by one-third in 1994. However, the Saudi government still provides education, health, and administrative services free of charge for its citizens.[118]

The government also faces the problem that it must create a much larger private sector if it is to raise Saudi employment and control public spending in ways which avoid causing internal unrest. Reducing subsidies may ease the Kingdom's financial problems, but it inevitably means a trade-off in terms of political problems.

It is privatization measures that will be the key to Saudi Arabia's success, and this is reflected in the Saudi five year plan announced in July, 1995. This sixth plan, which covers the period from 1996–2000, places heavy emphasis on the growth of the private sector. In December 1994, the government approved the sale of three-quarters of its 70 percent share in SABIC. Other possible candidates for privatization are Saudi Airlines and profitable sectors of the Ministry of Posts, Telephones, and Telegraphs.[119]

The Saudi government is actively encouraging private investment in metals industries, down-stream industries, and like manufactures. SABIC is a conglomerate with 16 affiliates and subsidiaries and a market capitalization of nearly $10 billion. One affiliate, Saudi Iron and Steel, is able to invest in $1 billion rolling mills. Saudi private steel mills and aluminum products companies also involve large-scale businesses. The Saudi Industrial Development Fund (SIDF) reports that it has financed some 1,700 factories so far, and has a 96% recoupment rate on its loans. Further, in spite of increased public borrowing, Saudi banks show very high private sector earnings, and are steadily increasing their loans to the private sector.[120]

At the same time, these measures do not yet have the speed and scale to restructure the economy at the rate Saudi Arabia needs. It is also unclear whether they have been accompanied by an adequate effort to determine ways of cutting Saudi Arabia's subsidy of domestic agriculture and the economic and ecological cost of underpricing water.

Further, it is difficult to ascertain if Saudi Arabia has given proper consideration to its present policy of subsidizing both state sector and private sector operations by providing gas and oil feedstocks well below world market prices. It is also unclear if either the prices for state sector services or fees and taxes will be raised to levels that allow Saudi Arabia to eliminate its future budget deficits during periods of low oil earnings and reduce its domestic public debt. In its 1996 budget, the Saudi government allocates more than $1.8 billion for domestic subsidies, or just over 4.5% of the total budget.[121] Saudi intentions are good, but the practice is still uncertain.

The Threat of Foreign Labor

Another problem that Saudi Arabia must firmly address is the interaction between its growing demographic problems and its over-dependence on foreign labor. Saudi Arabia's high population growth rate is making the current level of subsidy and welfare too expensive for the Saudi government to sustain. At the same time, its welfare economy has helped create a dependence on foreign labor that is expensive and unproductive and which has helped delay the "Saudiazation" of the labor force and the development of productive careers and realistic expectations among Saudi Arabia's native population.

Far too much of Saudi Arabia's population and labor force is foreign. The Saudi 1993 census calculated that Saudi Arabia had 4.6 million foreign residents out of a total population of 14.6 million, and more recent estimates put the foreign population at closer to six million, with five million of this total working in the labor force. These same estimates indicate that 85% of the foreign workers work in the private sector—50% in industrial and related jobs. They indicate that foreign workers repatriate between $13 and $15 billion a year. This is roughly 10% of the Saudi GDP, and compares with repatriations of around $8 billion a year in the early 1980s—when the Saudi GDP per capita was much higher.[122]

The CIA estimates that roughly 4.2 million foreign workers are employed in the government or the service sector. It estimates that as much as 60% of Saudi Arabia's labor force, and 31% of its total population, is still foreign. Saudi Arabia's total population now consists of about 21% Asian workers, 8% foreign Arab workers, 2% Africans, and 1% Europeans. The Saudi government has issued estimates of up to six million expatriate workers, with over 1 million Egyptians, 800,000 Indians, and 600,000 Filipinos.[123] At the same time, some 164,000 native Saudi males become old enough to enter the labor force each year, and 80,000–90,000 enter the private job market.[124]

This combination of population growth and dependence on foreign labor may be the greatest single threat to Saudi Arabia's stability, and poses a far more serious threat to the Kingdom's security than the threat from Iran and Iraq. Over-dependence on foreign labor threatens the structure of the Saudi economy, and the very fabric of Saudi society, because a rapidly growing native population and declining real per capita oil revenues call for major new measures to force reliance on native Saudi labor. It also almost certainly fuels the problem of Islamic extremism and many of Saudi Arabia's problems with its Shi'ites.

The Saudi Fourth Five Year Development Plan (1985–1990) attempted to reduce these problems by seeking a 600,000 man reduction in the Saudi labor force by 1990. In fact, though, the foreign labor force increased by

200,000, and increased by a rate of 8% to 10% per year during 1993–1994. As a result, foreign workers in Saudi Arabia sent home $15.25 billion in 1994 and an estimated $17.6 billion in 1995—an increase of 40% over total remittances in 1989. About 500,000 more work visas were issued in 1995 than in 1994, and the total number of expatriate workers and their families living in Saudi Arabia rose to 6.2 million.[125]

Studies by the ILO and World Bank also indicate that the Saudi educational system is failing to educate either male or female students for future jobs adequately, and is steadily deteriorating in quality and economic relevance. Further, the existing Saudi labor force is now grossly over-committed to the government and service sectors and much of it does not work at real jobs. A total of 34% of the entire labor force works for the government and 22% more in services. Only 28% works in industry and oil and 16% in agriculture. This represents a serious lack of productive employment within the private sector, and government and government-related jobs often employ three to four Saudis for every real job and then hire a foreigner to do the work. At least half of the Saudis now employed do not perform any real economic function. Their "jobs" are simply disguised unemployment, and most employed young Saudi males now have to face the frustration of working in a non-job.[126]

King Fahd recognized this problem as one of the issues Saudi Arabia had to deal with when he reorganized his cabinet in 1995, called for increased privatization, and provided guidance for review of the Kingdom's five year plan.[127] In July, 1995, Prince Naif, the Minister of the Interior, made a statement calling for major reductions in foreign labor. The Saudi government also announced it would take new measures to reduce foreign labor on July 20, 1995.[128] The Saudi government then issued major new directives calling for "Saudiazation" in October, 1995. For example, these directives required hotels to increase the Saudi portion of their labor force by 5% per year. They also established penalties for firms that do not "Saudi-ize," including denial of subsidies and loans, refusal of new applications to import foreign labor, and being barred from competition for government contracts.

The new Saudi development plan, issued in July, 1995, called for the creation of 191,700 new jobs, 148,700 vacancies as a result of turnover plans, and the creation of an additional 319,500 jobs by replacing non-Saudis with Saudis.[129] The government estimates that a total of 213,400 new jobs will be created between 1995–1999.

It is already clear, however, that the government is not really enforcing many of its measures to reduce Saudi dependence on foreign labor. It is also not doing anything to address the fact that its proposed salary scales, welfare charges, and regulations requiring the firing of Saudi employees create a major deterrent to hiring native labor. For example, the proposed salary scales for unskilled laborers call for a salary of 600–800 Rials for expatriates and 1,500–2,000 for nationals. The scale for skilled laborers is 1,500–2,000 Rials for expatriates and 3,000–4,000 for nationals. The scale for experienced employees is 3,500–4,000 Rials for expatriates and 5,000–7,000 for nationals, and the scale for engineers is 3,000–4,000 Rials for expatriates and 6,000–8,000 for nationals. Given the low work ethic and productivity of most Saudis, the only incentive to hire a national is usually that he is the son of a friend or relative or the employer must meet some quota.

Furthermore, even if Saudi development plans succeed, they will not create nearly enough jobs to accommodate the additional 574,800 young people who the government estimates will enter the job market during 1995–1996.[130] There is a similar lack of realism in the government's efforts to address the problems in Saudi education and their failed attempt to develop an effective work ethic by creating programs tailored to train Saudi males for jobs. Several Saudi Chambers of Commerce and Industry are beginning to create such programs, but the effort is minuscule relative to the need and Saudi Arabia is expanding non-economic Islamic education problems far more quickly than it is doing anything that makes native Saudis more employable.[131]

Redefining the Saudi Social Contract

No one outside Saudi Arabia, and perhaps no one within it, can be certain of just how serious the impact of these tensions within Saudi society really are. None seem to threaten the government, at present, and there are few signs that a cohesive opposition can emerge out of the different movements involved. Nevertheless, the Saudi government can scarcely ignore their importance, and it must be particularly careful to take Islamic sensitivities into careful consideration when moving towards internal reform, in modernizing Saudi society and military forces, and in dealing with the West.

Saudi Arabia must evolve if it is to preserve its internal stability. It must continue to expand the role of the Majlis, and find ways of allowing peaceful debate of social and economic issues and secularism versus Islam. It must allow popular debate and increasing popular control of its national resources. It must come to grips with the issue of defining a rule of law that applies to all its citizens, including the royal family, and which also provides for a uniform commercial code and fully competitive privatization, while resolving the inevitable tensions and conflicts between religious and secular law.

Saudi Arabia must redefine its "social contract." It must begin to tax directly at least its wealthier citizens, eliminate most subsidies and convert to market prices, diversify its economy, make a full commitment to privatization and adopt much more stringent restrictions on foreign labor that put far more native citizens to work.

Saudi Arabia must ensure that oil wealth is shared throughout its society. At the same time, it must move beyond a petroleum and service-based economy, and a subsidized welfare state. This is not simply a matter of dealing with declining oil revenues per capita. It is a matter of creating a work ethic and economy that employs young Saudis, giving them a real career and share in the future of the nation, and steadily reducing Saudi Arabia's dependence on foreign labor.

This means Saudi Arabia must take strong measures in several key areas. It must:

- Force radical reductions in the number of foreign workers, with priority for reductions in servants and in trades that allow the most rapid conversion to native labor. Eliminate economic disincentives for employers hiring native labor, and create disincentives for hiring foreign labor. Saudi Arabia's young and well-educated population needs to replace its foreign workers as quickly as possible, and it will only develop a work ethic and suitable skills once it is thrust into the labor market.
- Limit population growth.
- Reduce those aspects of state subsidies and welfare that distort the economy and discourage the native population from seeking jobs. It must steadily reduce dependence on welfare, and replace subsidies with jobs. Water, electricity, motor gasoline, basic foods, and many services need to be priced at market levels and subsidies to citizens need to be replaced with jobs and economic opportunities.
- Restructure the educational system to focus on job training and competitiveness. Create strong new incentives for faculty and students to focus on job-related education. Sharply down-size other forms of educational funding and activity, and eliminate high overhead educational activities without economic benefits.
- Reform the structure of the national budget to reduce the amount of money going directly to royal accounts, and ensure that most of the nation's revenues and foreign reserves are integrated into the national budget and into the planning process. Clearly separate royal and national income and investment holdings.
- Place limits on the transfer of state funds to princes and members of the royal family outside the actual ruling family, and transfers of unearned income to members of other leading families.
- Ensure that all income from enterprises with state financing is reflected in the national budget and is integrated into the national economic development and planning program.

- Freeze and then reduce the number of civil servants, and restructure and down-size the civil service to focus on productive areas of activity with a much smaller pool of manpower. Cut back sharply on state employees by the year 2000.
- Establish market criteria for all major state and state-supported investments. Require detailed and independent risk assessment and projections of comparative return on these investments, with a substantial penalty for state versus privately funded projects and ventures. Down-size the scale of programs to reduce investment and cash flow costs and the risk of cost-escalation.
- Carry out much more rapid and extensive privatization to increase the efficiency of Saudi Arabian investments in downstream and upstream operations, create real jobs and career opportunities for native Saudi Arabians, and open investment opportunities to a much wider range of investors. Privatization must be managed in ways that ensure all Saudi Arabians have an opportunity to share in the privatization process and not conducted in a manner that benefits a small, elite group of investors and discourages popular confidence and willingness to invest in Saudi Arabia.
- Stop subsidizing Saudi Arabian firms and businesses in ways which prevent economic growth and development, and which deprive the government of revenue. Present policies strongly favor Saudi Arabian citizens and Saudi Arabian-owned companies. Income taxes are only levied on foreign corporations and foreign interests in Saudi Arabian corporations, at rates that may range as high as 55 percent of net income. Individuals are not subject to income taxes, eliminating a key source of revenue, as well as a means of ensuring the more equitable distribution of income. Saudi Arabia needs to tax its citizens and companies and ensure that wealthier Saudi Arabian's make a proper contribution to social services and defense.
- Allow foreign investment on more competitive terms. Saudi Arabia currently allows only limited foreign investment in certain sectors of the economy, in minority partnerships, and on terms compatible with continued Saudi Arabian control of all basic economic activities. Some sectors of the economy—including oil, banking, insurance and real estate—have been virtually closed to foreign investment. Foreigners (with the exception of nationals from some GCC states) are not permitted to trade in Saudi Arabia, except through the medium of Saudi firms. Protection should not extend to the point where it eliminates efficiency and competitiveness, and restricts economic expansion. Saudi Arabia needs to act decisively on proposals such as allowing foreign equity participation in the banking sector and in the upstream oil sector.

- Create new incentives to invest in local industries and business and disincentives for the expatriation of capital.
- Avoid offset requirements that simply create disguised unemployment or non-competitive ventures that act as a further state-sponsored distortion of the economy.
- Tax earnings and sales with progressive taxes that reduce or eliminate budget deficits, which encourage local investment, and which create strong disincentives for the expatriation of capital, including all foreign holdings of capital and property by members of elite and ruling families.
- Shift goods to market prices. Remove distortions in economy and underpricing of water, oil, and gas.
- Establish a firm rule of law for all property, contract, permitting, and business activity and reduce state bureaucratic and permitting barriers to private investment.
- Place national security spending on the same basis as other state spending. Integrate it fully into the national budget, including investment and equipment purchases. Replace the present emphasis on judging purchases on the basis on initial procurement costs and technical features with a full assessment of life cycle costs—including training, maintenance, and facilities—and with specific procedures for evaluating the value of standardization and interoperability with existing national equipment and facilities, those of other Gulf states, and those of the US and other power projection forces.
- Saudi Arabia must redefine its support of Islam to preserve its traditional religious character without tolerating either domestic Islamic extremists or the funding of extremist movements overseas. Improved job opportunities and economic management can help deal with many social issues, and a peaceful debate over the evolution of Islam in Saudi Arabia is critical to peaceful social change. The government, however, cannot confuse a right to peaceful debate with a tolerance of violence or violent rhetoric, and it must be more careful to distinguish between the support of legitimate peaceful Islamic causes outside Saudi Arabia and the support of terrorism and violence.

Both the Saudi ruling elite and the West need to recognize that Saudi Arabia's key security challenge is not external threats, or internal extremism, but the need to come firmly to grips with its economy. The key economic challenge Saudi Arabia faces is not its current balance of payments or budget deficit, but to create a form of capitalism that suits Saudi social custom, that is run and staffed by Saudis, and that steadily expands the productive sector beyond oil and gas exports and large-scale downstream operations.

5

Oil and Petroleum Related Issues

Saudi Arabia's strategic position, economy, and ability to meet the expectations of its people all depend on oil and petroleum products. The US estimates that Saudi Arabia possesses at least 259–261 billion barrels of proven oil reserves, or a little over one-quarter of the world's total. Many analysts believe, however, that these figures sharply underestimate the country's potential. Saudi Arabia almost certainly has at least 42 billion barrels more and unofficial Saudi estimates put the total around 1 trillion barrels.[132]

Saudi Arabia had produced about 62.4 billion barrels of oil by the end of 1990, and had a high reserve-to-production ratio of 112/1.[133] In 1994, Saudi Arabia produced an estimated 8.15 million barrels per day of crude oil, down slightly from 8.2 million barrels per day in 1993. Production levels ranged from 8.12–8.41 million barrels per month in 1995. Saudi Arabia's 200,000 barrels per day share of the Neutral Zone is included in these estimates.[134]

IEA estimates of Saudi reserves are shown in Table Three and in Chart Twelve. Table Three also shows a typical projection of Saudi Arabia's growing importance as an oil producer. It indicates that Saudi production is projected to rise from around 8.0 million barrels per day (MMBD) in 1995 to 11.5 million barrels in 2000, 12.8 million in 2005, and 14.1 million barrels in 2010. This projection tracks closely with Saudi plans and is critical to meeting world demand. It is particularly critical because it now seems increasingly unlikely that Iran and Iraq can possibly make the investments in oil production necessary to reach the goals shown in Table Three, and because of growing uncertainties regarding future Russian and Central Asian production and the rate of increase in Asian demand.

Chart Thirteen shows the recent trends in Saudi oil and NGL production and exports. Saudi Arabia produced at a rate of about 8 million barrels per day during 1991–1995. This rate of production has made Saudi Arabia the largest oil producer in the Middle East and given it a GDP with a purchasing power equivalent to nearly $200 billion. Saudi Arabia

TABLE THREE   Comparative Oil Reserves and Production Levels of the Gulf States

Comparative Oil Reserves in 1994 in Billions of Barrels

Country	Identified	Undiscovered	Identified and Undiscovered	Proven	% of World Total
Bahrain	—	—	—	.35	
Iran	69.2	19.0	88.2	89.3	8.9
Iraq	90.8	35.0	125.8	100.0	10.0
Kuwait	92.6	3.0	95.6	96.5	9.7
Oman	—	—	—	5.0	NA
Qatar	3.9	0	3.9	3.7	0.4
Saudi Arabia	265.5	51.0	316.5	261.2	26.1
UAE	61.1	4.2	65.3	98.1	9.8
Total	583.0	112.2	695.2	654.1	64.9
Rest of World	—	—	—	345.7	35.1
World	—	—	—	999.8	100.0

(continues)

TABLE THREE (*continued*)

Comparative Oil Production in Millions of Barrels Per Day

Country	1995 Actual	OPEC Quota	DOE/IEA Estimate of Actual Production 1990	1992	2000	2005	2010	Maximum Sustainable 1995	2000	Announced Capacity in 2000
Bahrain	—	—	—	—	—	—	—	—	—	—
Iran	3,608	3,600	3.2	3.6	4.3	5.0	5.4	3.2	4.5	4.5
Iraq	600	400	2.2	0.4	4.4	5.4	6.6	2.5	5.0	5.0
Kuwait	1,850	2,000	1.7	1.1	2.9	3.6	4.2	2.8	3.3	3.3
Oman	—	—	—	—	—	—	—	—	—	—
Qatar	449	378	0.5	0.4	0.6	0.6	0.6	0.5	0.6	0.6
Saudi Arabia	8,018	8,000	8.5	9.6	11.5	12.8	14.1	10.3	11.1	11.1
UAE	2,193	2,161	2.5	2.6	3.1	3.5	4.3	3.0	3.8	3.2
Total Gulf	—	—	18.6	17.7	26.8	30.9	35.0	23.5	28.2	28.2
World	—	—	69.6	67.4	78.6	84.2	88.8	—	—	—

Source: Adapted by Anthony H. Cordesman from estimates in IEA, *Middle East Oil and Gas*, Paris, OECD/IEA, 1995, Annex 2 and DOE/EIA, *International Energy Outlook, 1995*, Washington, DOE/EIA, June, 1995, pp. 26–30, and *Middle East Economic Digest*, February 23, 1996, p. 3. IEA and DOE do not provide country breakouts for Bahrain and Oman. Reserve data estimated by author based on country data.

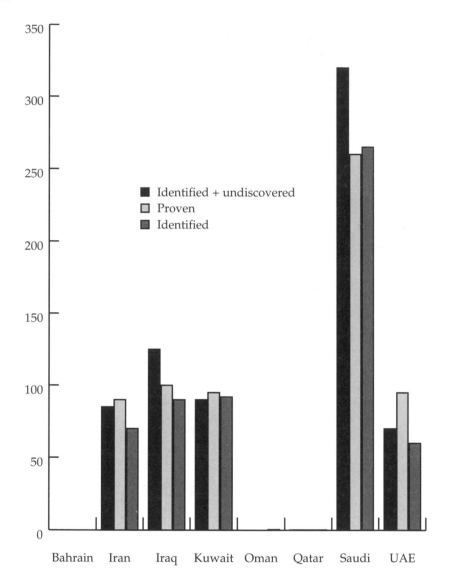

CHART TWELVE   Total Oil Reserves of the Gulf States in Billions of Barrels.
Source: IEA, *Middle East Oil and Gas,* Paris, OECD/IEA, Annex 2, and data
provided by Bahrain and Oman. Bahrain's reserves are only 350 million barrels
and do not show up on the chart because of scale.

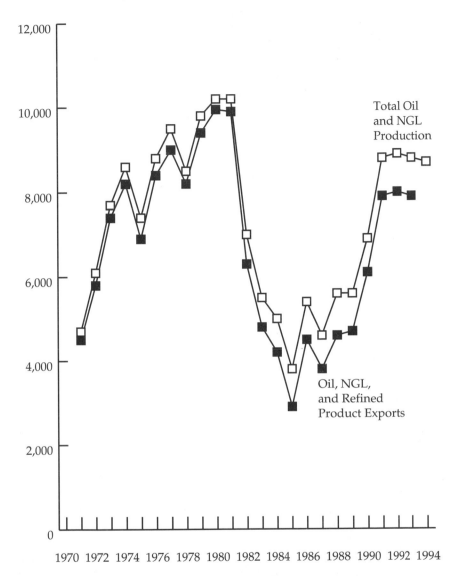

CHART THIRTEEN   Saudi Arabia—Oil and Natural Gas Liquids Total
Production and Exports in Thousands of Barrels Per Day. *Source:* Adapted by
Anthony H. Cordesman from International Energy Agency (IEA), *Middle East Oil
and Gas,* Paris, 1995, pp. 307–317.

has 1,862,500 barrels of condesate per day (B/CD) of refining capacity, as well as extensive downstream and distribution operations, and the US Department of Energy estimates that it will produce 11.0–14.0 MMBD of crude oil equivalent by the early part of the next century. Chart Thirteen also shows that domestic demand is rising, but not to an extent where it will make major further reductions in Saudi capability to export.[135]

Recent Oil Production

Oil production in Saudi Arabia occurs in 18 oil fields in Saudi Arabia and in five oil fields in the zone it shares with Kuwait. Over half of Saudi Arabia's current proven reserves are contained in eight fields, and 90% of all Saudi production comes from the four largest fields in Saudi Arabia—Ghawar, Safaniyah, Abqaig, and Berri. The Ghawar field alone has some 70–85 billion barrels and is the world's largest on-shore oil field. The Safaniyah field has 19 billion barrels and is the world's large off-shore field. The Abqaig field has 17 billion barrels and Berri has 11 billion barrels. Other major fields include Manifa (11 billion barrels), Zuluf (8 billion barrels), Shaybah (7 billion), Abu Safah (6 billion), and Khursaniyah (3.5 billion).[136]

Much of Saudi Arabia's oil potential is still unexplored and drilling rates have been limited through much of the 1990s. Saudi Arabia did, however, discover seven new oil fields in 1990 alone, with potential reserves of between 500 million and 3 billion barrels.[137] In 1994, a five-year exploration search was concluded which found new, ultra light crude oil reserves in the country's Central Area and additional fields on the northern and southern Red Sea coasts. Another major super-light crude field was found about 15 miles from Houta (100 miles south of Riyadh) in April, 1995.[138]

Three companies—Saudi Aramco, Saudi Arabian Texaco, and AOC—produce all Saudi crude oil. The 1976 nationalization of the Saudi Arabian petroleum industry led to Saudi Aramco's control over most of the country's upstream oil operations. Saudi Aramco produces more than 95% of all crude oil and NGL, and has played a major role in the world oil market. Saudi Aramco is a vertically integrated company with tanker and refinery operations. It has both cut its production levels to maintain its assigned OPEC quota level, and raised production to prevent possible price and supply crises or reduce their impact. The Saudi government's ability to use Aramco as a "swing producer" gives Saudi Arabia still further strategic importance.[139]

Saudi Arabia carried out major development activity during 1991–1995. It raised the production of 14 different fields during this period, and raised its sustained production capacity from 8.7 MMBD to 10.87 MMBD, with most of the increase taking place in the Ghawar field. The bulk of Saudi

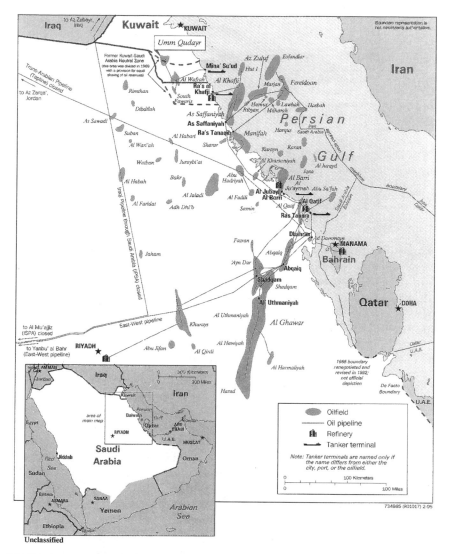

MAP TWO   Saudi Oil Facilities

Arabia's recent offshore capacity increases occurred in the Zuluf and Marjan fields. Their outputs were boosted to 1.2 million barrels per day and 600,000 barrels per day, respectively. Work at Zuluf entailed the completion of two 250,000-barrels per day gas/oil separation plants (GOSP). Construction of a 270,000-barrels per day GOSP at the offshore Safaniya field also boosted production in 1994. These fields are the primary producers of Saudi Arabia's Arab Heavy and Arab Medium, which have gravities of around 27° and 31° API, respectively. By mid-1994, total offshore Saudi oil output was estimated at 3.8 million barrels per day.

Expanding Oil Field Production

Saudi Arabia has announced plans to raise its production capacity to at least 12 MMBD by 2005, to increase the volume and share of light crude oil production, to increase the vertical integration of its oil companies, to refine 50% of its crude oil production, and carry 50% of its exports in Saudi-owned tankers. It is expanding its petrochemical production and marketing, and has developed plans to spend a total of $34 to 50 billion over the period between 1995 and 2007.[140]

In early 1995, Saudi Aramco announced new plans to develop Saudi Arabia's oil fields and to increase capacity above its present 10 million barrels per day. In April, 1995, former Saudi Oil Minister Hisham Nazer stated that the country's oil industry was undergoing a "restructuring" in an effort to ensure "stable petroleum revenues" and "an efficient oil industry capable of a timely response to the changing market." The new expansion plans he announced included five projects which ultimately could cost $3 billion. The foremost of these projects was the $2 billion Shaybah field development project, located in a remote area bordering the United Arab Emirates. The Shaybah field contains an estimated 7 billion barrels of 42¡ oil. As of April, 1995, Saudi Aramco officials were considering terms for possible foreign involvement in the field's development.

The Shaybah field, which has been called Saudi Arabia's "crown jewel," is located 400 miles from Abqaiq, the country's closest gathering center. Consequently, Saudi Aramco is discussing the use of Amoco's Indian Ocean export facilities in the UAE. However, observers feel Shaybah's oil may have to be blended to maximize revenues. In this case, the blended Shaybah crude would be exported from the Ras Tanura terminal. Shaybah is due to come on-line by 1999 with a projected maximum output of 500,000 barrels per day.

Other projects include bringing the Haradh field on line in 1996, with a capacity of 300,000 barrels per day, a $200-million upgrade of several offshore Arab Heavy and Medium fields. In addition, a new $1 million, 250,000-barrels per day GOSP unit for the Ghawar field's Haradh zone is planned as well as a 75,000-barrels per day GOSP at the smaller, onshore Nuayyim field.

Export Facilities and Distribution

Saudi Arabia is a key oil supplier for the United States, Europe, and Japan. Since 1988, it has been the largest single annual source of US oil imports. In 1994, it supplied 15.7 percent of US oil imports, down slightly from 16.7 percent in 1993, 20.3 percent in 1992, and 21.3 percent in 1991. The majority of Saudi Arabia's crude oil is exported through the Persian Gulf and the Red Sea via the processing facility at Abqaiq. The terminals in these locations have the capability of processing up to 14 million barrels per day. They play a major role in ensuring the supply of world oil exports, and are key potential targets for any attack on Saudi Arabia.

Saudi Arabia has the following major terminals, all holding significant strategic importance and posing a key potential target in a future war:

- Ras Tanura has a capacity of 5 MMBD, facilities to load crude oil and LPG, two piers, and 18 berths. It can handle ULCCs up to 550,000 dead weight tons (dwt) and has a 33 million metric ton tank farm.
- Ras al Juaymah has a capacity of 3 MMBD, facilities to load crude oil and LPG, six single buoy moorings, and 2 berths. It can handle VLCCs and has a 33 million metric ton tank farm.
- Yanbu has a capacity of 3 MMBD, facilities to load crude oil and LPG, one three-berth pier, and a two-berth LPG platform. It can load ULCC and LPG tankers.
- Jubail has four berths and can load ULCCs.
- Ras al-Khafji has four berths located three to seven miles off the Neutral Zone and can load 100,000 and 300,000 dwt tankers.
- Zuluf is the terminal for the Zuluf field and is 40 miles offshore.
- Rabigh has nine berths and can support tankers of up to 321,000 dwt with crude oil or product.

Saudi Arabia has a massive network of domestic pipelines and five pipelines to ports or other countries. It should be noted that none of these pipelines connect directly to a Red Sea port, and that they represent key areas of potential vulnerability.

- The 4.8-million barrel per day (bpd) East-West Crude Oil Pipeline (Petroline) was expanded to its present capacity in 1993. It is used predominantly to transport Arab Light and Super Light both to refineries in the Western Province and to Red Sea terminals for direct export to European markets.
- The 430,000 bpd Abqaiq-Yanbu natural gas liquids (NGL) pipeline runs parallel to the Petroline. It is used to carry NGLs to Yanbu for petrochemical processing.
- The 500,000 bpd Trans-Arabian Pipeline (Tapline) was constructed in 1950 to transport crude oil for export from Lebanon. However, since the 1970s, it has served only to supply a 60,000 bpd Jordanian refin-

ery and many components have been removed from the rest of the pipeline or are no longer operational. Shipment to Jordan was cut-off after the Gulf War, and the pipeline was mothballed.

- The Iraqi-Saudi Pipelines (IPSA-1 and IPSA-2) were closed indefinitely after the start of the Gulf War. The 500,000 bpd IPSA-1 transmits oil from Khor al-Zubair in Southern Iraq to a Petroline pipeline in Saudi Arabia. The 1.65-million barrel per day Iraqi-Saudi Pipeline (IPSA-2) transmits oil from a Petroline pipeline in Saudi Arabia to Yanbu.
- The Bahrain pipeline connects Abqaiq to Bahrain and has a capacity of 200,000 bpd.

Saudi Arabia is increasing its export capabilities, and protecting against market fluctuations and short-term damage to its facilities by acquiring new tankers, increasing its overseas crude oil storage capacities, and buying downstream operations in Europe and Asia.[141] In early 1994, Japan's Mitsubishi agreed to provide Saudi Arabia with 5 new double-hull, 300,000-dwt very large crude carriers (VLCC) by 1997. In addition Saudi Arabia received 14 of its 15 VLCC and ultra large crude carriers (ULCC) at the end of 1994. These were built in Japanese, South Korean, and Danish shipyards. The Saudi fleet currently comprises 22 such vessels.

Saudi Arabia maintains a strategic oil reserve and is boosting the size of its overseas storage facilities. In mid-1994, storage capacity was increased dramatically through a 34 percent acquisition of equity in Texaco's 17-million barrel Maatschap terminal. This acquisition in Rotterdam represented a move from Saudi Arabia's previous strategy of only leasing storage facilities. In December 1993, Saudi Arabia signed a long-term lease for a 5-million barrel facility on St. Eustatius in the Caribbean. Saudi Arabia's owned and leased storage facilities now have a capacity of over 30 million barrels.

Refining

Saudi Arabia is investing heavily in downstream operations. It has eight refineries with a total crude throughput capacity of 1.661 million barrels per day. Ras Tanura is the largest and oldest refinery with a capacity of 530,000 bpd, although a fire in 1990 reduced this capacity and it is still in the process of being restored to levels over 300,000 bpd. Two large refineries at Yanbu have a throughput of 315.2 and 190.0 bpd, the refinery at Rabigh has a throughput of 325,000 bpd, Jubail has a throughput of 284,000 bpd, Riyadh has a throughput of 140,000 bpd, and refineries at Jeddah and Ras al-Khafji have throughputs of 87,000 and 30,000 bpd respectively.

The country is able to meet roughly twice its domestic demand for refined products. In June, 1993, Saudi Arabian Marketing and Refining (SAMAREC) merged with Saudi Aramco in an attempt to vertically integrate the country's oil industry. This move placed all except for the 30,000 barrels per day Mina al-Khafji refinery in the Neutral Zone under Saudi Aramco's control.[142]

Prior to the merger, SAMAREC had planned to spend $4 billion over a ten year period to upgrade all of the country's refineries. After the merger, these plans were put on hold, except for the $1.6-billion upgrade of the 265,000-barrels per day Ras Tanura refinery, which previously had a capacity of 530,000 barrels per day until a 1990 fire destroyed one of its distillation towers. Work on the refinery, which is expected to meet the increasing domestic demand for gasoline and middle distillates, began in late 1994. Also, a $284-million expansion of the 190,000-barrels per day Yanbu refinery was begun by Japan's Chiyoda in late 1994. Yanbu is a primary supplier of gasoline, lubricants, and kerosene for the Western Province. A third upgrade, a joint venture between Saudi Aramco and Greece's Petrola, is currently on hold.

Saudi Arabia has taken measures to secure its outlets for refined products in the United States, Europe, and Asia. In 1988, it acquired a 50 percent stake in a joint venture with Texaco named Star Enterprise. Star Enterprise controls distribution networks in half of the United States and has contracts to purchase up to 600,000 barrels per day of Saudi crude oil for processing at its 3 refineries.

In 1991, Saudi Arabia bought a 35 percent share in South Korea's two 300,000 barrels per day Ssangyong refineries. In February 1994, a similar move was made to buy a 40 percent equity in a Philippines refinery. However, the Philippine Supreme Court was expected to nullify the deal sometime in 1995 on the grounds that the shares should first be made public. In 1994, Saudi Arabia made two more successful acquisitions. The first was a $1.2-billion deal to buy two 265,000 barrels per day refineries, owned by the Swedish refinery company OK Petroleum. The second was a 200,000 barrels per day joint refinery construction venture, which will be located north of Shanghai, China.

As of April 1995, Saudi Aramco was on the verge of acquiring a 50 percent stake in Motor-Oil Hellas valued at over $500 million. If purchased, Motor-Oil Hellas and a related company, Avinoil, would substantially increase Saudi Aramco's ability to market its products in Europe and the Balkans.

Saudi refinery expansion plans have been scaled back steadily since 1990, and are now much more market-oriented than in the past, and total Saudi refining capacity totaled 2.5 MMBD in 1995, with 1.6 MMBD of domestic capacity and 0.9 MMBD of Saudi-owned foreign capacity.

Saudi Arabia has, however, announced a goal of creating domestic and foreign-owned refining capacity equal to 50% of its crude oil production. This goal seems to be too high to offer secure rates of return on investment in the near and mid-terms, although it might be economically feasible by 2020.[143]

Petrochemicals

While a number of Gulf countries are involved in petrochemical operations, Saudi Arabia has created a massive new industry in this field. SABIC is the third largest petrochemical producer in the world and the largest exporter of Saudi Arabian petrochemicals. SABIC increased production by 35% in 1994, and plans to increase its production of methyl tertiary butyl ether (MTBE) from its current levels of 2 million tons per year to 2.7 million tons per year by the end of 1996. SABIC's profits reached $1 billion a year for the first time in 1994, and some estimates indicate they may reach $2 billion in 1995.[144] Future profits may be further enhanced by the December, 1995, privatization of SABIC's Arabian Industrial Fibre Company.[145]

Mobil Corporation also signed a contract in May 1996 to invest $1 billion in a joint venture with the Saudi government to create a major new petrochemical complex in Yanbu. The operation will be 70% Saudi owened and crete a complex capable of producing more than 1.6 million metric tons of ethylene per year. Construction is supposed to start in 1997 and be completed in early 2000.[146]

Saudi officials predict that world MTBE demand will rise by 20 percent per year and will reach 21 million tons in 2000. In order to meet this demand, Saudi Arabia indicated its willingness in October, 1994 to allow foreign companies to participate in petrochemical projects. This announcement followed a 1993 Saudi rejection of a planned $800 million joint venture with Mobil to construct a MTBE plant in Yanbu. In November, 1993, a 700,000 ton per year plant began operation in Jubail. In July, 1994, a 700,000 ton per year complex at Ibn Sina started operations. Also, there are plans for the construction of a fourth, $400 million, 700,000 barrels per day unit at the Sadaf plant to come on-line in late 1995. The Sadaf project is a venture between SABIC and Shell's subsidiary, Pecten Arabia.

Natural Gas

Saudi Arabia is a large exporter of LPG and Saudi Arabia produces about 1,158.6 billion cubic feet of natural gas per year.[147] Saudi Arabia has at least 185 trillion cubic feet (tcf) of natural gas reserves. This is about 3.7% of the world's reserves, and ranks Saudi Arabia fifth in the world.[148]

TABLE FOUR   Gulf and World Gas Reserves and Production

Nation	Reserves in 1995		Percent of World Supply	Production in 1993 (BCM)
	TCF	*BCM*		
Bahrain	—	—	—	—
Iran	741.6	21,000	14.9	60.0
Iraq	109.5	3,100	2.2	2.75
Kuwait	52.9	1,498	1.1	5.17
Oman	—	600–640	—	—
Qatar	250.0	7,070	5.0	18.4
Saudi Arabia	185.9	5,134	4.2	67.3
UAE	208.7	5,779*	4.2	31.63
Gulf	1,548.6	—	31.1	185.25
Rest of World	3,431.7	104,642	68.9	—
World Total	4,980.3	148,223	100.0	—

*Other sources estimate 6,320–7,280 BCM for Abu Dhabi only.

Source: The reserve and production data are adapted by Anthony H. Cordesman from IEA, *Middle East Oil and Gas*, Paris, OECD/IEA, 1995, Annex 2.

Saudi reserves are comparable to the former Soviet Union reserves of 1,977 tcf, Iranian reserves of 742 tcf, Qatari reserves of 250 tcf, and Abu Dhabi reserves of 188 tcf. The US, by comparison, has reserves of 162 tcf.[149] An IEA estimate of the relative size and ranking of Saudi gas reserves is shown in Table Four and Chart Fourteen.

The US Department of Energy estimates that the vast majority of Saudi Arabia's reserves are associated gas. The Ghawar oil field alone is estimated to account for one-third of the country's total gas reserves. New gas reserves have been discovered in the 1990s, largely in fields which contain light crude oil, mainly in the Najd region. Two such discoveries were made in 1994.

Saudi gas production has risen from 1.43 million tons of oil equivalent (Mtoe) in 1971, to 3.101 Mtoe in 1975, 8.51 Mtoe in 1980, 15.75 Mtoe in 1985, 25.36 Mtoe in 1990, and 29.32 Mtoe in 1993. At present, Saudi gas production totals about 6% of Saudi primary energy production, including crude oil.[150]

All of Saudi Arabia's natural gas was flared prior to the start-up of the Kingdom's Master Gas System (MGS) in 1982. This system currently gathers about 4.3 billion cubic feet (Bcf) per day of natural gas, primarily from the Ghawar field and the offshore Safaniyah and Zuluf fields. Associated gas accounts for 2.5 Bcf per day of this amount and non-associated

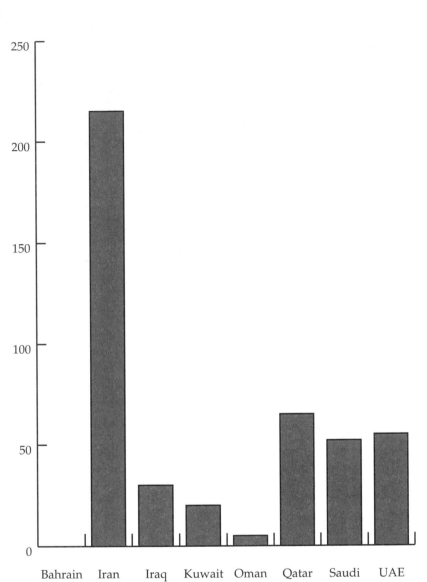

CHART FOURTEEN   Total Gas Reserves of the Gulf States in Billions of Cubic
Meters. *Source:* Adapted by Anthony H. Cordesman from IEA, *Middle East Oil
and Gas,* Paris, OECD/IEA, 1995, Annex 2, and data provided by Bahrain and
Oman. Bahrain's reserves are too small to show on the chart because of scale.

gas for 1.8 Bcf per day. Three processing facilities at Berri, Shedgum, and Uthmaniya are able to process up to 4 Bcf per day. There are also fractionalization plants at Juaymah and Yanbu.[151]

This gas production has done much to meet domestic energy needs and reduce demand for oil that is easier and more economical to export. Saudi Arabia is also steadily increasing its reinjection of gas. It still, however, loses over 20% of its total gas production through flaring, venting, and other losses. This is partly because the cost of increasing distribution capacity has been roughly $0.75 a Mbtu versus are market price of $0.50 a Mbtu and a flaring cost of $0.20 a Mbtu. Saudi Arabia has, however, recently begun to realize that it is wasting a major asset because this price for gas is the product of a subsidy that sharply underprices gas to the Saudi market. It is now seeking to expand the Master Gas System, and is at least considering selling gas at more realistic prices.[152]

During 1995, Saudi Aramco plans to begin a $200 million project to build a third fractionalization plant at Juaymah, a $100 million upgrade of the Berri plant, and a similar upgrading at Uthmaniya. A new pipeline network between gas plants is also under consideration.

Prognosis

Unlike many other oil and gas exporting states, Saudi Arabia has invested in downstream and other sorts of operations, which are based on a strategy of maintaining moderate prices and securing markets indefinitely into the future through high production. Saudi Arabia has been largely successful both in developing its existing fields and bringing new ones on line and in creating efficient refineries. There is little reason to assume that Saudi Arabia will be less efficient in the future.

The real issue affecting Saudi Arabia's future is not whether it will be a major oil producer, but just how large a producer it will be. Virtually any Saudi regime will confront the need to export at high levels to maintain high oil revenues, but most of the world's oil forecasts are heavily dependent on major increases in Saudi oil production capacity between 1995 and 2010. The US Department of Energy projects Saudi production capacity at 11.5 million barrels per day (MMBD) in 2000, with a range of 10.8–12.5 MMBD. It projects Saudi production capacity at 12.8 million barrels per day (MMBD) in 2005, with a range of 11.5–13.5 MMBD, and at 14.1 million barrels per day (MMBD) in 2010, with a range of 12.3–14.6 MMBD.

Given the growing likelihood that Iran, Iraq, and Russia will not meet their currently projected production goals, Saudi Arabia's willingness and ability to meet its goals will become increasingly critical in ensuring that world oil supplies and prices remain relatively stable. Saudi long-range plans, however, are uncertain as is Saudi Arabia's ability to provide the necessary investment to maintain and expand its oil fields and distribution system at the required level.[153]

Saudi Arabia has also invested in some very large petrochemical facilities, some of which border on the grandiose and have questionable profitability if their feedstock is priced at world prices. It has been slow to privatize and make its operations lean and more cost-effective. The resulting expenditures have increased Saudi Arabia's present economic problems. The focus on automation and expensive technology reflects only a limited effort to maximize the employment of native Saudi labor.

Saudi Arabia may need to reevaluate a number of its oil and gas development plans to further reduce dependence on government investment and management. This will involve increased privatization of some operations, the introduction of more effective management methods, and the development of more cost-effective operations in which all activities and feedstocks are priced at world market prices. At the same time, the government needs to focus its investment on labor intensive activities. The recent changes in the Saudi government seem designed to support such policies, and a shift from an OPEC-centered oil policy to one which is commercially oriented and focused on quality over quota.

Finally, Saudi Arabia may face near-term problems in adjusting to the changes in the market that will occur when Iraqi oil production comes back on-stream. It presently is seeking to retain its present share of roughly 12.5% of world output and 33.3% of OPEC production. This may not be possible if Iraq should suddenly provide a major increase in world export capacity.

6

Saudi Military Forces

The present military balance in the Gulf is shown in Table Five. It is clear from this balance that Saudi Arabia is a major military power by Gulf standards and that Saudi forces makes up a great deal of the total military strength of the Gulf Cooperation Council. At the same time, it is clear that Saudi Arabia cannot hope to match the total force strength of Iran or Iraq.

Saudi Arabia's military forces are currently divided into five major branches: the Army, the National Guard, the Navy, the Air Force, and the Air Defense Force. In addition, Saudi Arabia has large paramilitary and internal security forces, and a small strategic missile force. The military forces are directly under the control of King Fahd who is prime minister and commander-in-chief. Prince Abdullah, the Crown Prince and First Deputy Prime Minister, commands the National Guard. Prince Sultan, the Second Deputy Prime Minister and Minister of Defense and Aviation, commands the regular armed forces. Prince Naif, the Minister of the Interior, controls the Frontier Force, Civil Defense force, and police. Prince Turki al-Faisal controls Saudi intelligence. A number of other members of the royal family play key roles in the military. For example, Prince Abd al-Rahman is Deputy Minister of Defense and Aviation and Prince Badr bin Abd al-Aziz is Deputy Commander of the National Guard.

Most senior commanders are from families with long ties to the Saudi royal family, and many officers come from families and tribes that are traditionally loyal to the Saud family. At the same time, the level of education and experience of Saudi officers has changed strikingly since the mid-1950s—when most officers had a traditional background and a handful of others supported Nasser and other Arab radicals with little background other than an interest in politics.

The Saudi officer corps remains traditional in cultural background, but is increasingly well educated and has considerable technical proficiency. The Saudi military services have evolved relatively modern headquarters and management systems, with the support of Western advisors and

TABLE FIVE Gulf Military Forces in 1996

	Iran	Iraq	Bahrain	Kuwait	Oman	Qatar	Saudi Arabia*	UAE	Yemen
Manpower									
Total Active	320,000	382,500	10,700	16,600	43,500	11,100	161,500	70,000	39,500
Regular	220,000	382,500	10,700	16,600	37,000	11,100	105,500	70,000	39,500
National Guard & Other	100,000	0	0	0	6,500	0	57,000	0	0
Reserve	350,000	650,000	0	23,700	0	0	0	0	40,000
Paramilitary	135,000	24,800	9,250	5,200	4,400	0	15,500	2,700	30,000
Army and Guard									
Manpower	260,000	350,000	8,500	10,000	31,500	8,500	127,000	65,000	37,000
Regular Army Manpower	180,000	350,000	8,500	10,000	25,000	8,500	70,000	65,000	37,000
Reserve	350,000	450,000	0	0	0	0	20,000	0	40,000
Tanks	1,350	2,700	81	220	85	24	910	133	1,125
AIFV/Recce, Lt. Tanks	515	1,600	46	130	136	50	1,467	515	580
APCs	550	2,200	235	199	7	172	3,670	380	560
Self Propelled Artillery	294	150	13	38	6	28	200	90	30
Towed Artillery	2,000	1,500	36	0	96	12	270	82	483
MRLs	890	120	9	0	0	4	60	48	220
Mortars	3,500	2,000+	18	24	74	39	400	101	800
SSM Launchers	46	12	0	0	0	0	10	6	30
Light SAM Launchers	700	3,000	65	48	62	58	650	36	700
AA Guns	1,700	5,500	0	0	18	12	10	62	372
Air Force Manpower	20,000	15,000	1,500	2,500	4,100	800	18,000	3,500	1,000
Air Defense Manpower	15,000	15,000	0	0	0	0	4,000	0	0

(continues)

	Iran	Iraq	Bahrain	Kuwait	Oman	Qatar	Saudi Arabia*	UAE	Yemen
Total Combat Aircraft	295	353	24	76	46	12	295	97	69
Bombers	0	6	0	0	0	0	0	0	0
Fighter/Attack	150	130	12	40	19	11	112	41	27
Fighter/Interceptor	115	180	12	8	0	1	122	22	30
Recce/FGA Recce	8	0	0	0	12	0	10	8	0
AEW C4I/BM	1	0	0	0	0	5	0	0	0
MR/MPA**	6	0	0	0	7	0	0	0	0
OCU/COIN	0	18	0	11	13	0	36	15	0
Combat Trainers	92	200	0	11	22	0	66	35	12
Transport Aircraft**	68	34	3	4	14	5	49	20	19
Tanker Aircraft	4	2	0	0	0	0	16	0	0
Armed Helicoptors**	100	120	10	16	0	20	12	42	8
Other Helicoptors**	509	350	8	36	37	7	138	42	21
Major SAM Launchers	204	340	12	24	0	0	128	18	21
Light SAM Launchers	60	200	0	12	28	9	249	34	87
AA Guns	0	0	0	12	0	0	420	0	0
Navy Manpower	38,000	2,500	1,000	1,500	4,200	1,800	17,000	1,500	1,500
Major Surface Combatants									
Missile	5	0	3	0	0	0	8	0	0
Other	2	1	0	0	0	0	0	0	0
Patrol Craft									
Missile	10	1	4	2	4	3	9	10	7

(continues)

TABLE FIVE (continued)

	Iran	Iraq	Bahrain	Kuwait	Oman	Qatar	Saudi Arabia*	UAE	Yemen
Other	26	7	5	12	8	6	20	18	3
Submarines	2	0	0	0	0	0	0	0	0
Mine Vessels	3	4	0	0	0	0	5	0	3
Amphibious Ships	8	0	0	0	2	0	0	0	2
Landing Craft	17	3	4	6	4	1	7	4	2

Note: Does not include equipment in storage. Air Force totals include all helicopters, and all heavy surface-to-air missile launchers.

*60,000 reserves are National Guard Tribal Levies. The total for land forces includes active National Guard equipment. These additions total 262 AIFVs, 1,165 APCs, and 70 towed artillery weapons.

**Includes navy, army, national guard, and royal flights, but not paramilitary.

Source: Adapted by Anthony H. Cordesman from International Institute for Strategic Studies, *Military Balance* (IISS, London), in this case, the 1995–1996 edition; *Military Technology, World Defense Almanac, 1994–1995*; and Jaffee Center for Strategic Studies, *The Military Balance in the Middle East, 1993–1994* (JCSS, Tel Aviv, 1994).

technicians. As a result, there is a relatively high degree of military proficiency in many areas, although Saudi Arabia has been slow to develop systems of rotation that retire senior officers and systems which modernize the higher levels of command.

Saudi Arabia has one of the most complex military structures of any developing nation, and it operates some of the most advanced military technology in the world. In several cases, this technology is more advanced than that in developed NATO countries. At the same time, Saudi Arabia is just completing the final stages of massive infrastructure programs that have created some of the world's most modern facilities out of empty desert. It is beginning to produce its first full generation of other ranks with modern military training. Only a generation ago most of its troops were Bedouin with only limited education and technical background. Saudi Arabia is also moving from a nation whose military forces were almost entirely static and defensive in character to military forces with close collective security ties to the United States and growing ties to several other Southern Gulf states—most notably Bahrain and Kuwait.

The Saudi military forces have often been criticized for their weaknesses by those who have little appreciation of the challenges they have faced or of how much they have accomplished. There is no doubt that Saudi Arabia's military planning and management has been as imperfect as that of every other country that has tried to cope with the on-going revolution in military affairs. At the same time, Saudi Arabia has faced massive challenges in terms of manpower, infrastructure, and technology transfer and it is important to understand just how much the Kingdom has and has not accomplished in meeting its challenges.

Saudi Military Manpower

Manpower is the most important single challenge that Saudi Arabia has faced since it first decided to create modern military forces in the 1960s, and it is a challenge which it will continue to face until well after the year 2000. Saudi Arabia's total population is limited relative to its Gulf neighbors so its ability to recruit and trained qualified manpower is a serious problem.

There have long been debates over the size of Saudi Arabia's native population. During much of the 1980s, Saudi Arabia issued figures that exaggerated its total population because it felt a higher number gave it strategic and political value in dealing with the rest of the Arab world. In 1992, however, it completed a more accurate census which estimated its population at 16.9 million, with a population growth rate of 3.5% to 3.7% per year. The CIA estimate for 1995 is 18,730,000, which is close to the probable increase in the Saudi total, and the CIA estimates that 12,304,835 of this total consists of native citizens. The IISS estimates the current total population of Saudi Arabia at 18,613,000, of which 12,843,000—or 69%—is native.[154]

The CIA estimates that there are about 5.3 million males between the ages of 15 and 49, but this figure may include some foreign workers. About 2.9 million of this total are fit for military service. It estimates that the population is about 90% Arab and 10% Afro-Asian. It also estimates that 164,200 males reach age 17 each year, when they become eligible for military service.[155] The IISS estimates there are 1,128,400 males between the ages of 13 and 17, 907,400 between the ages of 18 and 22, and 1,396,200 between the ages of 23 and 32.[156]

Table Six shows that the total pool of 5.3 million Saudi men compares with roughly 14.6 million males of military age in Iran, 4.6 million males of military age in Iraq, and 3.1 million males of military age in Yemen.[157] Total population, however, is only part of the Saudi problem. Saudi Arabia has not mobilized its manpower as effectively as Iran and Iraq, both of which were able to place nearly one million men under arms during the Iran-Iraq War. Saudi Arabia currently has only a maximum of 162,500 men in its regular forces and the National Guard, compared with 513,000 for Iran and 382,000 for Iraq (which has a roughly similar population.)

In spite of massive improvements in Saudi education, it is still hard to recruit and retain skilled manpower, and Saudi Arabia still has to train its military manpower intensely. Saudi military forces are very well paid, but the armed forces cannot compete with the civilian economy. The Saudi military manpower base is also limited by continuing tribal and regional rivalries. Saudi Arabia is cautious about recruiting from the regions—like the Hejaz—that opposed the Saudi conquest in the 1920s and 1930s, and from rival tribes. The rise of Islamic fundamentalism among the poorer and more tribal Saudis, coupled with long-standing hostility among a number of tribes and the Hejaz, place additional serious limits on the Saudi recruiting base and the groups it can conscript. As a result, the armed forces has already drawn heavily on most of the tribal and regional groupings on which it can count for political support.

In the past, Saudi Arabia has tried to compensate for these manpower problems by:

- A heavy dependence on foreign support and technicians (now over 14,000 personnel);
- Using small elements of foreign forces in key specialty and technical areas—such as combat engineers— to "fill in" the gaps in Saudi land forces. It formerly had some 10,000 Pakistani troops to fill out one brigade (the 12th Armored Brigade) at Tabuk. These Pakistani forces

TABLE SIX Saudi Military Demographics Versus Those of Neighboring States (1995)

Country	Total Population	Males Reaching Military Age Each Year	Males Between the Ages of			Males Between 15 and 49	
			13 and 17	18 and 22	23 and 32	Total	Medically Fit
Saudi Arabia	18,730,000	164,220	1,128,400	907,400	1,396,200	5,304,000	2,950,000
Iran	64,625,000	615,096	3,844,400	3,159,000	4,828,600	14,630,000	8,704,000
Iraq	20,644,000	229,015	1,293,000	1,063,000	1,562,600	4,627,000	2,598,000
Yemen	14,728,000	181,057	800,400	707,800	1,120,400	3,135,600	1,771,226
Bahrain	575,900	4,346	25,600	20,800	40,800	210,725	117,414
Kuwait	1,817,000	16,710	102,000	78,400	140,800	610,205	363,735
Oman	2,125,000	26,065	105,600	83,400	127,800	520,428	294,993
Qatar	544,000	3,915	21,200	17,600	38,800	219,442	115,013
UAE	2,924,600	19,266	82,600	72,000	140,400	1,072,300	584,000
Egypt	62,360,000	648,724	3,264,000	2,739,600	4,650,200	16,113,000	10,456,000
Jordan	4,100,900	45,494	246,400	232,600	410,000	981,004	699,891
Syria	14,284,000	159,942	869,600	702,400	1,075,000	3,440,030	1,928,000

Source: CIA, World Factbook, 1995 and IISS, Military Balance, 1995–1996.

have not been replaced, although possible contingency arrangements may exist with Egypt.[158]

- Use of French and British internal security experts;
- Selective undermanning while it builds its training and manpower base;
- Concentrating on building a fully effective air force as a first line deterrent and defense; and,
- A *de facto* reliance on over-the-horizon reinforcement by the US, France, Egypt, Syria, or some other power to deal with high-level or enduring conflicts.

These measures have not, however, compensated for the quantitative and qualitative problems caused by the slow build-up of Saudi military manpower shown in Chart Fifteen. Saudi Arabia currently only has approximately 105,500 full time uniformed actives in its armed forces, plus 57,000 more full-time actives in its paramilitary Royal Guards and National Guard, 10,500 in its Frontier Forces, 4,500 in its Coast Guard, and up to 500 more men in its Special Security Forces and other special units. These figures produce a maximum of about 178,000 men, and much of this total includes men who are part-time or have assignments in forces with little military capability, except in internal security missions.

Saudi Arabia talked about expanding its total manpower to 200,000 men after the Gulf War, and Prince Sultan reiterated this goal in May, 1996. He stated that, "The sixth plan for our armed forces, which may begin next year, will be, God willing, a plan of expansion not only in purchases but in men and attracting Saudi school and university graduates."[159] It is far from clear, however, that Saudi Arabia can reach 200,000 full time actives of reasonable quality by the year 2002, and such an expansion would scarcely permit the doubling of Saudi Arabia's force structure or the creation of large numbers of additional combat units. Even by the standards of Iranian and Iraqi forces, it would take about 150,000 full-time actives to man the regular part of Saudi Arabia's force structure adequately. Saudi Arabia is also short of the skilled career manpower necessary to maintain its present forces, much less support major expansion plans.

At the same time, many of Saudi Arabia's manpower constraints will change during the next decade. Saudi Arabia's high population growth rate will sharply increase the number of eligible men; its educational system is becoming significantly superior to that of many of its neighbors, and military service is becoming more popular. Saudi Arabia has begun to pay more for new entrants relative to comparable civilian jobs, and the expectations of young Saudis are more modest than they were in the 1970s and 1980s.

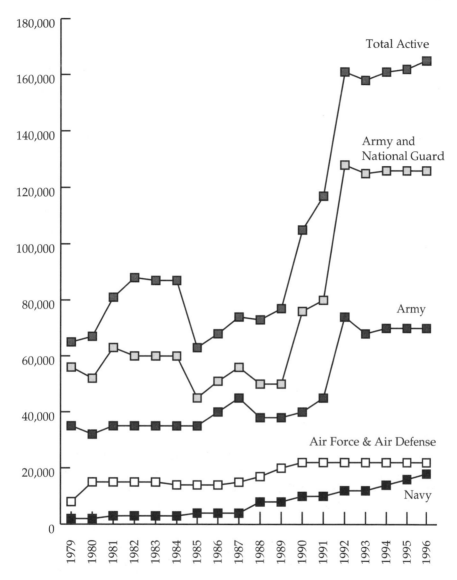

CHART FIFTEEN Saudi Military Manning—1979–1996. *Source:* Adapted by Anthony H. Cordesman from various editions of the IISS, *Military Balance,* the JCSS, *Military Balance in the Middle East,* and material provided by US experts.

The Gulf War also showed that Saudi Arabia can expand its forces in an emergency. It called for volunteers for the first time, expecting some 25,000 volunteers at most. It got 200,000 to 250,000. This is another indicator that Saudi Arabia probably could expand its manpower significantly in future years. At the same time, the internal political issues discussed earlier prevent Saudi Arabia from instituting conscription—the only way it can assure a stable supply of increased manpower. While Saudi officials have talked about conscription for more than a decade, Saudi Arabia's religious establishment opposes this as a violation of Islamic law, and any full-scale program would have unacceptable political and economic costs.[160]

As a result, Saudi Arabia must concentrate on the "Saudiazation" of its combat arms. It must allocate most of its output of skilled military manpower to operational forces and command roles, and it cannot hope to replace Western technical support. It has learned from the Gulf War, however, that it may be able to organize its land units to accept volunteers into support units with functions similar to their civil jobs, and shift regular military personnel to combat functions. This is now being studied as a possible alternative to conscription.[161]

It is difficult to make any estimate of the degree to which Saudi Arabia currently offsets its manpower shortages by the use of foreign troops and advisors. Further, the separation between formal military advisors and Western contractors is often more a matter of clothing than function. There are significant numbers of US, British, and French military advisors, and at least several thousand Western contract personnel—many handling critical service and support functions for Saudi Arabia's most modern weapons. There are small cadres from Brazil and other arms sellers, and at least several hundred PRC personnel servicing and operating Saudi Arabia's CSS-2 long-range surface-to-surface missiles. There no longer seem to be whole Pakistani formations in Saudi Arabia, but there may still be over 1,000 Pakistani troops there, some operating at the battalion level in the army.[162]

Saudi Military Expenditures

It is impossible to make precise estimates of Saudi military spending that take full account of all purchases of equipment, construction, and services. Saudi Arabia does not report many of its costs in its budget documents—particularly costs relating to the purchase of foreign defense goods and services—and Saudi Arabia often adjusts its flow of defense expenditures without reporting them. Saudi and outside sources report very different figures, and the problem is compounded by the difficulty of making accurate estimates of expenditures in constant Rials and constant dollars and Rial to dollar conversions, as well as pricing annual cash outflows for large purchases of defense goods and services.

Saudi Estimates of Saudi Military Expenditures

In FY1986, the Saudi defense and security budget was projected at 64.6 billion Rials ($17.7 billion), or 32% of the total budget.[163] The oil revenue deficit then led to spending cuts to about 64.09 billion Rials ($17.3 billion). The FY1987 defense and security budget was about 60.8 billion Rials, or $16.23 billion.[164] The FY1988 defense and security budget, which includes the National Guard and the Interior Ministry and its police forces, was originally projected at about 50.8 billion Rials or $13.6 billion. This was a cut of 9.9 billion Rials or $2.57 billion from FY1988.[165] The FY1989 budget seems to have been 55.0 billion Rials ($14.69 billion).

The Saudi government reports the FY1990 defense and security budget to have been 51.9 billion Rials ($13.8 billion), but actual expenditures may have been 119.216 billion Rials ($31.86 billion)—including $18 billion in Gulf War contributions to the US and UK. The FY1991 defense budget seems to have reached at least 100.4 billion Rials ($26.8 billion), including $13.73 billion in contributions to the US, France, Britain, Kuwait, and other members of the UN Coalition. It may have reached as high as $31.8 billion.[166] From FY1992 onwards, Saudi official defense budgets seem to be more accurate. As Table Seven shows, the FY1992 budget was 54.3 billion Rials ($14.47 billion), and the FY1993 budget was 61.64 billion Rials ($16.43 billion). The FY1994 budget was projected to be $13.9 billion and the FY1995 budget to be $13.2 billion.[167]

US and IISS Estimates of Saudi Military Expenditures

US estimates of Saudi military spending are different from those of Saudi Arabia, although many of the differences may reflect differences over exchange rates and reporting periods, rather than significant differences as to the value of goods and services. If one uses ACDA and CIA sources, Saudi defense expenditures were $9.6 billion in 1978, $12.4 billion in 1979, $15.0 billion in 1980, $18.4 billion in 1981, $22.0 billion in 1982, $24.8 billion in 1983, $20.4 billion in 1984, $21.3 billion in 1985, $17.3 billion in 1986, $16.2 billion in 1987, $13.6 billion in 1988, $14.7 billion in 1989, $23.2 billion in 1990, $35.5 billion in 1991, $35.0 billion in 1992, $20.5 billion in 1993, and $17.2 billion in 1994.[168]

US estimates of Saudi military spending in constant dollars are summarized in Chart Sixteen, along with similar data on the trends in central government spending, total exports (oil income), and arms imports. This chart shows that Saudi military expenditures are high relative to the size

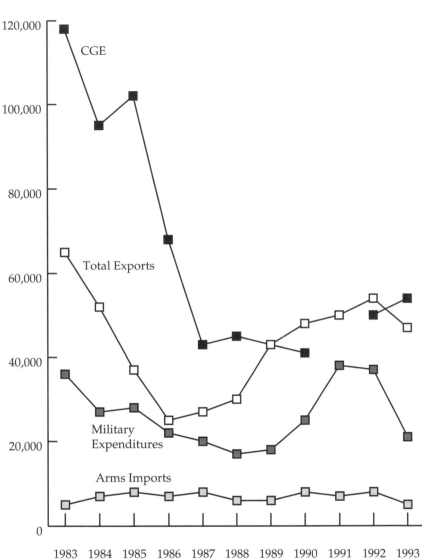

CHART SIXTEEN   Saudi Central Government Expenditures, Military Expenditures, Total Exports, and Arms Import Deliveries—1983–1993 (Constant $93
Millions). *Source:* Adapted by Anthony H. Cordesman from ACDA, *World
Military Expenditures and Arms Transfers, 1993–1994,* ACDA/GPO, Washington,
1995.

of the total Saudi central government budget. No other Southern Gulf state, and few other states world-wide, maintain this scale of military effort. As a result, Saudi military spending does compete directly with civil spending. These data also show that Saudi Arabia increased central government expenditures and military spending as a result of the Gulf War, but this increase was far smaller as a percent of total GDP than in the case of Kuwait. The burden of paying for the Gulf War—while significant—did not have a massive long-term impact on the Saudi economy.

"Guns" Versus "Butter" and Saudi Defense Expenditures as a Percent of Total Government Expenditures

Western policy-makers have sometimes tended to treat Saudi oil wealth as infinite when they have sought increased Saudi arms purchases or Saudi financial support in meeting their strategic objectives. Saudi Arabia's current political and economic problems are a warning, however, that there are growing limits to the extent to which Saudi Arabia can afford to sustain its economic development, share its oil wealth in ways that maintain internal economic stability, and modernize its military forces.

No nation can easily fund both "guns" and "butter," and Saudi Arabia has already had to pay exceptional costs to convert a nomadic society into one capable of operating modern armor, ships, and aircraft. It has only been able to do this by creating entire military cities, new ports, and major road networks. In fact, Saudi Arabia has had the highest ratio of expenditures to active men in uniform of any country in the developing world for more than a quarter century.

Saudi Arabia has had to spend several hundred billion dollars to create a modern system of bases, the ability to train and support soldiers capable of operating modern military equipment, and a pool of equipment modern enough to give it a potential edge over Iran and Iraq. It spent from $14 to $24 billion a year on defense during the later 1970s and the 1980s, although its full-time active military manpower only ranged from 79,000 to 84,000.

Much of this expenditure—probably on the order of 60–65%—was spent on infrastructure, foreign services and maintenance, and basic manpower training. It also took place at the cost of increases in civil and foreign investment, domestic and foreign borrowing, and led to drawing on foreign reserves. It has also helped lead to the budget deficit discussed earlier and created the relationship between total government spending and defense spending shown in Table Seven.[169]

The Gulf War sharply increased Saudi military and security expenditures as a percent of the total Saudi budget. This percentage rose from

TABLE SEVEN The Cost of Guns and Butter ($ Current Billions)

Fiscal Year	Total Saudi Budget			Defense and Security	Military Imports	
	Revenues	Expenditures	Difference		Orders	Deliveries
1982–1983	83.57	83.57	—	24.8	-2.8	
1983–1984	60.00	69.33	-9.33	20.4	-3.8	
1984–1985	57.09	69.33	-12.24	21.3	-3.3	
1985–1986	53.33	53.33	—	17.3	-5.5	
1987	31.25	45.33	-14.08	16.2	-7.0	
1988	28.08	37.65	-9.57	13.6	-2.7	
1989	30.93	37.60	-6.67	14.7	-4.2	
1990	31.46	38.13	-6.67	13.8	-31.9**	6.7–18.6
1991*	31.46	38.13	-6.67	13.0	-31.8**	7.1–7.8
1992	40.26	48.26	-8.00	14.5	4.5	4.5
1993	45.10	52.52	-7.41	16.4	-5.1	
1994	32.00	42.66	-10.67	13.9	—	
1995	36.00	40.00	4.00	13.2	—	

*Nominal budget. Actual expenditures higher due to Gulf War.

**Higher range includes aid payments to US and other Gulf War allies and special costs for Gulf War.

Source: Adapted by the author from materials provided by the Embassy of Saudi Arabia in Washington, and data provided by the Arms Control and Disarmament Agency and the Congressional Research Service.

36% in 1988, and 39% in 1989, to nearly 80% in 1990—although any such figures are highly dependent on what aspects of the cost of Saudi support to allied military forces during the Gulf War is included. The percentage reached around 70% in 1991—including the cost of aid to allied governments during Desert Storm—but has declined to around 30% since 1992.[170] US estimates indicate a similar trend for Saudi defense spending as a percentage of total GDP. Saudi Arabia spent about 20% of its GDP on defense during 1983–1986, reduced this to 16% during 1988 and 1989, and then increased this percentage to 21% in 1990, 29% in 1991, and 27% in 1992. This percentage dropped back to 16% in 1993.

There is no way to establish a "golden rule" as to what share Saudi military and security expenditures should consume of the total budget. It is clear, however, that the recent percentages have placed an increasing strain on the Saudi budget and economy, and that this strain will continue. At the same time, these percentages are not easy to cut. Saudi Arabia must spend about $10 to $13 billion a year, in 1995 dollars, if it is to maintain its present forces and rate of modernization. It should be noted that the military is apparently making an effort to save some money by increasing its electronics repair capability, which would reduce the number of spares normally required to be stockpiled while systems are enroute for overseas repair.[171]

Saudi Arms Imports

Saudi Arabia has long made massive expenditures on military imports—totaling $52.4 billion in new deliveries during 1985–1992, with $63.6 billion in new agreements. These expenditures, however, are not comparable to those of other Middle Eastern countries as a measure of arms or weapons imports.[172] Until the mid- to late 1980s, these military import figures included an exceptionally large portion of construction, and goods and services. While such imports do not include any weapons, they are classified as "arms imports" because they are funded as part of the US foreign military sales program and other foreign sales programs.

In contrast, the arms sales data on other countries in the Middle East have been dominated by the cost of actual weapons purchases. Further, the weapons that have made up such purchases have often been obtained at far lower prices per weapon than the weapons shipped to Saudi Arabia—particularly in the case of weapons supplied by states in the former Soviet Union, the PRC, North Korea, and Central Europe. This makes it impossible to relate data on Saudi purchases of military imports to the actual flow of arms into Saudi Arabia or to the data on other countries in the region. No other country in the developing world has received so few actual arms per dollar.

The Volume of Saudi Arms Imports

These problems in interpreting the data on Saudi Arabia have been compounded by the fact that Saudi Arabia does not provide statistics on its military imports, and most outside estimates are little more than rough guesses with little analytic reliability. Two sources are available, however, from the US government: The Arms Control and Disarmament Agency (ACDA), and the Congressional Research Service. These indicate the steady increase in Saudi expenditures that has taken place in reaction to the massive build-up of Iraqi and Iranian forces, the threats and uncertainties posed by the Iran-Iraq War, the cost of fighting the Gulf War, and other current threats.

ACDA estimates that Saudi Arabia imported $1.5 billion worth of military imports in 1978, $1.2 billion in 1979, $1.6 billion in 1980, $2.7 billion in 1981, $2.8 billion in 1982, $3.3 billion in 1983, $4.8 billion in 1984, 5.4 billion in 1985, $5.1 billion in 1986, $6.0 billion in 1987, $5.1 billion in 1988, $5.2 billion in 1989, $ 6.8 billion in 1990, $6.2 billion in 1991, $7.2 billion in 1992, and $5.1 billion in 1993.[173] The trends in these data have already been shown in Charts One and Three.

More recent data, issued by Richard F. Grimmett of the Congressional Research Service, are shown in Chart Seventeen, and reflect a major shift to the US market and a decline in orders from Europe and the PRC. They indicate that the rate of Saudi arms imports has not increased radically as a result of the Gulf War. In fact, new Saudi arms import agreements during 1991–1994 were only about two-thirds of the total during 1987–1990. However, recent Saudi orders are still extremely large by the standards of other countries.[174]

Sources of Saudi Arms Imports

ACDA reporting indicates that Saudi Arabia has obtained most of its military imports from three nations: The United States, France, and Britain. If one examines the period from 1979–1983—which covers the period from the fall of the Shah of Iran through the early years of the Iran-Iraq War—ACDA reports that Saudi Arabia took delivery on $12.125 billion worth of military imports. This included $5.1 billion worth of military imports from the US, $2.5 billion from France, $1.9 billion from the UK, $525 million from West Germany, $200 million from Italy, and $1.9 billion from other countries.[175]

Saudi Arabia took delivery on $19.530 billion worth of military imports during 1984–1988. This included $5.8 billion worth of military imports from the US, $7.5 billion from France, $2.5 billion from the PRC, $2.1 billion from the UK, $30 million from Italy, and $1.6 billion from other countries.[176]

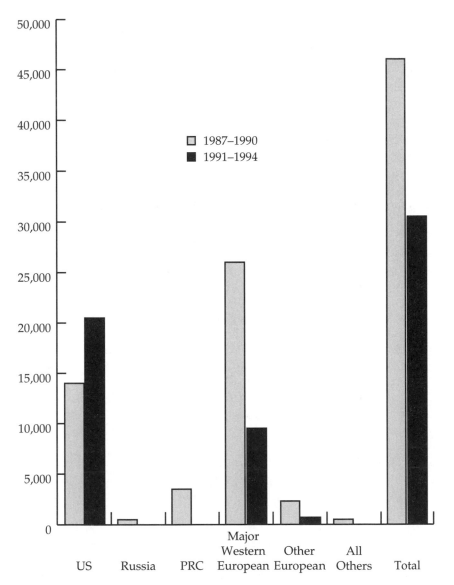

CHART SEVENTEEN   Saudi Arabian Arms Sales Agreements by Supplier
Country—1987–1994 ($Current Millions). *Source:* Adapted by Anthony H.
Cordesman from work by Richard F. Grimmett in *Conventional Arms Transfers to
Developing Nations, 1987–1994,* Congressional Research Service 95-862F, August 4,
1994, pp. 56–57.

During the period from 1985–1989—which covers the period from the most intense fighting in the Iran-Iraq War through the cease-fire in 1988—Saudi Arabia imported $23.04 billion worth of military goods, including $5.0 billion from the US, $7.0 billion from France, $7.7 billion from the UK, $2.5 billion from the PRC, $40 million from West Germany, $250 million from other European countries, $140 million from other East Asian states, $390 million from Latin America, and $20 million from other countries in the world.[177]

During 1992–1994—the period immediately after the Gulf War—Saudi Arabia imported $20.465 billion worth of military goods, including $8.6 billion from the US, $525 million from France, $9.4 billion from the UK, $170 million from the PRC, $30 million from Germany, $670 million from other European countries, $10 million from other East Asian states, $70 million from Russia, and $90 million from other countries in the world.[178] These totals for 1991–1993 are somewhat misleading, however, because they only reflect deliveries and were heavily influenced by past orders of British aircraft. Most new Saudi orders were placed with the US.

Reporting by the Congressional Research Service indicates that Saudi Arabia took delivery on $48.1 billion worth of arms during 1983–1989, and purchased 14.1% of all Third World military import agreements during 1982–1989.[179] If one looks at total transfers to the developing world, Saudi Arabia was the largest "arms" importer during 1984–1987 ($27.5 billion) and the largest during 1988–1991 ($26.8 billion). It must be stressed, however, that the figures for Saudi Arabia include substantial amounts of services, and the value of actual weapons transfers is around half the total reported.

The Gulf War forced Saudi Arabia to make major additional purchases of military imports. In 1990, the Congressional Research Service indicates Saudi Arabia ordered $18.6 billion worth of military imports, and took delivery on $6.749 billion worth. Saudi Arabia cut its new orders to $7.8 billion in 1991, but took delivery on $7.1 billion as its backlog of increased orders began to raise deliveries. Both new orders and deliveries dropped to $4.5 billion in 1992. Saudi military imports then began to rise again because of the perceived threats from Iran and Iraq. Saudi Arabia ordered $9.6 billion worth, and took delivery on $6.4 billion worth. In 1994, it ordered $9.5 billion worth of military imports and took delivery on $5.2 billion.

Saudi Arabia ordered a total of $30.2 billion worth of military imports during 1991–1994. A total of $20.2 billion came from the US, $9.5 billion from major West European countries, and $500 million from other European countries. Saudi Arabia took delivery on a total of $27.9 billion worth of military imports during 1991–1994. A total of $10.9 billion came from the US, $300 million came from China, $100 million came from Russia, $14.7 billion from major West European countries, $1.8 billion came from all other European countries, and $100 million came from other countries.[180]

The recent patterns in Saudi imports become clearer from other sources, which break out the source of Saudi imports immediately before and after the Gulf War in more detail. Saudi Arabia received a total of $25.5 billion in deliveries of military imports during 1989–1992. Its principal suppliers were the four major West European nations ($13.3 billion), and the United States ($8.8 billion). It also received $1.3 billion worth of military imports from other European countries, $200 million worth of military imports from Russia, $1.7 billion from the PRC, and $200 million from other countries.[181]

Saudi purchases during 1992–1994 were very similar. Saudi Arabia received a total of $20.465 billion in deliveries of military imports during 1992–1994. Its principal suppliers were the United Kingdom ($9.4 billion) and the United States ($8.6 billion). It also received $900 million worth of arms from Canada, $$525 million worth from France, $30 million worth from Germany, $900 million worth of military imports from other European countries, $170 million worth from the PRC, $10 million worth from other East Asian countries, and $80 million from other countries.[182]

The Changing Nature of Saudi Arms Imports

These are high levels of imports by any standard, but the total dollar value provides a misleading picture of the true nature of the Saudi military imports. Many of the Saudi imports counted in these figures were not arms, and a substantial portion went to the UN Coalition and preparation to support US power projection. Between 1989 and 1992, large amounts of the total arms deliveries to Saudi Arabia consisted of the in-kind support and arms that Saudi Arabia transferred to the UN Coalition during Operation Desert Storm.

There have been major qualitative changes in Saudi military imports since the mid-1980s, which have been further accelerated since the Gulf War. Until the mid-1980s, Saudi Arabia concentrated on building up its military infrastructure and basic military capabilities. Since the mid-1980s, Saudi military imports have shifted to include a steadily increasing number of first line weapons systems. If Saudi Arabia imported only a moderate amount of actual arms per military import dollar before 1988, and concentrated on building the foundation for modern forces, it has recently attempted to increase its pace of military expansion, even if this has meant increasing the burden on the budget and the budget deficit, and causing

TABLE EIGHT   Key Saudi Equipment Developments

- 315 M-1A2s, 30 M-88A1 tank recovery vehicles, 175 M-998 utility trucks, 224 heavy tactical trucks, 29 heavy equipment transporters, 268 five ton trucks, spares and support equipment, logistics support, ammunition, facilities design and construction, training aids and devices, and US military training services.
- 235 additional M-1A2 tanks, or Leclercs.
- 400 M-2A2s, 200 M-113 armored personnel carriers, 50 M-548 cargo carriers, 17 M-88A1 recovery vehicles, and 43 M-578 recovery vehicles.
- Additional Astros II and M-198s on order, better mobile fire-control and ammunition-supply equipment, and new target acquisition radars—such as the AN/PPS-15A, MSTAR, or Rasit 3190B.
- Considered order for 9 Multiple Launch Rocket Systems (MLRS), including vehicle mounted rocket launchers, 2,880 tactical rockets, 50 practice rockets, 9 MV-755A2 command post carriers, training and training equipment.
- 12 AH-64 Apache attack helicopters, 155 Hellfire missiles, 24 spare Hellfire launchers, six spare engines and associated equipment. Possible total of 48 AH-64s.
- Saudi National Guard has bought 400 to 450 versions of the Piranha light armored vehicle. Also 1,117 LAV-25s (light armored vehicles) from General Motors of Canada through the US Army Tank Automotive Command (TACOM).
- Two new Lafayette-class F-3000 frigates.
- More Sandown or Tripartite minelayers.
- Consider buy of several AEGIS-class warships to give it advanced battle management, Harpoon anti-ship missiles, Tomahawk strike capability, ASW, anti-aircraft, and anti-ship missile defense capabilities.
- 24 F-15S aircraft designed for air combat, and 48 F-15S aircraft dual-capable in both the air defense and strike/attack missions: 24 spare engines, 48 targeting and navigation pods, 900 AGM-65D/G Maverick air-to-surface missiles, 600 CBU-87 bombs, 700 GBU-10/12 bombs, and special mission planning systems.
- 20 more Hawk 65 jets and 20 more Swiss Pilatus PC-9 turboprop trainers.
- 20 Patriot batteries with 1,055 missiles.
- New Peace Shield system fully operational.

---

considerable turbulence in Saudi Arabia's force structure, shortages in skilled personnel, and overall undermanning in Saudi forces.

At the same time, the following analysis of Saudi military modernization efforts by service indicates that most of Saudi Arabia's actual purchase of arms have met valid military needs and remain important to Saudi strategic interests. Saudi Arabia is driven to match the military build-up in Iran, and increase its deterrent and war fighting capability against Iraq in preparation for the eventual lifting of UN sanctions. It must also continue to pay for the many costs of prepositioning munitions, supplies, and service facilities for the power projection capabilities of Britain and the US.

Saudi Arabia has no easy way to strike a balance between security and its domestic economic needs. It is unfair, and somewhat hypocritical, for the West to criticize Saudi Arabia for making purchases that not only serve the strategic interests of Saudi Arabia, but also those of the West.

Military Imports from the US

Table Nine shows the value of US military exports to Saudi Arabia since 1950, which total more than $81 billion worth of military goods. Saudi Arabia took delivery on $8.6 billion worth of this total during 1992–1994.[183] Saudi Arabia's purchases of actual weapons, however, have been far more modest than this total seems to imply. Saudi Arabia spent over $50 billion of this total on US military goods and services that did not include major weapons, and it had spent more on US military construction services than it had spent on major arms until the period shortly before the Gulf War.

There were also many problems in these US arms transfers to Saudi Arabia. The US sometimes declined to sell key weapons to Saudi Arabia because of political objections within the US Congress, or proposed arms sales packages that met US needs without meeting Saudi needs. Examples of such problems include a covert US arrangement with Britain where the US pressured Saudi Arabia into buying British Lightning fighters and surface-to-air missiles so that Britain could afford to buy US F-4 fighters. The problems included a refusal to sell more US tanks that led Saudi Arabia to buy low-grade French AMX-30s; a naval advisory and sales effort that sold Saudi Arabia low-grade, used US Navy ships that the US failed to properly support; and a series of long, bitter debates over the sale of the E-3A AWACS and F-15S. At the same time, the Saudi purchases shown in Table Nine went on to play a vital role in helping to support the US in Desert Storm.

The recent trends in Saudi orders of US military equipment are summarized in Table Ten. Reporting by the US Defense Security Assistance Agency shows that Saudi Arabia signed major new FMS sales agreements as a result of the Gulf War, and ordered $11.7 billion worth of arms in fiscal year 1991, about $1 billion worth in 1992, $11.6 billion worth in 1993, and $1 billion in 1994. Saudi Arabia has also placed significant orders for commercial sales from the US—although these orders were a small portion of its total FMS orders—and ordered significant US military construction services as a result of the Gulf War.

The value of US deliveries to Saudi Arabia shows less of a rise, but this is a result of long lead times between agreements and deliveries and the fact that Saudi Arabia has signed delivery schedules that avoid massive deliveries in any one year. All US sales to Saudi Arabia are cash transac-

TABLE NINE   US Arms Transfers to Saudi Arabia by Category ($US billions)

Category	1950–1990		1991–1993*		1950–1993	
	Ordered	Percentage	Ordered	Percentage	Ordered	Percentage
Weapons and ammunition	8.384	16	5.317	30	13.700	19
Support equipment	8.541	16	4.956	28	13.497	19
Spare parts, modifications	4.578	9	2.609	15	7.187	10
Support services	15.835	29	4.624	26	20.459	29
Construction	16.486	31	0.421	2	16.907	24
Totals	53.823	100	17.927	100	71.751	100

Notes: Amounts represent agreement, not deliveries. A total of $46.765 billion had been delivered as of March 31, 1993.
Percentages are for total arms transfers constituted by each of the five categories shown in the left hand column.
*Includes FY1991, FY1992, and the first six months of FY1993. It does not include a $9 billion order for 72 F-15S fighter aircraft signed in May, 1993.

Source: Adapted by the author from Alfred B. Prados, "Saudi Arabia: Post War Issues and US Relations," Washington, Congressional Research Service IB93113, November 3, 1994.

TABLE TEN   US Foreign Military Sales (FMS), Commercial Arms Export Agreements, Military Assistance Programs (MAP), and International Military Education and Training (IMET) Programs With Saudi Arabia—FY1985–1994 ($Current Millions)

	1985	1986	1987	1988	1989	1990	1991	1992	1993	1994
Foreign Military Financing Program Payment Waived	—	—	—	—	—	—	—	—	—	—
DoD Direct	—	—	—	—	—	—	—	—	—	—
DoD Guarantee	—	—	—	—	—	—	—	—	—	—
FMS Agreements	2,447.1	695.0	650.5	1,658.7	1,165.7	4,093.4	11,740.4	965.8	11,624.2	837.9
Commercial Sales	138.8	81.4	183.2	167.6	68.2	91.5	66.7	88.9	4.0	2.2
FMS Construction Agreements	927.7	6.0	—	18.7	—	165.5	323.8	538.0	780.0	—
FMS Deliveries	1,359.4	2,199.1	3,081.1	967.2	638.9	889.0	2,767.6	2,458.1	3,537.5	2,174.7
MAP Program	—	—	—	—	—	—	—	—	—	—
MAP Deliveries	—	—	—	—	—	—	—	—	—	—
MAP Excess Defense Articles Program	—	—	—	—	—	—	—	—	—	—
MAP Excess Defense Articles Deliveries	—	—	—	—	—	—	—	—	—	—
IMET Program/Deliveries	—	—	—	—	—	—	—	—	—	—

Source: Adapted from US Defense Security Assistance Agency (DSAA), "Foreign Military Sales, Foreign Military Construction Sales and Military Assistance Facts as of September 30, 1994," Department of Defense, Washington, 1995.

tions. Saudi Arabia does not make use of the International Military Education and Training (IMET), and has received no recent Military Assistance Program (MAP) aid.[184]

These Saudi purchases provide an important contingency capability for any future US intervention in the Gulf. This is not an argument for issuing Saudi Arabia a "blank check" to buy any US weapon or technology. There are good reasons to examine each US arms sale, and it has only been during the last few years that the Arab-Israeli peace process has advanced to the point where concerns that Saudi Arabia might use US arms directly or indirectly against Israel have diminished to the point where technology transfer has become a relatively minor issue.

The US also needs to work closely with Saudi Arabia to ensure that its FMS purchases remain affordable and that Saudi Arabia can meet its payment schedules without impacting too much on its budget deficits and civil expenditures. The total Saudi FMS debt will drop to $10 billion in FY1997, but Saudi Arabia still owes the US a great deal for a few major cases. In mid-1996, it still owed $6.5 billion out of a total of $9.0 billion for the 72 F-15Ss, $500 million out of $3.1 billion for 315 M-1A2s, $500 million out of $1.5 billion for 400 M-2A2s, and $2.2 billion out of $4.0 billion for 20 Patriot batteries. Saudi Arabia will continue to need some major new arms programs, but it must be careful to stick within its fiscal guideline of a maximum FMS debt of $10 billion, and it needs to give priority to funding the rounding-out of its partially field combat units and military organizations, to fully fund resource training, and the overall level of training and readiness necessary to make its present forces and arms orders fully effective.

The Financing of Saudi Military Imports

Saudi Arabia has faced growing problems in financing its military imports because of the costs of the Gulf War. A combination of Saudi Arabia's budget deficits resulting from the Gulf War, and lower oil revenues, forced Saudi Arabia to reduce its arms purchases after 1991. It then forced Saudi Arabia to limit its arms payments on existing orders in 1994. Saudi Arabia had to delay several major potential military import contracts—including purchases of $64 million worth of US multiple rocket launchers and a $1 billion contract for 150 more M-1 tanks. It was also forced to delay or defer a contract with Britain for the purchase of some aviation equipment and the construction of a new air base.[185]

As a result, Saudi Arabia had to reach an agreement with the US to restructure and defer some of its payments for past military imports because it faced unanticipated major payments to the US to cover the costs of deploying US forces during the Gulf War.[186] Saudi Arabia had to restructure its payments in early 1994. Saudi Arabia faced projected payments for US arms of about $4.1 billion in 1994 and $6 billion in 1995. This would have cost Saudi Arabia $10.1 billion over a period of only two years.

As a result, the US and Saudi Arabia agreed on January 29, 1994, to restructure the Saudi military sales program in ways that avoided the cancellation of any weapons programs, but stretched some purchases out and reduced the monthly procurement rate of F-15 fighters from two to one. This cut total arms purchases during 1994–1995 from $10.1 to $9.2 billion, and Saudi Arabia's payment for 1994 to $3.35 billion. In April, Saudi Arabia also arranged to borrow $1.85 billion of this total from three Saudi banks.[187]

The data are far less clear in the case of European purchases. It is clear, however, that Saudi Arabia slipped some or adjusted many payment schedules, and canceled some contracts.

These financial problems, however, must be kept in perspective. The Gulf War forced Saudi Arabia to make massive expenditures. Even so, Saudi Arabia did not halt major arms purchases after the war. It instead restructured its arms purchases to concentrate on funding key imports. It also seems to have recovered from much of the financial impact of the war by 1995. As a result, Saudi Arabia should be able to maintain a significant rate of military modernization even if it cuts back further on future arms purchases and does not transform some of its existing agreements and memorandums of understanding into actual orders.

Commissions and Special Fees

The Saudi Ministry of Defense and Aviation (MODA) is slowly improving its accounting and fiscal controls, but commissions and special fees remain a problem. In spite of efforts to eliminate profiteering in arms sales, many European arms sales to Saudi Arabia involve at least some special payments, kick backs, commissions and fees, or open bribes. In spite of US law, US companies and firms also find ways to make such payments—sometimes by rigging the offset programs required as part of arms sales to favor firms or agents favored by given princes. Commissions and fees are also more common for US commercial arms sales than for sales under the US Foreign Military Sales program.

Such commissions and special fees are scarcely unusual. Every Gulf state engages in such practices to some degree, including Iran and Iraq, and only Kuwait and Oman have made major progress in reducing such abuses. Commissions and special fees are a normal practice in foreign arms sales to the rest of the Middle East, most of the developing world, and even some European countries. They do, however, involve truly massive sums in the case of Saudi Arabia, and taint Saudi military purchases with corruption. Extremist opposition groups—and many moderate Saudis—are convinced that Saudi arms purchases are often made as a result of commissions and bribes and charge that many of Saudi Arabia's arms buys are simply a waste of money.

These problems are compounded by agreements that trade oil for arms, or which are funded by state funds that are not integrated into the Saudi national budget. These "off-book" arms buys make orderly accounting extremely difficult, and lead to still further charges of corruption. Further, there is no doubt that many offset programs are grossly overstaffed and far too expensive, regardless of whether they are actually corrupt. In at least some cases, four Saudis or more are hired for every real job and the actual work is done by foreigners. Such offset programs may seem impressive on paper, but they are yet another waste of state funds.

Both Saudi Arabia and the West need to pay more careful attention to this aspect of Saudi arms sales. Commissions and special fees damage the credibility and integrity of the Saudi armed forces, the Saudi Royal Family, and Western governments and arms sellers. They waste state funds at a time when Saudi Arabia can no longer afford such waste, and they encourage political arms buys of a kind that undercut Saudi efforts at interoperability and standardization. There is an urgent need to improve Saudi military accounting and contracting procedures at a far more rapid rate than is currently the case, to prosecute Saudis and Westerners who engage in such practices ruthlessly, and to integrate every aspect of Saudi arms purchases fully so they are visible in the regular Saudi national budget and subject to normal Saudi audit procedures and fiscal controls.

7

The Saudi Army

The Saudi Army emerged as a significant regional military force during the Gulf War. Both Arab task forces—Joint Forces Command (East) and Joint Forces Command (North)—were organized under the command of Lt. General Prince Khalid Bin Sultan al-Saud.[188] By the time the AirLand phase of the war began, the Saudi ground forces in the theater totaled nearly 50,000 men, with about 270 main battle tanks, 930 other armored fighting vehicles, 115 artillery weapons, and over 400 anti-tank weapons.

The manpower trends in the Saudi Army have already been shown in Chart Fifteen. The growth of its armor strength is shown in Chart Eighteen, and the growth of its artillery strength is shown in Chart Nineteen.[189] The Saudi Army has, however, encountered problems in expanding to the force levels required to secure Saudi Arabia's north borders, to help ensure the security of Kuwait, and to deal with potential problems in the south.

One key problem is manpower. The Saudi Army only had a total of 38,000–43,000 men in late 1988, with another 56,000 full-time and part-time men in the National Guard. Despite crash efforts to build up the army's manpower during the Gulf War—efforts which sometimes raised combat unit manning by as much as 20%—the army's force structure was still undermanned in 1991 by about 20–35%. Many individual units had even worse manning levels.

As of 1996, the Saudi Army seems to have reached a total of around 70,000 full time actives. The army was, however, continuing to experience significant problems in recruiting and training skilled technicians and NCOs. It could not fully man its present strength of 10 independent brigades: Three armored, five mechanized, one airborne brigade, and one Royal Guards regiment. It is experiencing difficulties in expanding its combat support forces to man five independent artillery brigades and create an aviation command.[190]

The Saudi Army's force structure and equipment pool now requires a minimum of 90,000–110,000 men for proper manning—a substantial

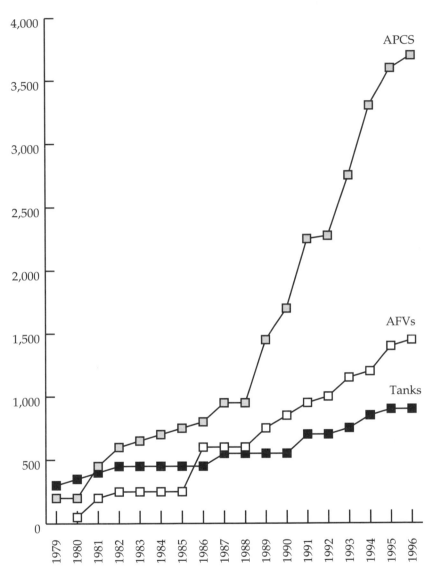

CHART EIGHTEEN   Saudi Armored Weapons Strength—1979–1996.
Source: Adapted by Anthony H. Cordesman from various editions of the IISS,
Military Balance, the JCSS, *Military Balance in the Middle East,* and material
provided by US experts.

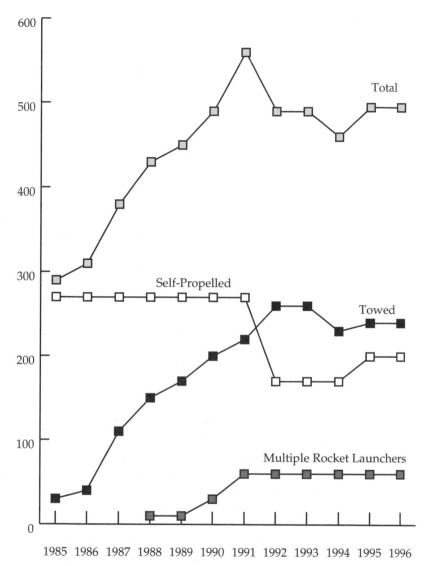

CHART NINETEEN   Saudi Artillery Weapons Strength—1985–1996.
Source: Adapted by Anthony H. Cordesman from various editions of the IISS,
Military Balance, the JCSS, *Military Balance in the Middle East,* and material
provided by US experts.

increase over the present total. While the Saudi Army may be able to build up to these numbers during the next few years, it will do so only at the cost of manpower quality. It will be hard pressed to build up to more than 100,000 fully trained and combat capable men by the year 2000. In the interim, it will experience turbulence and manpower allocation problems, and will have limited ability to sustain casualties. It will also remain heavily dependent on contractor support for many service support, maintenance, and logistics functions for the indefinite future.

Saudi Army Organization and Deployment

These manpower problems raise serious doubts about the kind of force expansion that has sometimes been discussed in the US and Saudi Arabia. For example, some reports indicate that a secret Saudi-US Joint Security Review, the Malcor Report, was carried out after the Gulf War in August, 1991. These reports suggest the plan called for a three corps Saudi force of seven divisions by the year 2000. Other reports indicate that it called for a nine division force of 90,000 men.[191]

The Saudi Army's current goals are more modest. Saudi Arabia now has a total of seven heavy combat brigades (three armored and four mechanized) and two light brigades. These are roughly equivalent to three full divisions (three brigades each) or four light divisions (two brigades each). According to Saudi sources, the Army would like to expand to a total of five divisions by the year 2000. This change would involve a conversion from a brigade-oriented command structure to a division-oriented structure. It would provide three divisions in the north to defend Saudi Arabia's Gulf Coast and border with Iraq. Another division would be deployed near al-Kharj or the capital, and a fifth division in the south—although some sources indicate that one brigade of this latter division would be in the south and the other would be at Tabuk.

Even these goals probably cannot be achieved.

- First, it is not clear that the Saudi command structure has yet adapted to the point where it can integrate combat operations at the divisional level.
- Second, even if all five divisions were lightly manned, the total manning of the combat units in the Saudi Army would still have to expand from about 40,000 full time regulars in 1995 to 50,000–65,000 by the year 2000.
- Third, Saudi Arabia would need more than nine heavy brigades to provide the combat elements for such a force. It currently has seven functional heavy brigades and plans to expand to nine, but it is

unclear if it has the trained manpower and equipment funds to create and sustain more than eight such brigades.

- Fourth, Saudi Arabia also plans to create another airborne brigade or major special forces units, and needs a school for airborne and special forces training. This requirement places a further strain on Saudi Army manpower and financial resources. A total Saudi force structure of about 10 brigades, plus some lighter independent formations, seems as large a force as Saudi Arabia can create and sustain until well beyond the year 2000.
- Fifth, Saudi forces currently lack all of the independent combat support and service support forces necessary to sustain and support the existing strength of the Saudi Army.
- Sixth, much of Saudi maintenance is already done by foreign contractors, and the quality of much of this work is mixed and declining. Over-stretching Saudi military manpower will further delay Saudi Army ability to provide an adequate Saudi ordinance corps and Saudi forces that can properly sustain combat equipment away from major bases, in extensive maneuver, or under conditions where combat repair and recovery are needed.
- Finally, the only way Saudi Arabia could field five divisions would be to create two-brigade units instead of the present three-brigade forces, and leave them without adequate combat support and service support forces. This change, however, would be more likely to waste manpower and financial resources on administrative staff than improve Saudi military effectiveness. The present three brigade structure is the most efficient way of organizing Saudi forces as long as they are going to be dispersed widely to the borders of the country.

Saudi Arabia has also talked about creating two to three additional light divisions and adding a mobilization or reserve component to its support forces. Such support forces would be limited in peacetime, but would use temporary duty civilians in their support forces in a major crisis. Such Saudi force expansion plans are more realistic than the Malcor plan, but still present a major challenge in terms of available manpower. Saudi Arabia will not have the necessary manning to create additional combat units, and there is little indication that Saudi Arabia has taken any steps to add a mobilization component to its support forces.

Regardless of how Saudi plans develop, no foreseeable expansion of Saudi forces will enable the Saudi Army to defend its territory in the upper Gulf from an all-out attack by Iraq, or to concentrate its forces quickly and effectively to aid Kuwait, unless Saudi Arabia has extensive US support. The Saudi Army will be hard pressed to deal with any sudden Iranian thrust across the Gulf to achieve a limited objective, such as the seizure of an oil platform or small island in the Gulf. Further, the threat from the northern Gulf is only part of the threat that Saudi Arabia must deal with. The Saudi Army must defend a territory roughly the size of the US east of the Mississippi. It must provide forces sufficient enough to defend its Western border area and Red Sea coast, while maintaining forces in the south to deal with a continuing low-level border conflict with Yemen.

As a result, the Saudi Army is normally dispersed over much of the Kingdom. It has brigade-sized casernes at Khamis Mushayt and Shahrurah in the southeast, a garrison at Najran and Jezan in the south, and brigade sized forces at King Khalid City in the north, Tabuk in the West, and Dammam in the East. The Gulf Cooperation Council Peninsular Shield Force is located at King Khalid City, which is near the border with Kuwait and Iraq. These deployments are partly a matter of internal security. Saudi forces are usually kept far away from key cities and political centers of power, but they are primarily a reflection of the fact that the Saudi Army cannot leave any of its border areas undefended.

These problems in expansion, planning, manpower, organization, and deployment are compounded by the need to operate a complex mix of equipment from many nations. The diversification of the Saudi Army's sources of army equipment has reduced its dependence on the United States, but it has also increased its training and support burden, and has raised its operations and maintenance costs. Saudi Arabia has also made some purchases of army equipment from its major oil customers that do not serve the army's needs.

Finally, Saudi weather and terrain conditions create still further problems. Much of the equipment the Saudi Army has purchased has required modification, or extensive changes to its original technical and logistic support plan, before it could be operated in large numbers. A few systems still present major servicing problems. Contractor support has sometimes been erratic, and all of these problems are compounded by the need to support equipment in remote and widely dispersed locations. The Saudi Army has tried to reduce such problems by creating an advanced logistic system, but some experts feel this effort has been overly ambitious and has lacked proper Saudi and US advisory management.

Saudi Tanks

The problem of standardization is clearly reflected in the current equipment holdings and modernization plans of the Saudi Army. In mid-1996, Saudi Arabia had about 1,055 main battle tanks and about 300 tank transporters. These tanks included 227 M-1A2s, 443 M-60A3s, and 290 French-made AMX-30s. Saudi Arabia was in the process of receiving another 88 M-1A2s, and about half of the AMX-30s were in storage.

Part of this tank force meets Saudi needs. Saudi Arabia found the M-60A3 to be a significant advance over the M-60A1 and converted all of its existing M-60A1s to the M-60A3 by 1990. Saudi Arabia's other M-60A3s are relatively new. Saudi Arabia bought 150 M-60A3s, along with 15,000 depleted uranium 105 mm anti-tank rounds, as part of an emergency order in August, 1990. The M-60A3 has shown it is capable of engaging any tank currently deployed in the region. Although it lacks a decisive technical superiority over the T-72 and the other first-line tanks in potential threat forces, it is likely to remain in the Saudi force structure through the year 2000. The M-60A3s have thermal sights, modern fire-control computers, laser range finders, and engine and air intake improvements. The M-60A3 does, however, present some operational problems—the crew compartment cannot be cooled effectively and it can develop internal temperatures of well over 120 degrees.[192]

Saudi Arabia's inventory of 290 French AMX-30s is a different story. The AMX-30 lacks the armor, firepower, and operational availability to be kept in service against threats armed with T-62s, T-72s, and modern tanks like the T-80, M-60, Khalid, Merkava, Chieftain, and Challenger. While the adoption of newer anti-armor round technology has made up for the lack of penetrating power in the Obus G rounds that France originally sold the Saudi Army, the AMX-30's fire control and range-finding capability is not able to help Saudi tank crews make up for their lack of experience. The AMX-30 also lacks the power, cooling, and filtration for desert combat. Saudi Arabia has needed to phase the AMX-30 out of its force structure for nearly half a decade. A substantial number of its AMX-30s are evidently now in storage, but Saudi Arabia is unlikely to fully phase the AMX-30 out of its forces before the late 1990s.

Saudi Arabia has long recognized the need to replace its AMX-30s, and has sought improved armor since the mid-1980s. It began by seeking to re-equip and expand its armored forces with US-made M-1 tanks. The M-1 offered the Saudi Army one of the world's most effective weapons systems, and one that could be fully supported and upgraded over time by the US Army. It not only offered Saudi Arabia a tank superior to any tank in Iranian and Iraqi forces, but also offered improved interoperability and standardization with the US Army and improved US rapid deployment capabilities. Saudi Arabia faced major uncertainties, however, over whether the US Congress would permit such sales.

As a result, Saudi Arabia examined alternative tanks—including Brazilian, British, French, and German models. It announced in February, 1988 that it had short-listed the M-1A1 and EE-T1 Osoro for some form of co-production in a purchase that might involve some 315 vehicles and a

$1 billion contract. Two issues that delayed a Saudi decision were uncertainty over whether the US was willing to sell the M-1A2 with a 120 mm gun, and whether Brazil could actually mass produce the Osoro, which then only existed in prototype form.

Saudi Arabia finally decided to buy 315 M-1A2s for a total cost of $3.1 billion in September, 1989.[193] The reasons for the Saudi decision become clear from an examination of the M-1A2s performance characteristics. The Saudis bought an advanced version of the 68.5 ton M-1 with a 120 mm gun, advanced armor, and thermal sights. It has full line-of-sight gun stabilization which provides full shoot-on-the-move capability. A digital ballistic computer provides quick aiming correction, based on automatic and manual inputs, such as wind velocity, vehicle cant, and gun tube deflection. A laser range finder provides target data for the ballistic computer. The thermal imaging sight improves target acquisition during both day and night at ranges in excess of 3,000 meters.

The M-1A2 does consume large amounts of fuel, but its 1,500 horsepower engine, automatic transmission, and two final drives give it a top speed of 43 mph on hard surfaced roads. An advanced torsion bar and long-stroke rotary shock absorber suspension give it cross country speeds of up to 33 mph. Crew survivability is enhanced by the compartmented storage of fuel and ammunition, and an automatic fire extinguisher system. The tank has a comparatively low profile and noise signature, and has external grenade launchers for rapid concealment.

Other key features of the M-1A2 tank include:[194]

- Added appliqué armor to protect it against future Soviet-made weapons systems, and potential upgradability to active armor.
- A commander's independent thermal viewer that allows him to acquire targets in the dark or haze, while the gunner is engaging other targets, and hand off such targets independently to the gunner.
- An improved commander's weapon station with excellent visibility and ballistic protection, an enlarged hatch, and protection against directed energy weapons.
- Precise position navigation and use of the satellite global positioning system (GPS).
- A carbon dioxide laser range finder that allows all-weather target engagement, reduces the risk of blinding friendly forces, and allows rapid enough calculation to engage helicopters.
- A systems integration package of features to reduce work load and crew fatigue.

Saudi Arabia bought other modifications of the M-1A2 that improved its capability for desert warfare. These included use of a

Jaguar radio to improve inter-tank communication, instead of a single channel ground/air system, a driver's thermal viewer to improve visibility through smoke and dust, a two-kilowatt external auxiliary power unit, countermine equipment, and hardware and software capable of displaying English and Arabic text, and Arabic labels.

This first M-1A2 sale was part of a package that included 30 M-88A1 tank recovery vehicles, 175 M-998 utility trucks, 224 heavy tactical trucks, 29 heavy equipment transporters, 268 five ton trucks, spares and support equipment, logistics support, ammunition, facilities design and construction, training aids and devices, and US military training services.[195] It also involved substantial offset programs, including the manufacture of radios, circuit boards, and wiring assemblies for the tank.[196] The US Congress approved the sale after it became clear that Israel did not view it as a threat.[197]

Saudi Arabia also bought advanced gunnery trainers like the EEC M-1A2 gun trainer, and began to train crews at the US Army armored warfare training center at Fort Knox. This training project is called Project Sword. It will cost $16.7 million, and the first of the 178 Saudi troops to be trained in the US to act as instructors in Saudi Arabia arrived in the US early in 1993. These Saudi troops received language training in San Antonio and exercise training at the US Army proving ground at Aberdeen.[198]

Iraq's invasion of Kuwait led Saudi Arabia to consider further purchases of M-1A2 tanks. On September 27, 1990, it signed a tentative agreement to buy a second armored vehicle package that included 235 M-1A2 tanks, 200 Bradley fight vehicles, 207 M-113 armored personnel carriers, 50 M-548 cargo carriers, 17 M-88A1 recovery vehicles, and 43 M-578 recovery vehicles. This agreement would have brought the total number of M-1A2s on order to 465 tanks, with delivery to begin in April, 1993, and to take place over a three year period.

However, Saudi Arabia delayed its order for 235 additional M-1A2s in late July, 1992, because Kuwait's purchase of the M-1A2 kept the M-1A2 production line open longer than had previously been estimated, and Saudi Arabia did not have to place its orders until production for Kuwait was completed. Saudi Arabia was then forced to continue delaying its order for financial reasons. These problems became so serious in early 1994 that it seemed in early 1994 that Saudi Arabia might have to delay taking delivery on its first orders of M-1A2s. The US planned deliveries of 175 M-1A2s in March, 1994, and another 140 in August, and these deliveries only went forward after Saudi Arabia rescheduled its arms payments to the US.[199]

There is still a debate over (a) exactly how many M-1A2s Saudi Arabia will buy, (b) whether it needs and can afford a second type of modern tank, and (c) whether it will buy surplus tanks that will provide *de facto* prepositioning for US forces.[200] Senior Saudi sources indicated in August, 1993, that the Saudi Army still planned to buy the additional 235 tanks, and was planning to create a total tank force of 1,200 tanks, with a total of 700 M-1A2s and 500 M-60A3s.[201] Such plans would meet a valid military requirement—given the projected size of the Saudi Army, the need to phase the AMX-30 entirely out of service, and the need to develop a decisive, qualitative edge over Iraq. Saudi purchases may, however, be cut back sharply because of their cost. A number of Saudi experts also wonder whether Saudi Arabia can absorb 700 M-1A2 tanks at reasonable levels of support costs.[202]

There has been growing European competition for such sales—a competition which has been heightened by Saudi Arabia's history of buying major equipment from a number of suppliers, the concern of some Saudi officers about becoming over-reliant on the M-1A2, an intense political lobbying effort, and the payment of commissions. A number of Saudi officers have advocated the purchase of the French Leclerc, which completed extensive trials in Saudi Arabia in August, 1995, to fill the vacancies left by the retirement of the AMX-30.[203] According to some US experts these trials were successful enough for the Saudi Army to consider replacing its present French tanks with the Leclerc, and Saudi Arabia called for further tests of the Leclerc in April, 1996.[204]

The British have also been invited to participate in the competition for Saudi tank purchases, and will be sending the Desert Challenger to the Kingdom during the summer of 1996 for firepower and mobility trials. The Desert Challenger is still somewhat developmental and production samples have exhibited some performance problems with the turret system, drive train, and power pack.[205] It is also unclear that Saudi Arabia will make a major buy of British military equipment as long as the CDLR is allowed to operate from British soil.

The Desert Challenger does, however, have a number of improvements over the original Challenger 2, including a German MTU powerpack capable of matching the Leclerc's 1,500 hp. The Desert Challenger will also be accompanied by a Challenger Armored Repair and Recovery vehicle. The British hope to persuade the Saudi army to conclude a $4.7 billion contract for 150–300 Desert Challengers, and possibly to buy Desert Warrior armored fighting vehicles and AS-90 self-propelled guns for British equipped units. The British may, however, encounter political problems in their sales effort because Britain allows Saudi dissidents to operate from its territory.[206]

Speculation that an entire brigade of AMX-30s is due for early retirement has also prompted General Dynamics Land Systems, the manufacturer of the M-1A2, to offer to retrofit the entire Saudi M-1A2 inventory with an auxiliary power unit and crew compartment cooling system. According to GDSL the retrofit could be done relatively easily at a facility in the region. GDSL has indicated that it hopes such actions would be followed by the purchase of additional M-1A2s.[207]

The practical problem created by this competition between the M-1A2, Leclerc, and Desert Challenger is that it could result in the Saudi Army buying two or even three different types of advanced main battle tanks with different training, support, maintenance and tactical requirements. It could also create additional problems in terms of power projection and the defense of the upper Gulf. Saudi Arabia has refused US requests to preposition armored division equipment sets in Saudi Arabia, and efforts to create stronger Gulf Cooperation Council forces to defend Kuwait and the Upper Gulf have failed.

The US M-1A2 tank may or may not be better than its European counterparts, but this is not really the issue in ensuring military effectiveness. The improved Saudi standardization and interoperability that would result from buying US equipment would help compensate for the weakness of Saudi land forces and the failures of the Gulf Cooperation Council. Recent British force cuts mean that the British Army cannot deploy the kind of armored forces to the Gulf that it deployed in 1990, and France has never had a significant capability to project armored forces. Purchases of these tanks as an alternative to US armor cannot meet Saudi military needs.[208]

Saudi Other Armored Vehicles

It is not possible to separate all of the Saudi Army's holdings of other armored vehicles (OAFVs) from those of the National Guard, Frontier Force, and other paramilitary forces. As of mid-1996, however, the Saudi Army's holdings of armored infantry fighting and command vehicles seem to have included 400 M-2A2 Bradleys, 150 M-577A1s, 170 AMX-10s, and 200 Camillinos. It had 390–420 AML-60, AML-90, and AML-245 reconnaissance vehicles. It had 430–550 AMX-10P and 250 VAB/VCI mechanized infantry combat vehicles, command vehicles and special purpose vehicles.

The Saudi Army also had 1,700 variants of the M-113, including 950–850 M-113A1s and M-113A2s. It had 30 EE-11 Brazilian Urutu, 110 German UR-416, 120 Spanish BMR-600 and 270–290 Panhard M-3/VTT armored personnel carriers. Saudi Arabia also had 250 to 300 armored mortar carriers, including M-106A1s and M-125s. Unlike most Middle Eastern armies, the Saudi Army was fully equipped with armored support vehicles. It had large numbers of French and US-made armored recovery vehicles, armored bridging units, and large numbers of special purpose armored vehicles.[209]

It is obvious from these totals that the Saudi Army's holdings of OAFVs present problems in standardization and modernization. Saudi Arabia has bought a wide variety of types and sub-types of OAFVs. Many types are highly specialized and difficult to properly integrate into Saudi forces in small numbers. Some types are the result of political efforts to give foreign suppliers a share of the Saudi market, regardless of military need. The end result is that the Saudi army has so many different types of other armored vehicles that this is a major training, maintenance, logistic, maneuver, and readiness problem.

Saudi Arabia has attempted to deal with these problems by buying more modern US armored vehicles—including the M-113 and M-2A2 Bradley. During the Gulf War, it ordered 400 M-2A2 armored fighting vehicles for a cost of $1.5 billion. It also bought 200 M-113 armored personnel carriers, 50 M-548 cargo carriers, 17 M-88A1 recovery vehicles, and 43 M-578 recovery vehicles.[210] Saudi Arabia has also contracted with FMC-Arabia for logistic support of the M-2A2.[211]

In 1996, the Saudi Army had 400 Bradley M-2A2s in service. The purchase of the M-2A2 gives the Saudi Army an OAFV with the speed, protection, and firepower to keep pace with Saudi tanks and outmatch the Soviet armored fighting vehicles in most potential threat armies—many of which have better protection and firepower than many of the armored vehicles in service with Saudi forces. The M-2A2 is heavily armed, equipped with TOW-2 missiles and a 25 mm cannon. It has air conditioning which provides protection against gas warfare and allows extended operation at desert heats.

Saudi sources indicated in August, 1993, that Saudi Arabia might buy a total of 550–700 M-2A2s, and then standardize on the M-113A1 for the rest of Saudi Arabia's armored fighting vehicles. Like the M-1A2 buy, such standardization would both improve Saudi army capabilities, and provide a high degree of interoperability and standardization with US Army forces. The M-113, and various combat versions of the M-113, are acceptable armored vehicles, although they lack the speed and armor to fight armored forces equipped with the most modern tanks and armored fighting vehicles.

It seems increasingly unlikely, however, that Saudi Arabia will buy more M-2A2s in the near future. Further, even if Saudi Arabia did buy 700 M-2A2s this would not totally eliminate the need to support many types of vehicles which are dependent for parts and technical support on so many different countries, and Saudi Arabia continues to buy other types of OAFVs. It has 36 German Fuchsia chemical defense vehicles and additional French armored vehicles on order, and is examining possible purchases of other armored vehicles from Brazil, Britain, and Germany.[212]

Saudi Anti-Tank Weapons

The Saudi Army has an excellent mix of small arms, light weaponry, and anti-tank weapons. These include massive stocks of mobile, crew-portable, and man-portable TOW, HOT, and Dragon anti-tank guided missiles. In 1996, Saudi Arabia had some 200 TOW launchers mounted on VCC-1 armored fighting vehicles and an additional 300 mounted on M-113A1s or other US supplied armored vehicles. It also had 90 HOT launchers mounted on AMX-10P armored fighting vehicles.

The Army had large numbers of TOW crew-portable and Dragon man-portable anti-tank guided weapons systems. It also had 300 Carl Gustav rocket launchers, 400 M-20 3.5" rocket launchers, thousands of M-72 LAWs, and extensive numbers of 75 mm, 84 mm, 90 mm and 106 mm rocket launchers and recoilless rifles. Saudi Arabia ordered 4,460 TOW-2 missiles in April, 1987, and 150 more TOW-2A missile launchers with night vision sights and support equipment on September 27, 1990.[213] The Saudi Army ordered French Apilas anti-tank weapons in 1991.

This inventory gives the Saudi Army missiles that can kill T-72A, T-72M1, T-80 and other modern tanks. Individual crew and operator training has reached moderate proficiency, although it still lacks consistency and realism. Units equipped with anti-tank weapons mounted on armored vehicles also sometimes lack maneuver and combined arms training. Crews and men using older weapons are often less proficient than those with the latest weapons, and anti-tank units often lack aggressiveness in employing anti-tank weapons in exercises.

Saudi Artillery

The Saudi Army has large numbers of modern artillery weapons. In 1996, these holdings included 60–70 ASTROS II multiple rocket launchers, and 110–120 M-109A1/A2 and 90 GCT 155 mm self-propelled howitzers. The Army had 24 Model 56 and 90–100 M-101/M-102 105 mm towed howitzers, 40 FH-70 and 90 M-198 155 mm towed howitzers, 5–10 M-115 203 mm towed howitzers, and some older towed weapons in storage. It also had some 200 M-106 and M-125A1 120 mm self propelled mortars and large numbers of towed mortars. These included over 400 120 mm and 4.2" weapons, over 1,000 81 mm weapons, and large numbers of light 60 mm weapons.[214]

The Saudi Army has more Astros IIs and M-198s on order, and is steadily acquiring better mobile fire-control and ammunition-supply equipment. Saudi Arabia has, however, ordered new target acquisition radars—such as the AN/PPS-15A, MSTAR, or Rasit 3190B—to replace 1960 vintage systems, and is steadily improving its counterbattery radars and fire control systems.[215]

These Saudi orders will steadily improve the Saudi Army's artillery capabilities. At the same time, Saudi artillery units will suffer from manpower quality, mobility, and support problems well after the year 2000. The Saudi Army will only have a limited-to-moderate ability to use artillery in maneuver and combine arms warfare, to target effectively in counter-battery fire or at targets beyond visual range, and to shift and concentrate fires.

Saudi Arabia has considered ordering the Multiple Launch Rocket Systems (MLRS) to help deal with these problems. On September 27, 1990, it announced its intention to order a package of 9 Multiple Launch Rocket Systems (MLRS), including vehicle mounted rocket launchers, 2,880 tactical rockets, 50 practice rockets, 9 MV-755A2 command post carriers, training and training equipment, and 20 AN/VRC-46 radio sets. Such an order for the MLRS rocket might have given Saudi Arabia an important potential force multiplier. The MLRS has a highly sophisticated warhead which mixes anti-armor and anti-personnel bomblets. Each MLRS launcher is capable of inflicting more destruction on an area target or large maneuver target than a battalion of regular tube artillery or multiple rocket launchers and can do so at ranges in excess of 40 kilometers. This allows the MLRS to out-range most of the weapons in potential threat forces.[216] The MLRS proved to be too expensive, however, when Saudi oil revenues declined and the Saudi Army has delayed any purchase of the MLRS for at least several years.

Saudi Army Air Defense

It is not easy to separate the Saudi Army's air defense assets from those in the Saudi Air Defense Force, and sources disagree over which force operates given systems. However, the Saudi Army seems to have had 17 anti-aircraft artillery batteries in mid-1996. Total Saudi holdings of short-range air defenses included 45–50 Crotale radar guided missiles on tracked armored vehicles, 73 Shahine radar guided missiles on tracked armored vehicles, 700 Mistrals, over 300 Stingers, and 570 obsolescent Redeye man portable surface-to-air missiles. Saudi Arabia bought 50 Stinger launchers and 200 Stinger missiles on an emergency basis in August, 1990, and had ordered additional Crotales and 700 French Mistral launchers and 1,500 missiles.[217]

It is equally difficult to separate the army's air defense gun holdings from those of the Air Defense Force and National Guard, but Saudi Arabia's total holdings of light anti-aircraft weapons seems to include 10 M-42 40 mm, 50–60 AMX-30SA 30 mm self-propelled, and 92 Vulcan M-163 anti-aircraft guns. It also seems to have 150 Bofors L-60/L-70 40 mm and 128 Oerlikon 35 mm towed guns, and possibly 15 M-117 90 mm towed anti-aircraft guns. This is a strong mix of air defense assets, but training and readiness levels are moderate to low. The Air Defense Force is also a relatively static force that cannot easily support the army in mobile operations. Saudi land forces remain heavily dependent on air power for air defense.

Saudi Army Aviation

Saudi Army helicopter forces are another important area for force improvement. Much of the Saudi Army is now deployed at least 500 miles from the Kingdom's main oil facilities in the Eastern Province, although a brigade is stationed in the new King Fahd military city in the Eastern Province, and the combat elements of a another brigade deployed to the new Saudi Army base at King Khalid City, near Hafr al-Batin, in 1984. For the foreseeable future, the Saudi Army will be dispersed so that much of its strength will be deployed near Saudi Arabia's borders with the angles located at Tabuk, Hafr al-Batin, and Sharurah-Khamis Mushayt.

Helicopters offer a partial solution to these deployment problems. They can provide rapid concentration of force and allow Saudi Arabia to make up for its lack of experience in large-scale maneuver. These factors first led the Saudi Army to seek attack helicopters in the early 1980s. In the mid-1980s, the Saudi Army studied plans for developing a sizable helicopter force by the mid-1990s. It initially considered buying 60–100 US AH-64 attack helicopters, plus additional Blackhawk utility and support, and Chinook CH-47 transport helicopters from the US. However, Saudi Arabia initially experienced political problems in obtaining such helicopters from the US, and this led it to obtain an option to buy 88 Sikorsky-designed S-70 Black Hawk helicopters from Westland in Britain. Roughly 80 of these Westlands were to be attack helicopters equipped with TOW-2. The rest were to be configured for SAR missions. The order was divided into batches of 40 and 48 aircraft.

The Gulf War, however, created the political conditions in which Saudi Arabia could buy the AH-64 from the US.[218] On September 27, 1990, Saudi Arabia ordered 12 AH-64 Apache attack helicopters, 155 Hellfire missiles, 24 spare Hellfire launchers, six spare engines and associated equipment from the US. At the time, it indicated an interest in buying a total of 48 AH-64s, and that it was examining the purchase of more attack and support helicopters from the US, Italy, France, or a Franco-German consortium. The Saudi Army has not placed any additional orders of this kind, but in June, 1992, it bought 362 more Hellfire missiles, 3,500 Hydra-70 rockets, and 40 HMMWV vehicles and US support services for its Apaches. It also bought eight S-70 Sikorsky medevac helicopters.[219]

The AH-64s began to enter Saudi service in 1993, and the Saudi Army now has a helicopter strength of 12 AH-64 attack helicopters, 15 Bell 406CS attack helicopters, 11 S-70A1 Sikorsky Blackhawk transport helicopters, 6 SA-365N medical evacuation helicopters, and 10 UL-60 Blackhawk medical evacuation and transport helicopters.[220] The AH-64s are a major force multiplier for the Saudi Army, and will give the Saudi Army still further interoperability with the US Army. At the same time, the Saudi Army will need extensive US support to absorb such aircraft. It has some maintenance problems with its existing helicopter fleet, and modern combat helicopters require almost as much support and training as a light jet combat aircraft.[221]

More generally, the Saudi Army has excellent support facilities, and logistic and support vehicles and equipment. The Saudi Army is one of the few forces in the developing world which is organized to provide as much sustainability as maneuver and firepower. As has been noted earlier, Saudi Arabia has made major purchases of support equipment, along with the purchase of its M-1A2s and M-2A2s. It is improving its field support vehicle strength and ordered 10,000 support vehicles from the US on September 27, 1990, including 1,200 High Mobility Multipurpose Wheeled Vehicles (HMMWVs).

Saudi Arabia has long had US Army support for its Ordnance Corps, logistic system, and technical services. This contract was renewed on June 1, 1992, and not only aids Saudi Arabia, but improves the ability of Saudi forces to support US reinforcements and work with them on an interoperable basis.

Saudi Army Readiness and Warfighting Capabilities

The Saudi Army showed during the Gulf War that it can fight well against Iraqi armored forces and the kind of threats it faces in the Gulf region. It is in the process of expanding its forces and is steadily improving its effectiveness. Nevertheless, the Saudi Army faces continuing problems in many areas. It will not have the manpower and training to operate its new major equipment orders properly as they are delivered. It is still an army that normally operates near its peace-time casernes, and which will experience serious problems in redeploying major combat forces unless it has extensive strategic warning. It would take the

Saudi Army a minimum of 7–10 days to redeploy a brigade to a new front or city.

Training has been a problem, and will continue to be one in the future. US advisors helped bring Saudi forces to a level of readiness during the Gulf War that they had never before experienced, and gave them their first real experience with large scale unit and combined arms training. Many Saudi officers absorbed this training quickly, and the Saudi Army did well during Operation Desert Storm—very well if its low pre-war readiness is considered. The Saudi Army's training plans since the war have not always been properly executed, and maneuver training has been mediocre. Saudi Arabia has, however, leased the US Army Multiple Integrated Laser Engagement Systems (MILES) for advanced realistic combat training, and delivery is expected in July, 1996.[222] These deliveries will help the Saudi Army create the only modern land warfare training capabilities in the Southern Gulf. It has also carried out further joint training and exercises with the US.

This illustrates a broader need to create land warfare training facilities for all the land forces in the Southern Gulf with the sort of automated advanced training capabilities used by the US at Fort Irwin, and used by Israel in a cheaper and less sophisticated form. Manpower and equipment are only effective to the extent they are integrated into forces with realistic war-fighting training. High technology training offers Southern Gulf forces still another potential force multiplier over potential threats from the Northern Gulf. They also provide a way of making up for a lack of combat experience, by standardizing training so as to make Gulf forces more interoperable, and improving interoperability with the US and British armies. The smaller Gulf countries cannot afford such training facilities, but joint use of Saudi facilities would provide them with the capabilities they need and reduce costs to the Saudi Army.

The Saudi Army needs to improve its command, control, communications, and computer (C^4) and battle management capabilities. Saudi Army command and communications are too rigid and over-centralized and better long-range communications are needed. It is also essential that promotion at senior command levels should be based on professional merit, not politics.

It is not clear that the Saudi Army is effectively organized, trained, and equipped to provide land-based air defense for its maneuver forces. The creation of a separate air defense force may have had benefits in ensuring that the air defense units would achieve proper attention and suitable amounts of training manpower, but a separate air defense force is best suited to a static and defensive concept of warfare.

Finally, the Saudi Army is still too static and defensive in character and lacks strategic focus. Saudi Arabia needs to emphasize the ability to redeploy forces and meet an attacker as far forward as possible. This is especially true in the case of joint operations with Kuwaiti and US land forces against a land threat from the Northern Gulf, although Saudi performance was much better in joint exercises in 1995 than in previous years. It may be that the Saudi Air Force can act as a substitute for land-based air defenses under such conditions, but modern joint operations require fully integrated air defense as part of the maneuver forces.

These changes require the Saudi Army to fundamentally re-think its war fighting concepts and to concentrate fully on the ability to concentrate its heavy forces for the defense of Kuwait and Saudi Arabia against Iraq, to concentrate on developing its capabilities for joint maneuver warfare, and to give rapid maneuver and sustained high-intensity operations the proper priority. They require the Saudi Army to limit its future procurements to equipment with the proper degree of standardization and interoperability, and they require the Saudi Army to make existing units fully effective before making major equipment buys for force expansion purposes.

8

The Saudi National Guard

Saudi Arabia divides its land force manpower between the Army and the National Guard, and keeps roughly 25% of its full-time military manpower in the Guard. The National Guard was used to deal with the Shi'ite uprising in the Eastern Province, the siege of the Grand Mosque in Mecca in 1979, and put down the Iranian riots in Mecca in 1987. It also helped secure the Eastern Province during the Iran-Iraq War and Gulf War.[223]

The National Guard is the successor of the Ikhwan or White Army. It is a tribal force forged out of those tribal elements loyal to the Saud family. It is a counterweight to any threat from the regular military forces, and a counterbalance within the royal family to Sudairi control over the regular armed forces. The National Guard is under the command of Prince Abdullah, who is descended from another wife of Abdul Aziz and is currently the Crown Prince.

Estimates of the current strength of the National Guard differ sharply. The most recent IISS estimate is 57,000 actives, and 20,000 tribal levies. A more realistic estimate may be 30,000–35,000 full-time actives, 15,000 part-time actives and tribal levies. The training of the professional forces has improved steadily in recent years, but varies by commander and unit. The men in the part-time tribal forces often have little training and are usually a mix of retired military personnel, descendants of the troops that fought with King Abd al-Aziz, or the sons or relatives of tribal leaders.

The Organization of the National Guard

Sources differ regarding the current organization of the professional units. The IISS reports that the Guard is organized into two mechanized brigades with four combined arms battalions each, four infantry brigades, and one ceremonial cavalry squadron. Other sources indicate that the Guard also has an engineer battalion, and a special security battalion. One source suggests that its strength is two mechanized brigades and two special forces units.[224]

The full-time professional forces have been organized into modern military formations over the last decade, with extensive help from the Vinnell Corporation in the US. They began to hold significant training exercises for their first 6,500-man Mechanized Brigade, the Imam Mohammed bin-Saud Brigade, during the early 1980s. They established a brigade-sized presence, and a limited oil-field security force in the Eastern Province, and the Mohammed bin Saud brigade held its first major exercise in the desert about 250 miles west of Riyadh in early 1983. Units moved from as far away as the Eastern Province, and the key mechanized elements performed relatively well. While the Guard experienced problems in translating tribal discipline into regular military discipline, and the force was well below its authorized manning level, the set-piece maneuvers performed were successful.

The National Guard inaugurated its second mechanized "brigade" in a ceremony on March 14, 1985. This new unit was called the King Abd al-Aziz Brigade, which was formed after another relatively successful round of set-piece exercises called "Al Areen," which were held near Bisha. Prince Abdullah then spoke of expanding the Guard to 35,000 men, and succeeded in building up a force of three mechanized "brigades" by 1989.

The Equipment of the National Guard

In mid-1996, the Guard's forces were equipped with about 1,000–1,100 V-150 Commando wheeled armored fighting vehicles—some 50% of which were in storage. These vehicles are part of a family of vehicles with a number of different configurations and weapons systems, including anti-tank guided missile carriers, cannon turrets, and main guns. While estimates differ, current holdings seem to include 100–120 V-150s configured as AIFVs, 20–30 with 90 mm guns, 130–140 armored command vehicles, 70–80 81 mm mortar carriers, 45–50 armored recovery vehicles, 30 special purpose vehicles, and 325–375 configured as APCs.

The National Guard seems to have ordered 400 to 450 versions of the Piranha light armored vehicle, 65 of which have been delivered. The Saudi National Guard has bought up to 1,117 LAV-25s (light armored vehicles) from General Motors of Canada through the US Army Tank Automotive Command (TACOM). The total order for LAVs seems to include ten different types of LAV-25s, including 111 anti-tank weapons vehicles with TOW, 74 120 mm mortar carriers, 182 command vehicles, 71 ambulances, 417 APCs, together with ammunition carriers, recovery vehicles, engineer vehicles. Some 384 LAVs will be armed with two man turrets with the 25 mm McDonnell Douglas chain gun and thermal sights. An additional 141 LAVs will be fitted with 105 mm guns. About 262 LAVs were in service in early 1996.[225]

The Guard also had 40 M-102 105 mm towed artillery weapons, 30 M-198 155 mm howitzers, and 81 mm mortars. It had large numbers of TOW anti-tank guided missiles, rocket launchers, and recoilless rifles, a limited number of helicopters, and 30 M-40 Vulcan 20 mm anti-aircraft guns. At least 100 TOW fire units are mounted on V-150s.[226] The National Guard had 27 M-198 howitzers, 116 TOW launchers and 2,000 missiles, and HMMWV light transport vehicles on order.[227] It had also signed a $52 million contract with the Harris Corporation for RF-5000 Falcon digital high-frequency radios for its vehicles and base stations, and Arabic-language data terminals, turn-key logistical support, and technical assistance.

The National Guard has the tightest fiscal management and controls of any of the Saudi military services. Prince Abdullah does not like the commissions and special charges the other services often pay for major procurements, and has often insisted that National Guard contracting avoid any such fees and payments.

The Readiness and Effectiveness of the National Guard

The National Guard's professional forces have had mixed success. They helped secure the Eastern Province during the Iran-Iraq War, but their capabilities were never really tested. They were given special training and additional manning during the Gulf War, but were unable to deal with the initial Iraqi assault on Khafji, and required extensive reinforcement by US air and artillery support during the battle to retake the city. They fought reasonably well during the rest of the battle of Khafji, but did not play a significant role in Desert Storm.

The National Guard has done a reasonably good job since 1991 in dealing with low-level problems with the Shi'ites in the Eastern Province and Islamic extremists. It has not, however, developed a high capability for sophisticated internal security operations in dealing with well organized cells or sophisticated hostile groups that hide under political cover. It is also not particularly well organized to deal with high technology forms of infiltration, terrorism and sabotage. Saudi Arabia must rely heavily on its intelligence services and foreign advisors in such missions.

The tribal forces of the National Guard are grouped and deployed in five to seven regions, covering every critical urban and populated area in the country. They are useful in securing Saudi Arabia's key facilities in a way that limits the ability of the army to conduct a coup, and its leaders are carefully chosen for their loyalty to the regime. The Guard balances tribal factions to reduce the risk of feuding, and provides a means through which the royal family can allocate funds to tribal and Bedouin leaders.

The Guard helps key princes to maintain close relations with the tribes, and is an extension of the Majlis system, as well as a means of maintaining internal security. This organization makes the tribal portion of the Guard politically vital to ensuring the integration of Saudi Arabia's tribes into its society. This does not mean it can adequately defend Saudi oil fields or other critical facilities against any well-trained or sophisticated threat.[228]

The changes in the organization and equipment of the Guard's full-time forces are slowly improving their quality, but the Guard's mechanized brigades lack the firepower, heavy armor, air defense, and maneuver capability to take on mechanized infantry or armored forces. The Guard's full-time forces also lack the overall force structure and equipment, air mobility, specialized units, logistics, and maintenance capabilities to deal with a Northern Gulf opponent. Its leadership is far better trained for paramilitary operations and internal security than combat with regular forces.

As a result, the National Guard is ill-equipped to expand beyond its present level. The Guard's professional full-time forces remain dependent on outside contractors for service support, maintenance, and logistics. This support is delivered through a 22-year-old, $5.6 billion modernization program financed by the Saudi government and run by the US Army Materiel Command. It was this program's headquarters which was the target of the car bomb in Riyadh on November 13, 1995. Currently, the program is administered through the Office of the Program Manager-Saudi National Guard by the US Army Materiel Command and the Vinnell Corporation, which in January, 1994, signed an $819 million, four-year contract to provide support services.[229]

The program involves 87 US military personnel, 175 US government civilian employees and some of the 1,200 employees that Vinnell Corporation maintains in-country to support this and other programs. The Guard signed an additional contract with Vinnell, valued at $163.3 million, for additional training support in 1995. The Guard's full-time active forces also require the support of the Saudi army and air force—or of foreign military forces—for any operation involving significant armor, maneuver operations, firepower, or sustainability in combat. The Guard's tribal levies are suitable only for light internal security missions and ensuring the loyalty of Saudi Arabia's traditional tribes.[230]

There have been reports that Prince Abdullah planned to build up the Guard in spite of these problems, and even that he has considered plans to bring the Guard up to a strength of 11 full time brigades, with tanks, self-propelled artillery and other heavy equipment. Fortunately, these reports seem exaggerated. Prince Abdullah evidently asked the Guard's foreign advisors to study an expansion to 100,000 regulars by the early 2000s.

A manning level of 100,000 men could double the Guard's present major combat units by creating two more mechanized brigades. It could create up to two more infantry brigade equivalents (the Guard now has six lightly manned infantry brigades), and a new mix of battalion sized formations for its part-time forces. Even this force goal, however, does not seem likely to meet either Saudi Arabia's overall force modernization needs or the needs of the National Guard. It would mean the Army would receive less manpower, and the National Guard is already having problems in creating a third mechanized brigade and creating the improved artillery and air defense units it needs.[231]

At present, the National Guard contributes to the Saudi Army's lack of strategic focus. It helps to create an overall mix of land forces that represent a highly expensive and duplicative effort, but do not provide the kind of rapidly deployable, mobile, and sustainable forces necessary to deal with key threats like Iran. Ideally, much of the Guard's manpower should be allocated to the Army but there is little prospect of such reform because the Army and Guard are under the control of different princes and the Saudi royal family has long feared that unified ground forces might become the source of a coup attempt.

9

The Saudi Navy

The Saudi Navy has grown steadily over the last ten years, and now has East and West fleets for its Gulf and Red Sea coasts. At the same time, the Saudi Navy still has only limited effectiveness, even in defensive roles.[232] Its force level has risen from an active strength of 6,000 men in the mid-1980s, to a strength of 17,000 men, including 1,500 marines. The 1,500-man marine force was organized into tow light brigades, and equipped with 140 BTR-60Ps. Saudi Arabia plans to expand its Marine forces to 2,400 men.[233]

Current Saudi Naval Forces

Chart Twenty shows the strength of the Saudi Navy relative to other Gulf navies. In mid-1996, the Saudi Navy was comprised of four Madina-class (F-2000) frigates, four Badr-class missile corvettes, nine Al Siddiq-class guided missile ships, 3 Dammam-class (German Jaguar) torpedo boats, 20 Naja 12 inshore fast craft, 17 Halter-type coastal patrol craft, four Safwa-class (ex-US MSC-322 Bluebird) mine warfare ships. There were also four Afif-class LCU amphibious craft, 4 LCMs, two other amphibious craft, 2 10,500-ton Boraida-class (French Durance) support ships, 4 smaller support vessels, 14 tug boats, and large numbers of small patrol boats including 40 Simmoneau Type 51 inshore patrol boats. Two large royal yachts are based at Dammam.

Various sources report different holdings for Saudi naval aviation. In 1996, it seems to have included 20 operational SA-365F Dauphin ASW and anti-ship missile helicopters with AS-15TT missiles, and 4 SA-365Ns for the search and rescue mission. These SA-365Fs have only limited ASW capability, and are configured primarily for the surface search and attack roles. Each combat-equipped SA-365F carries four missiles and has an Agrion search/attack system. They have Crouzet MAD systems and can carry two Mark 46 torpedoes. The Saudi Navy also had 3 Westland Sea King Mark 47 ASW helicopters, and 21 land-based AS-332SC Super

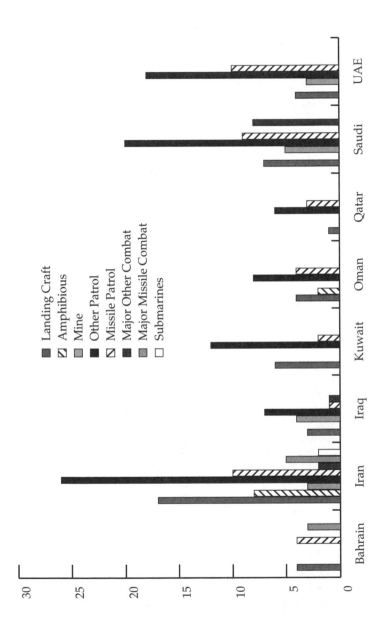

CHART TWENTY Gulf Naval Ships by Category in 1996. *Source:* Adapted by Anthony H. Cordesman from the IISS, *Military Balance, 1995–1996.*

CHART TWENTY (continued)

	Bahrain	Iran	Iraq	Kuwait	Oman	Qatar	Saudi	UAE
Submarines	—	2	—	—	—	—	—	—
Major Surface Combat								
Missile	3	5	—	—	—	—	8	—
Other	—	2	1	—	—	—	—	—
Patrol Craft								
Missile	4	10	1	2	4	3	9	10
Other	—	26	7	12	8	6	20	18
Mine Vessels	0	3	4	—	—	—	5	3
Amphibious Ships	0	8	0	0	2	0	0	0
Landing Craft	4	17	3	6	4	1	7	4

Puma helicopters. These AS-332s included 12 with Omera search radars, nine with Giat 20 mm cannon, and 12 with Exocet or Sea Eagle air-to-ship missiles.[234]

The 4,500 man Saudi coast guard has two large Yarmouk-class patrol boats, two fast missile attack craft with AS-15TT missiles, four large Al-Jouf-class patrol boats, two large Al Jubatel-class patrol boats, 25 Skorpion-class patrol boats, 13 other coastal patrol boats and four SRN-6, Model 4 Hovercraft, 16 Slingsby SAH 2200 Hovercraft, large numbers of inshore patrol craft, three royal yachts, three small tankers, fire fighting craft, and three tugs. [235]

The Saudi Navy has completed the construction of two major, fully modern naval bases at Jeddah and Jubail. Its deployments are divided into a Western Fleet with its main facilities at Jeddah, and an Eastern Fleet with its main facilities at al Qatif/Jubail. The Navy has additional facilities at Jizan, Ras Tanura, Dammam, Yanbu, Ras al Ghar, and Ras al Mishab.[236]

Saudi Naval Development

The major deliveries under the US phase of the Saudi naval expansion effort have been completed for several years.[237] The US delivered nine 478-ton Al Siddiq-class patrol-gunboat, guided missile (PGG) craft, armed with two twin Harpoon missile launchers, 1 76 mm gun, and light AA weapons. It also delivered four larger patrol-chaser missile (PCG) craft, or Badr-class, ships which the Saudis class as frigates and other sources class as corvettes.[238] These vessels displace 1,038 tons fully load, and have two quad Harpoon missile launchers, one 76 mm gun, Vulcan and 20 mm guns, and six 324 mm torpedo tubes. They are all based at Jubail on Saudi Arabia's east coast.[239]

The US delivered four MSC-322-class coastal mine sweepers, two large harbor tugs, two utility landing craft, and 4 LCM-6, 4 LCU-1610, and 4 LCM landing craft. Other US deliveries included Harpoon missiles, Mark 46 torpedoes, and ammunition for the Saudi Navy's 76 mm guns and other weapons. The Saudi Navy also took delivery of three Dammam-class torpedo boats from Germany, each with four 533 mm torpedo tubes each.

Saudi Arabia turned to France as the major source of its naval ships and weapons in the early 1980s partly because of dissatisfaction with the US Navy advisory effort, and partly because it felt French ships were better suited to its mission requirements. The Saudi Navy signed its first major contract with France in 1980 in an effort to accelerate its modernization, obtain better support, and obtain more advanced ships than it could purchase from the US. It signed a modernization package worth

$3.4 billion, and then another contract that effectively made France its primary future source of support and modernization for future Saudi orders. This follow-on French program, which began in 1982, is called Sawari (Mast) I. It has a minimum value of 14 billion French francs, or $1.9 billion, and may have escalated to $3.2 billion.

France delivered all four missile-equipped Madina-class or Type F-2000S frigates by August, 1986. These are 2,870 ton vessels when fully loaded. They have eight Otomat 2 missile launchers, eight Crotale surface-to-air missile launchers, 1 100 mm gun, 4 twin Breda 35 mm guns, 4 533 mm torpedo tubes, and 1 SA-365F helicopter.[240] France also delivered two modified Durance-class fuel supply/replenishment vessels (Boraida class), Otomat missiles for the frigates, 24 SA-365 Dauphin 2 helicopters (20 missile-equipped and 4 SAR-equipped), AS-15 missiles for the helicopters, and additional training services. The Otomat is the longest range anti-ship missile in Gulf service, with a range of 160 kilometers.[241]

These vessels are all based in Jeddah on Saudi Arabia's Red Sea coast and so far have had limited operational value. Saudi crews trained in France to operate the vessels and helicopters, but the ships are only at sea for a few weeks a year, and at least one ship has had a severe engine room fire that has evidently not been fully repaired. One F-2000 has had to return to France for a major refit, and ship wear and maintenance problems are a serious problem with this class of Saudi vessels.[242]

The Saudi Navy then began to study plans for a new Sawari II program, which was initially estimated to cost $1.6-$2.12 billion. Prince Sultan met with France's President Francois Mitterrand and Defense Minister Charles Hernu to discuss this program in May, 1983. The program he discussed would have provided Saudi Arabia with at least two more 2,000-ton frigates and possibly 4,000-ton frigates as well. It included selling mine-sweeping helicopters and maritime patrol aircraft as the first step in the procurement of much larger forces, including lift and troop-carrying helicopters, surveillance and intelligence equipment, and special warfare equipment.

While Saudi Arabia ordered 12 Super Pumas and 12 more patrol boats from France in the 1980s, it did not place major additional orders until 1990. Saudi Arabia did not agree to the Sawari II program because of funding problems and because the Saudis experienced growing problems with their French ships that were more severe than those experienced with American vessels. These maintenance and support problems were so serious in the late 1980s that Saudi Arabia even approached the US to provide support for the French vessels.

The situation slowly improved, however, and Saudi Arabia made a decision to keep France as its major naval supplier. The Saudi Navy signed a new support agreement with France in 1989. The Saudi Navy ordered 6 additional Super Pumas in 1989, and decided to raise its order for French patrol boats to 20 ships.

Saudi Naval Infrastructure and C⁴I Capabilities

The Saudi Navy C⁴I system was still unable to support effective combat operations when the Gulf War began. As a result, the Saudi Navy purchased a $307 million upgrade of its C⁴I system on September 27, 1990.[243] Even so, Saudi Navy C⁴I remains inadequate and could present problems in any complex combat operation.

Saudi naval facilities are excellent. The Saudi Navy's bases are exceptionally capable and well stocked. The main bases will eventually have up to five years of stocks on hand, and will have initial deliveries of two years worth of inventory. The Jubail base is now the second largest naval base in the Gulf and stretches nearly eight miles along the coast. It already has its own desalinization facility, and is designed to be expandable up to 100% above its present capacity. The Saudi Navy is also steadily improving its exercise performance, and has begun to conduct joint exercises with the British, Egyptian, and US navies.[244]

The Saudi Navy is procuring an automated logistic system similar to the systems used by its other services, and extensive modern command and control facilities. The first major links in this C⁴I system became operational, along with hardened command centers at Riyadh, Jubail, and Jeddah, by the end of 1985. The system was supposed to have automated data links to the E-3A by the late 1980s, and be able to transfer data to Saudi ships by secure digital link from the Saudi E-3As as they operated in the ocean surveillance mode.

The Saudi Navy has purchased other US designed facilities, including a meteorology laboratory, a Harpoon missile and Mark 46 torpedo maintenance facility, an advanced technical training school, and a Royal Naval Academy. Saudi Navy maintenance, however, is poor to very poor and these maintenance problems are compounded by the fact that Saudi Arabia cannot hire foreign maintenance personnel to go to sea, as it can hire foreigners to work at air bases and army depots. The resulting lack of maintenance at sea places a strain on contractor facilities on shore, and leads to the relatively rapid degradation of Saudi naval readiness after ships have been at sea. This situation is not improving.

Saudi Navy Force Expansion Plans

During the Gulf War, Saudi Arabia placed a tentative order for three F-3000 frigates. These orders were then delayed, however, because Saudi Arabia gave priority to new orders for its air and land forces, and because of its economic problems. The Saudi Navy did renew its maintenance agreements with France in February, 1994, but only signed firm contracts for new frigates on November 22, 1994.[245]

Even then, the Saudi Navy ordered only two of the frigates. The Saudi Navy instead concentrated on improving its infrastructure, training, and support capabilities. It contracted for a new naval base and training for 750 personnel to crew the ships. Saudi Arabia also placed orders with the French Direction des Construction Navales (DCN) for the overhaul of its four existing French supplied frigates and two supply ships—a step which should both modernize these ships and restore all of them to full operational status.[246]

The two new Lafayette-class F-3000 frigates will displace 3,700 tons fully loaded, and will be 128 meters long. They will each have 8 Exocet MM-40 Block 2 missile launchers, 1 octuple Crotale NG surface-to-air missile launcher, 1 100 mm gun, 2 twin 30 mm gun, 4 324 mm torpedo launchers, 1 SA-365F helicopter, Castor fire control systems, and Thomson-CSF Tavitac combat systems.[247]

Saudi Arabia is now examining a SNEP II program that would spend roughly $10 billion to expand and modernize the Saudi Navy over the next 10 years. It also is studying a $23 billion program to expand its Marine and naval special forces during the next 10 years—although it is far from clear how serious this latter program really is.

The Saudi Navy is considering plans to expand its mine warfare units, and ways to expand its ASW capabilities in response to Iran's purchase of Soviet Kilo-class submarines. The Saudi Navy now has four obsolescent US MSC-322 mine vessels of the Addriyah class. Saudi Arabia agreed to lease two Hunt-class mine vessels from Britain in July 1988, and placed an order for six to eight Vosper Sandown-class MCMVs, training by the Royal Navy, and new port facilities for mine warfare vessels from Ballast Nedam, as part of its $18 billion al-Yamamah 2 program.

The Al-Jawf class is a 500 ton ship with a crew of 40, built by Vosper-Thorneycroft, with a computerized ship positioning system accurate to one meter, and a Plessey-Marconi variable depth sonar. It has Saudi enhancements including twin 30 mm Emerson Electric guns and a Contraves fire control system, larger engines, and uprated Voith-Schneider propulsors.[248] According to press reports, two British Sandown class mine countermeasure craft (Al Jawf class) are nearing delivery, and the Saudi Navy has one more Al-Jawf class mine hunter in construction and options to buy three more.[249] The Saudi Navy may also be considering purchase of French-built Tripartite mine hunters.

These Saudi orders could set an interesting precedent for standardization and interoperability, since Kuwait, Bahrain, Oman, Qatar, and the UAE are also examining orders of the Sandown or Tripartite mine warfare vessels.[250] At present, however, Saudi Arabia has no operational effective mine warfare vessels, and can only conduct minimal local mine warfare operations with older types of mines.

Saudi Arabia has indefinitely deferred plans to buy coastal submarines. Saudi Arabia sought to buy six to eight submarines during the 1980s, and discussed programs costing $4 billion to $6 billion—including one submarine base for each fleet. Saudi Navy representatives visited several European manufacturers in 1986 and 1987—including the builders of the Walrus-class boats in the Netherlands, Vickers Type-2400 in the UK, and ILK 209/2000 and Kockums 471 in West Germany.

This deferral is a wise decision and any Saudi purchase of submarines would result in a gratuitous waste of money. Saudi Arabia lacks the manpower and maintenance resources to operate submarines. The Gulf and Red Sea are poor operating areas for such vessels, Saudi Arabia could not use such submarines to fight Iranian submarines effectively, and the high salinity of the Gulf could present problems in terms of long-term operating life.

Saudi Arabia also seems to have deferred an order for two AND-BA Atlantique 2 (ANG) maritime patrol aircraft, and the order of two more Atlantique 2, Fokker F-27 Maritime Enforcers, or Lockheed P-3 Orions as part of a GCC maritime surveillance force. The AND-BA Atlantique 2 (ANG) maritime patrol aircraft proved to be too expensive. The aircraft supplemented the existing maritime surveillance coverage provided by Saudi E-3As and were intended to cover the rest of the Southern Gulf. A Saudi purchase for this mission depended on GCC cooperation, and partial funding of the aircraft. Neither was forthcoming.[251]

These again appear to be sound decisions. Saudi Arabia has a valid need for both modern mine warfare and maritime patrol (MPA) aircraft, but the requirement for submarines is dubious at best. Iran's deployment of Kilo submarines has increased the submarine threat, but coastal submarines are not ideal hunter-killers, and it is unclear how the Saudis could make cost-effective use of submarines as a strike force in either the Gulf or Red Sea.

At a more speculative level, Saudi Arabia has begun to consider plans for the purchase of several AEGIS-class warships to give it advanced battle management, Harpoon anti-ship missiles, Tomahawk strike capability, ASW, anti-aircraft, and anti-ship missile defense capabilities. The AEGIS-class ships are highly effective, but they cost roughly $900 million to $1 billion each, and require highly trained crews. As a result, it would be at least 1998 before Saudi Arabia could order such a ship and 2002–2003 before one could be delivered. Saudi Arabia would also confront problems in obtaining release of some of the weapons and technologies involved.[252]

It seems likely that Saudi Arabia will acquire more advanced large surface ships in the future, but such an acquisition is not a high priority. The US Navy has ample capability to provide such support to Saudi Arabia, and investing similar amounts of money in added air and land capabilities would probably give Saudi Arabia more overall contingency capability.

Saudi Naval Readiness and Warfighting Capabilities

The Saudi Navy has enough equipment on hand and on order to be a relatively powerful force by regional standards, but is a long way from making that equipment fully effective. Its readiness is improving, and has been helped by crash training efforts during Operation Earnest Will (1987–1989) and the Gulf War. However, its current equipment mix requires a force of close to 15,000 men, the Navy is badly undermanned, and training standards are still low. It is dependent on foreign maintenance and logistic support, and is still having problems operating its new French frigates, although it has gradually become fairly effective in operating its older and less sophisticated US-supplied vessels.

Even with automation and foreign support, the Saudi Navy will not be able to operate all of its present forces properly by the late 1990s. While the Saudi Navy has made significant progress in recent years, it faces a decade of expansion before it can become a true "two sea" force capable of covering both Saudi Arabia's Gulf and Red Sea coasts. Even then, it will depend heavily on air support, and will be dependent on reinforcement by USCENTCOM and the British, French, and/or US navies.

The Saudi Navy also suffers from a lack of strategic focus. It needs to emphasize maritime surveillance, defending offshore facilities and coastal installations, dealing with unconventional threats like the naval branch of Iran's Revolutionary Guards, and threats to maritime traffic like mine warfare. Instead, a substantial part of its limited resources are devoted to manning frigates that attempt to duplicate the capabilities of large US and British surface ships, and at least some of its planning has focused on efforts to buy submarines, advanced anti-submarine warfare capabilities, and even larger surface ships that do not suit either Saudi Arabia's overall defense needs or the current capabilities of its navy.

10

The Saudi Air Force

Chart Twenty-One shows the trends in Saudi air strength and it is important to realize that the Royal Saudi Air Force has been in a period of constant transition for most of its existence. This expansion of the air force is still Saudi Arabia's foremost defense priority. The Royal Saudi Air Force (RSAF) is the only service that can cover Saudi Arabia's 2.3 million square kilometers of territory. It represents the investment most capable of cross-reinforcement with the other services. It also has the most impact in terms of regional prestige, and the most credibility in terms of being able to support other GCC states or to operate with USCENTCOM forces in a major crisis.[253]

The RSAF did a good job of creating effective air defenses to meet a threat from Iran during the Iran-Iraq War. It established the "Fahd Line," which created an Air Defense Identification Zone and forward air defense system off the Saudi coast. Saudi Arabia defended its air space and shot down an Iranian F-4 which tested Saudi defenses on June 5, 1984.

The RSAF was the most effective single element of Arab forces in the UN Coalition during the Gulf War. It flew a total of 6,852 sorties between January 17, and February 28, 1991—ranking second after the US in total air activity, and flying about 6% of all sorties flown. These sorties included 1,133 interdiction missions, and 523 battlefield air interdiction missions, for a total of 1,656 offensive missions. The RSAF flew 2,050 defensive counter-air missions, 129 offensive counter air missions, and 102 escort missions for a total of 2,281 air defense sorties. The RSAF flew 118 reconnaissance sorties, 85 E3-A AWACS sorties, 485 refueling sorties, and 1,829 airlift sorties.[254]

During the slightly longer period from January 16 to February 28, Saudi Air Force F-15C units flew 2,088 sorties (over one-third the total F-15C sorties flown by the USAF) and 451 Tornado ADV sorties. Saudi pilots were as capable in these air defense sorties as most pilots in NATO. The RSAF also flew 665 Tornado GR1/IDS strike sorties, 1,129 F-5 sorties, and 118 RF-5 sorties. Saudi F-15Cs shot down three Iraqi

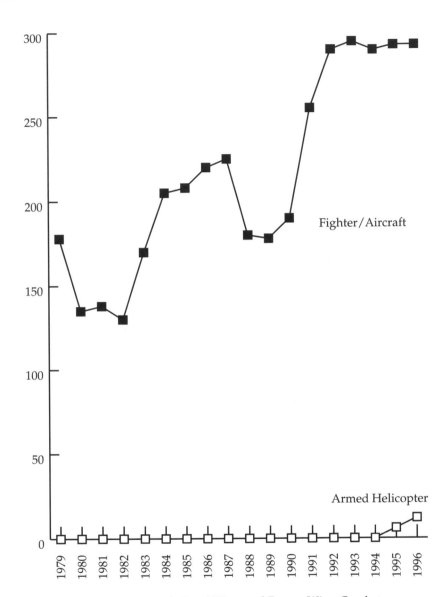

CHART TWENTY-ONE   Saudi Fixed Wing and Rotary Wing Combat
Air Strength—1979–1996. *Source:* Adapted by Anthony H. Cordesman from
various editions of the IISS, *Military Balance,* the JCSS, *Military Balance in the
Middle East,* and material provided by US experts.

Mirage F-1s with air-to-air missiles—including the only double kill by a single fighter in the war on January 24, 1991. The RSAF lost only two aircraft—one Tornado GR1 to anti-aircraft fire and one F-5 to unknown causes.[255]

The Current Size of the Saudi Air Force

In 1996, the RSAF had about 18,000 men, and six wings with a total of 15 combat squadrons and about 295 combat aircraft. It was shifting from a command structure that went from Air Force command to air base command to squadron to one that went from Air Force command to sector command to base command to wing or group command to squadron. This new command structure was designed to give certain sectors more freedom and flexibility at the local command level.

Saudi Arabia's total inventory of major combat aircraft include 8 F-15Ss, with 63 more in delivery, 93 F-15Cs, 93 F/RF-5s, 42 Tornado IDSs, 24 Tornado ADVs, and 6 Tornado IDS-Rs. It had 30 Hawk Mark 65 jets, and 36 BAC-167 turboprop COIN and training aircraft, and its US-supplied major non-combat air assets included 5 E-3As, 7 KE-3As, 1 KE-3B (EW), and 58 C-130s.

The RSAF aircraft strength included five fighter-attack squadrons with 56 F-5Es and two squadrons with 42 Tornado IDS. The IDS squadrons had dual-capable trainer aircraft. These seven squadrons comprised the offensive strength of the Saudi Air Force. They were equipped with modern attack munitions, including AS-15, AS-30, AGM-45 Shrike, and AGM-65 Maverick air-to-surface missiles and the Rockeye, Sea Eagle, and Alarm air-to-ground weapons. Saudi Arabia had MQM-74C Chukar II and Banshee remotely piloted vehicles for reconnaissance and target acquisition.

The RSAF also had included six interceptor squadrons for defensive missions. There were four squadrons with a total of 98 F-15C/Ds, including 78 F-15Cs and 20 F-15Ds. F-15Ds were deployed to each F-15 squadron to perform both training and operational missions. There were two Tornado ADV squadrons with 24 aircraft, which also included dual-capable trainer aircraft. Saudi fighters were equipped with modern air-to-air missiles, including AIM-9L and AIM-9P infrared guided missiles, AIM-7F Sparrow and Skyflash radar guided missiles

The RSAF had two reconnaissance squadrons with 10 RF-5Es and 6 Tornado IDS-Rs, an airborne early warning squadron with five E-3As, and two multipurpose squadrons with 7 F-5Fs and 14 F-5Bs. These latter two squadrons have both a training and combat mission. There were also 30 Hawk Mark 65 jets, and 36 BAC-167 turboprop, training aircraft capable of performing COIN and light attack functions with machine guns, cannons, and rockets, and 12 Cessna 172 and 30 PC-9 training aircraft not armed for combat.

The support units in the air force included a tanker squadron with 8 KE-3As and 8 KC-130Hs, and three transport squadrons with 7 C-130Es, 34 C-130Hs, 8 L-100-30HSs (hospital aircraft), and 35 C-212As. There were two helicopter squadrons with 25 AB-206Bs, 22 AB-205s, 27 AB-212s, and 20 KV-107s.

There was a Royal Flight with 1 B-747 SP, 1 B-737-200 1 Jetstream, and 4 BAe 125-800s. A Saudi "Special Flight" that the Air Force could drawn upon included 4 AB-125s, 4 CN-235s, 2 Learjet 35s, 2 C-140s, 6 VC-130Hs, 1 Cessna 310, and 2 Gulfstream III fixed wing aircraft, and 3 AS-61, AB-212, and 1 S-70 helicopters.

Saudi Arabia had excellent stocks of air munitions and spares. For example, it ordered 101 shipsets of F-15 conformal fuel tanks, 909 AIM-7F and AIM-9P/L air-to-air missiles, 100 Harpoon and 1,600 Maverick air-to-surface missiles, JP-233 and BL-755 bombs and munitions, before Iraq's invasion of Kuwait. It also ordered large numbers of additional Aim-9Ls and Aim-7Fs in August, 1990, and 2,000 Mark 84 2,000 pound bombs, 2,100 CBU-87 cluster munitions, 770 AIM-7Fs, and components for laser guided bombs in July, 1991. While there is no way to estimate current Saudi air munitions stockpiles, they are almost certainly large enough to support both the Saudi Air Force and a major reinforcing deployment by the US Air Force for a mid-intensity conflict.[256]

The Saudi Air Force has long been backed by excellent foreign support. During the 1970s and early 1980s, Saudi Arabia was able to draw on US Air Force and contractor support to create some of the most modern air facilities in the world. No US or NATO base has sheltering or hardening equal to the Saudi bases at Dhahran and Khamis Mushayt, and similar facilities will be built at all of Saudi Arabia's main operating bases. Saudi Arabia now performs most of the support and service for its Lockheed C-130s and its F-5E/F units have also reached proficiency levels approaching those of many Western squadrons.

Growing Saudi Air Force Proficiency

The first Saudi F-15C/Ds were operational in Dhahran by early 1983. A second squadron was formed at Taif by the end of 1983, and a third became operational at Khamis Mushayt in July 1984. Saudi aircraft attrition levels were significantly higher than those of the US, but overall training levels were good. The Saudis had an aircrew to aircraft ratio of 1.5:1 and the Saudi 34th Squadron became the most experienced F-15 squadron in the world, with pilots who have 700–900 hours each. Saudi pilots flew 22–33 hours per month versus 18 hours in Israel and 2 1/2 hours in Egypt. Saudi live firing exercises met NATO standards, and Saudi Arabia routinely fired off older missiles and munitions for training.

By late 1984 and early 1985, the Saudi Air Force was conducting major joint exercises in both the Gulf and Red Sea areas, and conducting Red-Blue or aggressor exercises similar to those employed by the US Air Force. Saudi Arabia maintained these proficiency levels, and began joint exercises with other members of the GCC. Its F-15 units scored 1st and 2nd place in three exercises with NATO forces.

Saudi Arabia also began to crew its five E-3As. The 5 E-3A AWACS aircraft were steadily upgraded to replace their main computer memories, and substitute semiconductors and bubble memories for their magnetic drums—tripling their memory capacity. Major radar system improvements were made to improve data handling, sensitivity, and provide both real time data to each console and the same range coverage against smaller cross section targets. Electronic support measures were installed in the aircraft for passive detection, location, and identification of electronic emitters. The software for the E-3As was updated beyond bloc 30/35, and infrared countermeasures were added to the engines. The E-3As has also been given global positioning systems and five additional operator consoles.[257]

While Saudi Arabia lacked some of the C4I/BM systems, advanced avionics and electronics, munitions, and attack capabilities the USAF used to achieve its high proficiency levels, it demonstrated a high level of squadron readiness. It performed much of its own major support on the F-5, and provided some of the support for the F-15 at its bases in Dhahran and Khamis Mushayt.

The Saudi Tornado Buy and Al-Yamamah Agreement

Saudi Arabia did, however, face problems in developing a modern offensive strike capability. It tried for nearly five years to buy more F-15s, and to acquire an advanced attack mission capability from the US. In July 1985, however, President Reagan sent King Fahd a letter stating that he could not obtain Congressional approval of the sales Saudi Arabia sought. As a result, the Saudi Air Force initiated talks with Britain. These talks led to an agreement in September, 1985 that Britain would provide 60 Tornado ADV air defense fighters, 60 Tornado IDS/GR.1 attack strike-fighters, light attack aircraft, trainers, helicopters, munitions, and British support services.

That same month, Saudi Arabia signed a series of memorandums of understanding (MOUs) with Britain that gave Saudi Arabia the option of turning each MOU into an individual contract. These MOUs were called the al-Yamamah agreement. Saudi Arabia's first major contract under the MOUs cost $8 billion, but the total value grew to a total of $29 billion by 1992. This figure included training, support, construction, naval vessels, etc. It was worth roughly $4 billion a year to Britain by the early 1990s. Saudi Arabia agreed to pay for al-Yamamah by bartering 600,000 barrels of oil per day. This gave Saudi Arabia a guaranteed market and allowed it to bypass some of the constraints imposed by OPEC quotas.[258]

The first phase of the al-Yamamah program called for the purchase of 24 Tornado ADV air defense fighters; 48 Tornado IDS/GR.1 ground attack fighters; 30 BAe Hawk 65 trainers; 30 Pilatus PC-9 trainers; and two Gulfstream aircraft, air weaponry, and ground support and training services.

The Tornado ADV did not prove to be a successful air defense fighter for either the British Royal Air Force or Saudi Arabia. It turned out to be under-powered. While its limited dogfight performance might not have been important in areas where long-range missile combat is critical, the short distances and reaction times affecting many potential threats to Saudi Arabia require dogfight superiority. Its radar warning receiver was not fully effective, and the Tornado's radar and air defense avionics experienced development and performance problems, as did efforts to fully integrate and qualify advanced air-to-air missiles with the aircraft.

Such problems are scarcely unusual in new aircraft, but they were severe enough in the case of the Tornado ADV to prompt the RAF to talk about converting its air defense Tornadoes to reconnaissance, strike, or electronic warfare missions, or dropping them from service the moment it could obtain some form of Eurofighter. The RSAF's experience with the first eight Tornado ADVs was also negative. It converted some to the reconnaissance role, and converted the rest of its orders for ADVs to IDS strike-attack aircraft.

These problems did not prevent additional Saudi orders for British aircraft. In July, 1988, Saudi Arabia signed a letter of intent for a second phase of al-Yamamah. According to Saudi sources, the second phase included 48 more Tornado strike-attack fighters, 40 Hawk 100 and 20 Hawk 200 trainer-fighters, 3–6 Vosper Thorneycroft mine counter measure vessels, C4I systems, and additional weapons, spares, ground support, and training. The Hawk 200 has combat radars—unlike the trainer version. It was also ordered with Sea Eagle anti-ship missiles. Munitions included the Skyflash, ALARM, Sea Eagle, and AIM-9L missiles, and JP-233 and BL-755 bombs.[259]

The new series of MOUs included the order for 80 Sikorsky Black Hawk helicopters for the army discussed earlier. The RSAF had already ordered 12 Black Hawks through the US, but these were transport versions of the aircraft and it was concerned that the US Congress would not sell it armed or attack versions. Accordingly, it ordered the 88 Black Hawks from Westland in Britain. According to some reports, it ordered them with TOW air-to-surface missiles.[260]

The total value of the memorandums of understanding that made up the second phase of al-Yamamah was approximately $18 billion. The deal included light transport aircraft (12 BAe 125s and 4 BAe 146s), and two major military cities and air bases for the new Tornado forces, complete with British support.[261] The new British-built military cities and air bases were to be located at Taiba (about 290 kilometers southwest of Tabuk) and at al-Sulayyil (on the edge of the Empty Quarter). The air bases were to be equipped with at least 25 hardened multiple aircraft shelters. Saudi Arabia felt that its existing bases were adequate in the Eastern Province and near the PDRY, but were not suited for a force of nearly 400 combat aircraft. This brought the potential total value of the two phases of al-Yamamah to $60 billion, projected over a 15 year program.[262]

There were good reasons for the Saudi purchase of the first phase of al-Yamamah package. Saudi Arabia's 12 BAC-167 trainers were only armed with 7.62 mm machine guns. They no longer could be used in anything other than light support functions. Saudi Arabia had bought its Lightning fighters from the UK under pressure from former Secretary of Defense Robert S. McNamara. The US effectively forced Saudi Arabia to buy the Lightning as part of a then-covert three-cornered deal, in which the Lightning sale to Saudi Arabia was designed to allow the UK to buy the F-111 from the US.[263] Even when first delivered, however, the Lightning never had the range, dual capability, and avionics Saudi Arabia needed.

The status of the al-Yamamah package could be in doubt, however, if Crown Prince Abdullah ascends to the throne, as he nearly did in 1995. Abdullah was not included in the 1986 negotiations which led to the signing of the first part of al-Yamamah, and is said to have been concerned with some aspects of the agreement. In particular, some former US officials indicate he did not favor the arrangement by which al-Yamamah was able to escape budgetary pressures while these constraints increased on other military forces, such as his National Guard. This could lead to al-Yamamah being placed within the overall Saudi budget, thereby adversely affecting the level of purchases by Saudi Arabia.[264]

There is also additional tension between Britain and Saudi Arabia concerning the status of Britain as a base for Saudi dissidents, specifically the CDLR. Following the November, 1995, car bombing in Riyadh, the Saudi government made it quite clear that its purchases of British equipment were dependent on a less hospitable climate for Saudi dissidents in Britain. The British government, well aware of Saudi displeasure, ordered the expulsion of Mohammed al-Mas'ari, the head of the CDLR, after he made statements seemingly condoning the November car bombing.[265]

Saudi Modernization After the Gulf War: The F-15S

Saudi Arabia made significant new aircraft purchases as a result of the Gulf War. It purchased 24 additional F-15C/Ds from USAF stocks, 8 C-130Hs, and 2 C-130H-30 aircraft and large numbers of Aim-9Ls, and AIM-7Fs from the US in late August, 1990. It also bought the Falcon Eye electronic warfare aircraft, although it knew that this plane lacked the sophistication and capability of US and Israeli ELINT aircraft.[266]

Saudi Arabia made these purchases because it needed additional modern strike aircraft. Its F-5E-IIs and F-5Fs were relatively advanced models of the F-5E/F, equipped with INS, refueling probes, and the ability to fire Mavericks (the F-5F can also fire laser guided bombs). The oldest of these F-5 aircraft, however, were nearing the end of their useful life, and the F-5 production line had long been closed. The F-5Es were not cost-effective to upgrade and they required more than twice as much Saudi and foreign technical support manpower per plane as an F-15. The F-5E/Fs were also too short-ranged and limited in avionics and payload to cope adequately with the kind of advanced-threat aircraft being introduced into the region, or to deploy from one Saudi air base in support of another. As a result, the F-5Es needed to be phased down into a training and light support role. Some 20–30% of Saudi Arabia's F-5 strength was already devoted to full-time training missions by 1990.

Saudi Arabia's F-15C/Ds were likely to be able to fulfill the role of first-line air defense adequately until well after the year 2010. The F-15C/D showed during the Gulf War that it could do an excellent job in air-to-air combat against the most advanced aircraft in service in potential threat nations. The Saudi F-15C/Ds, however, were configured as a one-mission aircraft and can only be used for air combat.

The US Air Force had recommended that the Saudi Air Force be given an advanced dual-capable fighter as early as 1977—when it conducted the original studies that led to the US sale of the F-15—but the US could never obtain Congressional permission to sell Saudi Arabia the bomb racks and attack systems necessary to make the F-15C/D effective in the air-to-ground role. As a result, a key part of Saudi Arabia's total first-line fighter strength was unable to perform effective attack missions, or provide attack support to Saudi land and naval forces.

The Gulf War showed the Saudi Air Force the importance of offensive air power, and demonstrated that the Saudi Air Force could use the Tornado in long-range strike missions. The Tornado proved during Desert Storm that it could be an effective strike fighter, once it was equipped with new FLIR and laser designator pods. The Tornado delivered over 1,000 laser guided bombs and ALARM missiles, and it was clear that the Tornado could help meet Saudi Arabia's need for a long-range deterrent to Iraq and Iran. However, the Tornado lacked the flexibility, maneuverability, and avionics to fly demanding missions using precision guided munitions against advanced air defenses in the forward battle area, and did not meet all of Saudi Arabia's needs for a first line strike aircraft.

Saudi Arabia's solution was to buy 72 more F-15s in 1992. This purchase was possible because of the tacit improvement in Saudi-Israeli relations and the strengthening of US and Saudi ties during the Gulf War. It included 24 more F-15 aircraft designed for air combat, and 48 F-15 aircraft dual-capable in both the air defense and strike/attack missions. All 72 F-15s were designated the F-15S, although they involved two configurations of aircraft.

The sale involved a total of $5 billion worth of aircraft, and up to $4 billion worth of other arms and supplies—including $800 million worth of construction. It also included 24 spare engines, 48 targeting and navigation pods, 900 AGM-65D/G Maverick air-to-surface missiles, 600 CBU-87 bombs, 700 GBU-10/12 bombs, and special mission planning systems.[267]

The 24 air defense versions of the F-15S were air defense aircraft based on the F-15E air frame. They cannot use navigation and targeting pods, or laser illuminators, and can only drop general purpose bombs. Their radars are better than those on the F-15C/D, however, and have a resolution of 60 feet at 20 nautical miles versus resolution of 530 feet in the F-15C/D. They use the same AIM-7F and AIM-7M radar guided air-to-air missiles used by existing Saudi F-15C/Ds, and the AIM-9S, which is the export version of the radar guided AIM-9M air-to-air missiles. They also have the technical capability to use AMRAAM, although the transfer of this missile has not been approved. When they are all operational and added to Saudi Arabia's 93 F-15C/Ds, they will give Saudi Arabia a total of 168 deployed F-15s and 120 advanced air defense aircraft.

The 48 F-15S strike/attack variants of the F-15E Strike Eagle differ from the US Air Force version of the F-15E in several important ways. They use the AAQ-20 Path Finder navigation pods, the AAQ-20 Sharpshooter targeting pods, and a laser illuminator. The Path Finder pods have a terrain-following radar, but have reduced ECCM capabilities that allow them to be tracked by US types of fighters. The Sharpshooter pods for the F-15S only have limited cluster bomb delivery capability. They will deliver the A/B version of the electro-optical Maverick and the D/G version of the IR Maverick, but will not have a missile boresight correlator. They only have a single-fire capability for Maverick, rather than multiple fire capability, and are not equipped to deliver the HARM anti-radiation missile.

The F-15S is not being supplied with conformal fuel tanks of the kind supplied on the F-15E, depriving it of two extra tangential stores stations for carrying extra munitions and some of its ability to carry precision guided weapons. The change will not affect Saudi Arabia in launching defensive missions against Iran and Iraq, but will force it to trade range for payload in any missions flown against Israel.

The F-15S includes several other changes from the F-15E. It has a detuned version of the APG-70 radar on the 15E. The radar on the F-15S has only 60% of the bandwidth of the regular APG-70, and only has 16 channels, rather than the regular 32. It does not have a computerized mapping capability, and only has a resolution of 60 feet at 15 nautical miles versus 8.5 feet at 20 nautical miles in the F-15E. The F-15S has altered software for the AWG-27 armament control system. It lacks a data transfer module, and its ASW-51 auto flight control does not include the terrain following mode. It uses a commercial-grade secure voice and global positioning system navigation system.

Most importantly, the F-15S's electronic warfare suite is only missionized for use against non-US aircraft and threats in the Gulf and Red Sea area. This means substantial modifications to the ALQ-135 internal countermeasures set, the ALR-56C radar warning receiver, the ALE-45 countermeasures dispenser, and MX-9287 interference blanker set. The ALQ-135 does not have the capability to jam friendly aircraft by type, and the radar warning receiver does not identify friendly aircraft by type.

These modifications have no impact on Saudi capability to deal with any threat aircraft in Iran and Iraq, but they preclude effective penetration of Israel's air space because Israeli fighters, surface-to-air defenses, and electronic warfare assets all use US or Israeli designed systems, and none of the electronic warfare assets on the F-15S will be tuned to counter such systems.[268]

The potential risk of the F-15S being used in an attack on Israel, or being used by an unfriendly regime in the event of some unforeseen coup, was also limited by the fact that Saudi Arabia was not going to conduct depot level maintenance for either the overall aircraft or the APG-70 radar. Saudi Arabia accepted a reliance on US technicians and technical support to keep the aircraft operating, knowing that reliance would continue well beyond the year 2005, and nearly 1,000 technicians from McDonnell Douglas were in Saudi Arabia by early 1996. As Iran showed during the first weeks of the Iran-Iraq War, even a relatively sophisticated air force can lose much of its operational strength in a few days if it lacks sophisticated technical support. Iranian F-14s had even lost their ability to use the Phoenix missiles by the time the Iran-Iraq War started.[269]

Equally important, the performance of the F-15S was determined by the software that its computer and other avionics used to recognize threats, launch air combat and attack munitions, counter enemy sensors and weapons, and navigate to target. No nation other than the US could alter the software on the F-15S, and it had no software optimized to attack US or Israeli air and air defense systems. It could not be modernized to deal with any changes in existing systems, operate a single new weapon, or deal with a single new threat without US approval. It also could not be upgraded as part of the US Air Force multi-stage improvement programs (MSIPs) planned for the F-15E without US support. Given the probable 20 year operating life of the F-15S (1995–2015), this placed a critical constraint on Saudi use of the F-15S for missions against Israel or US forces, although it in no way restricted the value of the F-15S for any of the missions for which Saudi Arabia needed the aircraft.

A combination of these factors, and a US commitment to provide Israel with enough technology superior to that of any potential Arab threat, allowed the Bush Administration to move the sale forward. President Bush and Defense Secretary Cheney made such a commitment to provide advanced technology at the time they announced the sale of the F-15S, and Israel's new Labor government indicated that it did not pose the same objections to the sale as did the Likud. As a result, Congressional leaders assured President Bush that they had the votes to ensure that Congress would not block the sale, and the President sent the proposed sale forward to Congress for approval on September 14, 1992.

The willingness of Congress to support the sale was reinforced by the Bush Administration's willingness to provide $10 billion worth of loan guarantees to Israel following the election of a Labor government. On September 24, 1992, more than thirty senators—led by Senator John McCain of Arizona and Joseph Lieberman of Connecticut—wrote to President calling for a six point program that included (a) providing the $10 billion in loan guarantees, (b) maintaining the existing level of military and economic aid to Israel in constant dollars on a long-term basis, (c) providing long-term military and economic aid to Egypt to ensure the safety of the Camp David accords, (d) giving

Israel the same technology sharing arrangements as our NATO allies, (e) establishing cooperation in civil space activities, (f) improving cooperation in intelligence, (f) improving other aspects of military cooperation, and (g) promptly implementing prior agreements to pre-position $300 million worth of equipment in Israel and provide Israel with $700 million worth of military equipment made surplus by the end of the Cold War.

Two days later, the Bush Administration stated publicly that Israel would continue to be given an edge in electronic warfare, munitions types and warheads, software, satellite intelligence, and a wide range of other capabilities. It also agreed that the US would soon preposition $300 million worth of US munitions and equipment in Israel, and transfer the $700 million worth of surplus military stocks that the US no longer need-ed for NATO—including additional Apache AH-64 attack helicopters and Black Hawk special mission helicopters, and other systems. As part of this effort, the US and Israel established special working groups on prepositioning; transferring stocks of surplus US military equipment to Israel; intelligence-sharing; expanding high-technology military coopera-tion; and developing a global protection system against missile attacks through a combination of intelligence sharing, ground and space-based early warning systems, and use of the THADD or Arrow to intercept the-ater-range missiles.[270]

Congress approved the guarantees on October 1, 1992, and this removed the last obstacle to a sale that provided major strategic bene-fits for both the Royal Saudi Air Force and the US. The US and Royal Saudi Air Forces had already proved they could cooperate closely. They had worked together during the Iran-Iraq War before the US reflagging operation, and then during Operation Earnest Will. They fought together during the war with Iraq, and are currently cooperat-ing in the enforcement of the "no fly zone" over southern Iraq in Oper-ation Southern Watch.

The F-15S is a far more advanced strike-fighter than any aircraft in ser-vice in Iran and Iraq. It will give Saudi Arabia a decisive edge over Iraq and Iran well beyond the year 2000. It will fully meet Saudi Arabia's desire for an F-15E-like aircraft that can attack deep into Iraqi or Iranian territory, defend itself in air-to-air combat, and launch air-to-ground ord-nance from outside the range of short-range air defense missiles. The F-15S can also be rapidly upgraded in an emergency if Iran or Iraq should acquire new types of fighters with advanced avionics.

Saudi operation of the F-15S will ensure interoperability between the US and Saudi Air Forces. Saudi Arabia will buy additional service and training facilities, munitions, spare parts, and specialized electronics facilities that can support both Saudi and USAF F-15 strike-attack aircraft—as well as Saudi and US F-15 air defense fighters. Such facilities and munitions stocks will vastly improve US rapid deployment capabilities in the Gulf, and give the US the ability to deploy and support well over 72 F-15E attack aircraft in a matter of days. More broadly, the Saudi F-15S buy will also ensure Saudi and US interoperability at every level of operations from the individual sortie to large-scale command and control and battle management.

Although Saudi Arabia's economic problems later threatened its delivery schedule for the F-15S, Saudi Arabia gave a high priority to funding the F-15S, and its funding problems have been eased by the rescheduling of US arms purchases discussed earlier. The roll-out of the first F-15S took place in the US in late September, 1995, and the RSAF began to receive the F-15Ss at the rate of one squadron a year. The first full squadron of F-15Ss became fully operational in Saudi Arabia in 1996. The second should be operational in 1997, and the third in 1998.[271]

Saudi Modernization After the Gulf War: More Tornadoes

The Saudi Air Force also went ahead with the purchase of additional Tornado and trainer aircraft. In April, 1992, Britain announced that Saudi Arabia had agreed to a financing package for the $2.7 billion sale, and indicated that the deal would again be financed "off-budget," by shifting oil revenue directly to a London account. This purchase of the additional aircraft was made financially possible by deciding not to turn other MOUs into firm contracts. On August 24, 1992, Saudi Arabia cut the number of new air bases it would buy from two to one.

This decision was a result of Saudi Arabia's discovery during the Gulf War that its existing facilities could sustain the build-up of some 500,000 foreign troops, and that they had substantial over-capacity. This decision saved Saudi Arabia $15.6 to $19.5 billion, and released funds it could use to complete the buy of 48 Tornado IDS/GR.1s It signed a contract with Britain in early February, 1993, which included shelters, maintenance, weapons, and training for the aircraft. The aircraft were to be delivered in configurations similar to those used by the RAF, and had Turbo-Union RB-199 engines, Sky Shadow ECM pods, and GEC-Marconi flight control systems, radars, and radar homing and warning receivers.[272]

The order did not include more Hawks and mine-countermeasure vessels, but negotiations continued on these purchases. When oil prices increased in 1994, Saudi Arabia ordered 20 more Hawk 65 jets and 20 more Swiss Pilatus PC-9 turboprop trainers, at a cost of $750 million. This purchase was essential to provide training for the new pilots Saudi Arabia needed to crew its F-15Ss and Tornadoes, although it meant Saudi

Arabia would not buy enough of the advanced Hawks to replace its F-5s and would rely more on the lower-performance, tandem-seat, Hawk 100 variant of the aircraft.[273]

The Saudi Air Force in the Late 1990s

These purchases of F-15Ss and Tornadoes will give Saudi Arabia the most modern air force in the Gulf, but they will not solve all of its major modernization problems. The Saudi Air Force still faces four major problems:

- First, the F-15S sale will cost nearly $9 billion, and the Tornado sale will cost $7.5 billion. Saudi Arabia will face significant problems in finding this money, despite a slow payment schedule and some concessionary terms.[274]
- Second, the F-15S and Tornado purchases still leave the Saudi Air Force with some hard decisions to make about the replacement of the F-5E II. Saudi Arabia had talked previously about buying Hawks, F-16s, and F-18s as direct replacements for 95 of its F-5s. However, the purchase of 72 F-15S aircraft, and 48 more Tornado IDS/GR.1s, plus some additional Hawks, seems to have convinced Saudi Arabia that it could phase out its F-5s without a major new purchase of additional aircraft. The sheer cost of any additional aircraft purchase was a key factor in deciding against a follow-on to the F-5, but Saudi Arabia also found that major diseconomies of scale arose in trying to make a limited buy of a new advanced fighter like the F-16 or F-18. It takes about 50% to 100% more Saudi and foreign manpower to support a new type than it does to add an additional F-15 or Tornado. It also creates major problems in terms of additional facilities and maintenance stockpiles.[275]
- Third, it is one thing to train pilots and another to reshape an entire air force. The purchase of the F-15Ss and additional Tornadoes requires the Saudi Air Force to focus on creating advanced offensive war-fighting capabilities. This is not an easy conversion to accomplish, even with US and British support. It means rethinking many aspects of Saudi command and control, reconnaissance and targeting, combined operations, support, and training.
- Fourth, by the time the RSAF fully absorbs all its F-15S aircraft into its force structure in 1998–1999, Saudi Arabia will be in the process of phasing out its F-5EIIs. All of Saudi Arabia's F-5s will be over twenty years old by 1999, and its initial F-15C/Ds will be 12 to 18 years old.[276]
- Finally, Saudi Arabia's C4I/BM assets are much better structured for air defense than air offense. Saudi Arabia needs to rethink its C4I/BM

needs for theater interdiction and large-scale attack missions comprehensively and acquire the necessary systems.

The Readiness and Warfighting
Capabilities of the Saudi Air Force

The Saudi Air Force has considerable experience with defensive operations. During the Iran-Iraq War, the Saudi Air Force worked closely with the US Air Force, and developed a patrol line called the Fahd Line near the center of the Gulf, a scramble line where aircraft on alert took off the moment an intruder came close, with inner defense lines covered by its Improved Hawk missiles. This air defense system was modified during the Gulf War to initially cover both the north and south, because of the possible risk of hostile air attacks from Yemen and the Sudan. During the rest of the war, Saudi Arabia steadily refined its system, working with the US Air Force and other UN Coalition forces to develop a layered system of land and airborne sensors and defense lines that could cover threats from Iraq as well as Iran.

Saudi F-15C pilots performed well in air defense missions during Desert Storm. The Saudi Air Force flew some 6,800 sorties during the Gulf War (January 17, 1991 to February 28, 1991), and some 2,000 sorties over the Kuwaiti Theater of Operations and Iraq. These sorties were largely counter-air. Saudi F-15C pilots proved to be competent and aggressive in air-to-air combat during the brief period when Iraq actively challenged Coalition fighters, and one Saudi pilot scored a double kill. Saudi Arabia was also the only Southern Gulf country that had a modern concept of air defense operations.

At the same time, the Gulf War showed the Saudi Air Force still had some serious weaknesses:

- The RSAF did well in flying air combat interdiction, airlift, and AWACS sorties, but it had weak mission planning and could not plan or control large-scale offensive operations. It had no force-on-force doctrine, or ability to operate beyond the squadron level. There were language, communications, inter-service cooperation, and mission planning problems. Coordination problems often emerged between the RSAF and the Ministry of Defense (MODA).
- The RSAF lacked the pilot numbers to operate all its British-supplied aircraft properly and some Saudi Tornadoes were flown by British pilots. Additional foreign technicians had to be brought in to maintain reasonable sortie rates with the F-15s and Tornadoes. The war showed that the RSAF will be dependent on such technicians for at least the next decade.

- The Saudi Air Force initially had difficulty in finding the manpower to operate its AWACS, and could not easily integrate AWACS data into its Command Operations Center in Riyadh, and Sector Operating Centers (SOCs) throughout the Kingdom. The Air Force operates these centers, although the Air Defense Force has responsibility for some functions and the radars and equipment at surface-to-air missile sites and some other formations.
- The Saudi air force did not do well in electronic warfare, and reconnaissance missions. The Saudi RF-5 force proved largely useless in seeking out targets and rapidly processing information, and Saudi Arabia was almost completely dependent on the US for reconnaissance and intelligence.
- Saudi Arabia learned it needed the passive ELINT systems that are being fitted to US AWACS. These electronic intelligence systems are called the AN/AYR-1, and provide the ability to detect, locate, and identify the radar emissions of ships, aircraft, and ground systems—often indicating their precise type and location. Saudi Arabia may also need the upgraded CC-2E central computer, GPS navigation system, and Class 2H version of the secure Joint Tactical Information Distribution System (JTIDS). These upgrades to the E-3A, however, will only be available for US aircraft during 1995–1999, and it is unclear whether and when they will be provided to Saudi Arabia.

Saudi Arabia is trying to solve these problems through a mix of new acquisitions and improved organization and training. It is seeking to upgrade some of its reconnaissance and targeting problems by improving the reconnaissance equipment on its aircraft, and by buying a relatively high resolution satellite imaging capability from the US. This satellite imaging service will be provided by Orbital Sciences of the US, and will be the first time the US has sold such precision imaging abroad.[277] As the following section indicates, the Saudi Air Force is also improving its land-based C^4I/BM system, and acquiring automated mission planning support. Mission planning has been a key weakness in Saudi operations.

Saudi Arabia found that flying a full air defense and air control and warning screen against a Northern Gulf state like Iraq or Iran can require up to four simultaneous orbits by AWACS aircraft, or a total of 9–12 aircraft. Saudi Arabia can only fly two orbits with its current five E-3As. Saudi Arabia is currently studying the purchase of four more AWACS aircraft, based on either a B-767 air frame or a modified Saudi B-707. These aircraft would allow Saudi Arabia to support continuous air defense and maritime surveillance coverage over both coasts. This purchase may prove too expensive, but it would also greatly ease US deployment problems in reinforcing Saudi Arabia or its smaller Southern Gulf neighbors.[278]

Saudi Arabia needs to both replace its F-5E IIs and improve its training aircraft. In the past, it has focused on the F-15 or F-16 as possible replacements for its 105 F-5E/Fs, but this may again be too expensive a solution. As a result, Saudi Arabia seems to be considering a mix of more US fighters and a buy of an advanced trainer like the Hawk 100/200.

The Gulf War also showed that the Saudi Air Force needs far more extensive exercise training in offensive operations at the mid- and high-command level. It began such exercise activity in January, 1996, when it held the Flag of Glory exercise. This exercise was one of the first force-wide exercises by any Gulf military service and involved 150 Saudi aircraft flying from bases at Dhahran, Khamis Mushayt, Tabuk, and Taif. It involved Saudi E-3As, F-5Es, F-15C/Ds, and Tornadoes, and involved combined offensive and defensive maneuver to deal with a threat like an Iraqi invasion. The Saudi Air Force also improved its performance in joint exercises with US and Kuwaiti forces in 1995 and 1996, and demonstrated that Saudi, Kuwaiti, and USAF aircraft could operate jointly using US and Saudi E-3As, the US JSTARS, other US C^{4}I/BM systems, and digital data links.

There are some areas where the Saudi Air Force is not making major progress. It needs to give still more emphasis to high-intensity, 24-hour-a-day operations against a threat like Iran and Iraq. It needs to raise its sortie rates sharply, and to improve its targeting and force-wide C^{4}I and battle management capabilities for offensive operations. This may require more dynamic leadership at the top.

The Saudi Air Force found during the Gulf War that it lacked many of the capabilities it needed for joint operations with the army and navy. While the Saudi Air Force could fly against fixed, lightly defended, interdiction targets, it could only do so with foreign planning and support. The Saudi Air Force proved to have limited operational flexibility in adapting from range training to actual close air support missions, and communications between the Saudi Air Force and Army presented major problems.

The Saudi Air Force still needs more extensive joint training and joint operations activity with the Saudi Army, although the lack of initiative and leadership in this area seems to be more the fault of the Army than the Air Force. The Air Force needs to develop a coordinated operational concept with the Saudi Navy, practice making more effective use of the maritime surveillance capabilities of the E-3A, and conduct joint training with the Navy. Here, however, the Air Force will have to wait until the Saudi Navy begins to transform its equipment strength into military effectiveness. At present, the Navy is more a showpiece than a force.

At the same time, these weaknesses in Saudi Air Force warfighting capability must be kept in perspective. They are common to even the best air forces in the developing world. They do not prevent the Saudi Air Force from being the most effective air force in the Southern Gulf, and one of the most effective air forces in the Arab world. At the same time, they indicate that Saudi Arabia will have major problems in defending against Iraq or Iran unless it has extensive foreign support. It will be a minimum of ten years before the RSAF can adequately match their offensive and defensive capabilities. The RSAF will need at least a decade more of US and British assistance to become an effective air force capable of force-on-force operations and combined operations.

11

The Saudi Air Defense Force

Saudi Arabia has a separate Saudi Air Defense Corps to provide fixed and mobile land-based air defense of key targets throughout Saudi Arabia. This force was created to establish a separate professional service, dedicated to the relatively high technology air defense mission, and to reduce the manpower quality and leadership problems that emerged when these air defense forces were subordinated to the army. The Air Defense Corps has since been given command over Saudi Arabia's Patriot theater anti-ballistic missile defenses and its PRC-supplied CSS-2 surface-to-surface missiles. It is subordinate to the Air Force for C^4I and battle management in time of war.[279]

The Current Strength of Saudi
Land-Based Air Defense Forces

Estimates of the current strength and equipment of the Air Defense Force differ according to which specific surface-based air defense units are included in the total, and which forces are counted as being in the ADF versus the Air Force, Navy, and Army. It is clear that the Air Defense Force controls all of Saudi Arabia's Improved Hawk missiles, and most of its medium surface-to-air missiles, but its exact lines of control are unclear. Some sources indicate that it controls all mobile and crew-powered weapons, and that the Army controls all man-portable Mistral, Stinger, and Redeye teams. Other sources indicate the Army also controls Saudi Arabia's Crotale missiles. Control of given deployments of anti-aircraft guns is also unclear.

The Saudi Air Defense Force appeared to have a strength of 4,000 men and some 33 surface-to-air missile batteries in mid-1996, although some sources indicate Saudi Arabia's total air defense manning exceeded 10,000 men. Its total major surface-to-air missile strength included 15 Improved Hawk batteries with 128 fire units, 9 Crotale batteries with 48 Crotale fire units (currently being modernized), 16 air defense batteries with 72 Shahine fire units, and 50 AMX-30SA 30 mm self-propelled guns.[280]

Most of Saudi Arabia's Shahine units were deployed in fixed locations for the defense of air bases and key targets. All of the Shahine systems were being upgraded as the result of an agreement with France signed in 1991. These units provide close-in defense capability for virtually all of Saudi Arabia's major cities, ports, oil facilities, and military bases.

Total Saudi holdings of man-portable surface-to-air missiles included 500–700 Mistrals, 350–400 Stingers, and 500–600 Redeyes. Saudi Arabia also had 92 M-163 Vulcan 20 mm anti-aircraft guns, 30 V-150s with Vulcan 20 mm guns, 30 towed 20 mm Vulcans, 128 35 mm AA guns, and 150 L/70 40 mm guns (most in storage).[281]

There were also six Patriot fire units or batteries, with 384 Patriot long-range air defense missiles, six AN/MPQ-53 radar sets, six engagement control stations, and 48 launcher stations deployed in Saudi Arabia. These systems are currently manned by US forces. They greatly improve Saudi Arabia's low to high-level air defense capability, and provide substantial defense against medium-range and theater ballistic missiles.

Saudi Arabia has its own Patriot units on order. It purchased its first Patriot units on September 27, 1990, as part of its Gulf War arms package. Saudi Arabia signed a $1.03 billion contract for the first part of this force in December, 1992. This contract included 13 launchers, 671 missiles, and associated equipment. It then bought 14 more Patriot fire units (with 64 Patriot long-range air defense missiles, 1 AN/MPQ-53 radar sets, 1 engagement control station, and 8 launcher stations each) to defend its sites, military bases, and major oil facilities. Saudi Arabia now has a total of 20 batteries on order, and Saudi and US Army studies indicate that Saudi Arabia might eventually require a total of 26. Saudi Arabia has already paid $2.2 billion out of a cost of $4.0 billion for the 20 batteries it already has on order.[282]

The Patriot units Saudi Arabia has bought are the PAC-3 version, with greatly improved software, radar processing capabilities, longer range missiles, better guidance systems, and more lethal warheads. Unlike the PAC-1 and PAC-2 systems used during the Gulf War, they are designed to kill missiles at comparatively long ranges and to discriminate fully between warheads and decoys and parts of the missile body. Saudi Arabia signed a $580 million support contract for its new Patriots and its existing IHawks with Raytheon in March, 1993.[283]

Integrating Saudi and Southern Gulf Air Defense

Saudi Arabia has steadily improved the organization of its ground-based air defense. It made significant improvements during the Gulf War.

However, the Air Defense Force has been slow to acquire the manpower quality and training it needs. It still lacks the systems integration, battle management systems, and C^{4}I software and integration it needs for effective operation. Moreover, contractor efforts to improve the integration of the Saudi Air Defense Corps' Improved Hawks, Shahines (Improved Crotale), anti-aircraft guns, and land-based radars and C^{4}I systems have not been fully effective, and the Saudi air defense system is not easy to restructure.

The Saudi Arabian air defense network was first developed in the 1960s and used US and British radars. Saudi Arabia then added a number of bits and pieces over the years. It bought a Thomson CSF air command and control system, and four Westinghouse AN/TPS-43 three dimensional radars in 1980. It ordered AN/TPS-43G radars to modernize its system as part of the Peace Pulse program in 1981, and updated its system to provide command and data links to its E-3A AWACS.[284]

Although these systems improved Saudi capabilities, Saudi Arabia still had major communications and C^{4}I integration problems, which it attempted to solve by giving new contracts to Litton and Boeing.[285] The Litton contract involved a $1.7 billion effort to provide C^{4}I, sensors, communications systems, and handle the interface between missiles and other air defense systems, as well as build sites and train personnel. Key elements involved 17 major communications links installed in S-280C militarized transportable shelters, and included both line-of-sight and tropospheric scatter links of 72 channel capacity. The field phase involved 34 low-level and 34 high-level shelters. While there is some dispute as to responsibility, the system was only partially operational when the contract was due to be completed. The Litton supplied system still seems to be experiencing operational problems, some of which may be the result of a lack of trained Saudi personnel.[286]

The Boeing contract, which was called the "Peace Shield" project, and had a total cost of $5.6 billion. It involved a far more ambitious effort to give Saudi Arabia a system of 17 AN/FPS-117(V)3 long-range, three-dimensional radar systems fully netted with its AN-TPS-43 and AN-TPS-72 short and medium-range radars. It was to have (a) a central command operations center (COC) at Riyadh, (b) five sector command centers (SCCs) at Dhahran, Taif, Tabuk, Khamis Mushayt, and Al Kharj to cover the country, and (c) additional sector operations centers (SOCs) at each major air base. It was to use a tropospheric scattering and microwave communications system to integrate Saudi Arabia's surface-to-air missile defenses, some anti-aircraft gun units, its radars, its E-3A airborne warning and control systems (AWACS) aircraft and fighters, and six major regional underground operating centers and numerous smaller sites—all of which were to be managed by a command center in Riyadh.

This system had considerable potential importance in giving Saudi Arabia the ability to provide battle management for high-intensity air combat and beyond-visual-range combat, and in providing the base for a system to integrate the six Southern Gulf countries in the GCC—Bahrain, Kuwait, Oman, Qatar, Saudi Arabia, and the UAE. However, the software and systems integration efforts required to make Peace Shield effective were years behind schedule at the time of the Gulf War. Contractor performance was so bad that the US Air Force Electronic Systems Division issued a "show cause notice" and then terminated Boeing's work on the program in January 1991.

Senior US advisors in Saudi Arabia regard the combined failure of Boeing and the US Air Force to deliver a useful Peace Shield program as the worst single arms sale in the history of US sales to developing countries and the worst managed arms sale in the history of the Gulf. One senior US officer described it as, "a disaster on the part of the contractor and the Air Force from start to finish . . . A model of what should never happen."

As a result, Saudi Arabia had to begin again with a new contractor. It shifted the contract from Boeing to Hughes in July, 1991, at a cost of $837 million, and this time the program made solid progress.[287] The new Peace Shield system began to become operational in January, 1995, and performed well in the Flag of Glory exercises that Saudi Arabia held in January 1996. The Peace Shield system uses Hughes AND-44 workstations, Hughes HDP-6200 large screen displays, a modern data processing architecture, and far more advanced software. It will have some 300 individual sites and integrate a mix of Saudi radars that now includes 28 AN/TPS-43s, 17 AN/FPS-117s, and 35 AN/TPS-63s. The system makes extensive use of modern optical fiber technology, although it has the limitation that no provision was made for advanced data links to neighboring states like Bahrain and Kuwait.

The system has adapted the concept of layered defense that Saudi Arabia developed during the Iran-Iraq War. There will be a patrol line like the Fahd Line near the center of the Gulf, or covering the forward area on other borders, a scramble line where aircraft on alert take off the moment an intruder comes close, and inner defense lines covered by its Improved Hawk missiles. It is now being used by Saudi commanders in local operations and exercises, and to train Saudi junior officers, although most of the work stations are still foreign-manned. Saudi Arabia has also ordered 27 mission planning systems from the Sander Corporation that should provide the mission planning support that the RSAF lacked during the Gulf War.

Saudi Arabia purchased another C⁴I/BM integration and system in March, 1989, called Falcon Eye. This is a tactical radar system which involves the supply of Westinghouse AN/TPS-70 radars with related computers, software, communications systems, and systems integration, and is to be managed by Ferranti. Falcon Eye is supposed to integrate data from ground radars and the E-3A force, and down-link data to the 14 Skyguard/Gun King batteries in the Saudi Air Defense Force that are used for close-in defense of air bases and vital military installations. It is supposed to be compatible with Peace Pulse and Peace Shield. The first phase of the system was supposed to become fully operational in 1992.

The Effectiveness of the Saudi Air Defense Force and Options for GCC and Southern Gulf Cooperation

The success of the Peace Shield and Falcon Eye systems will be critical to determining how well the Air Defense Force can absorb the Patriot missile units Saudi Arabia is buying. Peace Shield will not be fully operational until February, 1996 as opposed to an original target date of 1993. Like all of Saudi Arabia's sophisticated air systems, it will be heavily dependent on US technical assistance (and *de facto* assistance in operating the weapons) until well after the year 2000.[288]

More generally, the question arises as to whether the existence of a separate Air Defense Corps is the right long-term solution to Saudi Arabia's military needs. The existence of a separate Saudi Air Defense Corps reduces the possibility of any kind of coup attempt by creating a separate check on air force operations, but its ability to fight in defensive positions against superior forces will depend heavily on the quality of its air cover, the ability of the Saudi Air Force to provide overall command of the Air Defense Force in wartime and link its operations with those of the army, and its ability to provide close air and interdiction support. In the long run, integrating smaller and mobile systems into the army, and the larger missiles and C^4I system into the air force, might be more successful.[289]

Further, Saudi Arabia clearly needs to integrate its air defense and airborne maritime patrol system with those of other Gulf states. This is crucial to both Saudi Arabia's future security and the ability of the West to reinforce Bahrain and Kuwait effectively, because of their small size and air space. Kuwait is particularly vulnerable because of its common border with Iraq, and its proximity to Iran. It desperately requires a survivable air defense and land and maritime surveillance system. No Kuwaiti-based system can provide such characteristics unless it is integrated into a Saudi system, preferably with close links to Bahrain, Qatar, and the UAE.

At the same time, the air defense systems of Qatar, Oman, and the UAE need to be fully integrated with the Saudi air defense and airborne maritime patrol system to deal with potential threats from Iran and Yemen, and to enhance their beyond-visual-range air defense combat capability. The smaller Gulf states have no hope of providing effective air defense on a piecemeal basis, or developing the kind of air combat training and exercise experience necessary to interoperate effectively with US and Saudi fighters and E-3As. They need to standardize and exercise operational procedures and IFF capabilities, and develop the kind of aggressor training needed to cope effectively with mass raids. In the long run, such cooperation will also be critical to linking the Patriot and follow-on ATBM systems that will be needed to deal with the risk of proliferation.

12

Saudi Paramilitary and Internal Security Forces

Saudi Arabia has several paramilitary forces in addition to its National Guard. This reflects a system of layered forces designed to protect the regime. The regular army provides external security, but is kept away from urban areas. The National Guard provides internal security using loyal tribes and groups under a different chain of command. There is a separate Frontier Force, and the Ministry of Interior—under the direction of Prince Naif Bin Abdul Aziz—and other groups provide internal security at the political and intelligence levels. The Frontier Force has done much of the fighting with Yemen in recent years, and has taken some significant casualties.

The 10,500 man Frontier Force covers Saudi Arabia's land and sea borders. It performs a host of patrol and surveillance missions, and can act as a light defensive screen. It is equipped with four wheel drive vehicles and automatic weapons. About 4,500 men in the Frontier Force are assigned to a Coast Guard. The Coast Guard is equipped with two Salwa-class SA26 patrol boats, four Al Jouf-class inshore medium patrol craft, 15 Scorpion-type coastal patrol boats, 12 Rapier-type coastal patrol boats, 50 Huntress-type inshore patrol boats, 16–24 BH-7 and SRN-6 Hovercraft, the Royal Yacht and numerous small boats. It is unclear how many of these craft and boats are fully operational.[290]

Saudi Arabia is considering building a border surveillance system that would use patrol aircraft, remotely piloted vehicles, and early warning systems to detect intruders and border crossings. There would be a 12 kilometer-deep security zone around all 6,500 kilometers of the land and sea borders, with a mix of acoustic, seismic, radar, magnetic, and infrared sensors to detect movements of men and vehicles in the border area. It would be supported by small manned patrol aircraft, and unmanned remotely piloted vehicles, wherever some threat from an intruder might exist. Thomson CSF completed a $5 million feasibility study for this system in early 1990, and two consortiums—one led by E Systems and the other by Thomson CSF—submitted bids to Saudi Arabia in May, 1991. The estimated cost of the system is around $3 billion and would take several years to complete.[291]

The Ministry of Interior maintains a security service called the General Directorate of Investigation or "Mubahith," and a Special Security Force with 500 men and UR-416 APCs. Little is known about this force, which seems to be designed to deal with terrorism and hijacking. Other Saudi special forces include its regular Army airborne brigade, its Royal Guard Brigade, and its Marine Regiment.

There is a large special investigations force, something like the British CID, but with political as well as criminal justice functions. There is also a General Intelligence Directorate, with some security and anti-terrorism functions, which is led by Prince Turki al-Faisal. Saudi Arabia has a large Gendarmerie or national police force with more than 15,000 men. The "Mutawwa'in" are a volunteer religious police under the semi-autonomous Organization to Prevent Vice and Promote Virtue, which perform some security functions against religious extremists.[292]

It is impossible for an outsider to appraise the effectiveness of these forces, or even identify their precise functions. Saudi Arabia is a tightly closed society, but it tolerates a great deal of peaceful discussion and dissent. Reports of mass arrests, large numbers of political prisoners, torture, and other human rights abuses have not been confirmed by the US State Department. [293]

At the same time, Saudi Arabia shows no tolerance for open opposition to the government, major deviations from Wahhabi orthodoxy, or organized violence. Saudi security forces do conduct arbitrary arrests, detain prisoners for more than 24 hours without charge, conduct their own investigations, and fail to notify the public prosecutor. Security suspects can be held incommunicado for weeks or even months. The security forces have cracked down firmly on internal Islamic extremist movements, like the CDLR, and its spokesman Mohammed Al Mas'ri. They have arrested leading clerical critics like Salman Al-Awdah and Safar Al-Hawali, and 157 protesters who demonstrated against these arrests—although 130 were released soon after. The security force shows no tolerance for any hostile political activity by foreign labor. The military justice system also does not tolerate political or Islamic extremist activity by Saudi military personnel, who are tried by court-martials.[294]

Saudi Arabia has also been slow to control the flow of money from Saudi private citizens to various Islamic extremist groups—although it began to take action against conspicuous cases, like that of Osama Bin Laden, in 1994. Saudi Arabia has often chosen to ignore Islamic extremist activity when it is not directed towards the Kingdom. Saudi Arabia has, for example, maintained a dialogue with Libya, and has permitted

Libyan aircraft to fly pilgrims to the Haj, despite UN sanctions. Saudi Arabia conspicuously failed to cooperate with the US in arresting Imad Mughniyah on April 7, 1995. Mughniyah was a suspect in the killing of 241 Marines in a barracks in Lebanon in 1983 and the highjacking of an airliner in 1985 that resulted in the death of a US Navy diver. It did so in part because the US attempted to have FBI agents arrest Mughniyah on Saudi soil with minimal notice, despite the fact that the US and Saudi Arabia have no extradition treaty. This incident illustrates that Saudi Arabia is still trying to accommodate hard-line Islamic movements.[295]

13

Saudi Missile Capabilities

Saudi Arabia has supported arms control limits on biological, chemical, and nuclear weapons, and there have been no indications that it has sought weapons of mass destruction or funded such efforts outside Saudi Arabia. Saudi Arabia has, however, purchased Chinese CSS-2 (DF-3) long-range surface-to-surface missiles, which are deployed as part of the Air Defense Force. The Saudis have also bought a package of 50 to 56 missiles, 10–15 mobile launchers, and support from the PRC at a cost of about $3 billion to 3.5 billion.[296]

The CSS-2 missiles sold to Saudi Arabia have a special large conventional warhead. They are mobile, and one-third are normally kept armed and near-launch-ready on transporters, one-third are kept half fueled, and one-third are normally empty and being serviced. They are currently deployed in two battalions. One is located at the As-Sulayyil Oasis, roughly 475 kilometers south to southwest of Riyadh. As-Sulayyil will also be the site of one of Saudi Arabia's new air bases for its Tornado fighter-bombers. A second battalion is located at Al-Juaifer near the Al-Kharj air base south of Riyadh. A further training facility, that may have a launch capability, seems to exist in southwestern Saudi Arabia at al-Liddam.

Commercial satellite photos of the site at As-Sulayyil show a headquarters and transportation complex with 60 buildings or tents; a transportation center; a command and control complex with roughly 40 buildings and tents; a secure area; a construction area; a bunker which may be a fixed launcher site; other launch areas with bunkers for missile storage; an additional launch area, and three 150 meter-long white buildings that may be missile assembly facilities.[297]

The Saudis cannot maintain or fire the missiles without Chinese technical support, and Chinese technicians are operating the missiles under Saudi supervision. Ballast Nedam, a subsidiary of British Aerospace, has recently extended the runway at the As-Sulayyil air base to 3,000 meters. There are some signs that Saudi Arabia may be deploying surface-to-air missiles to defend the facility.[298]

None of the Saudi missiles are now armed with weapons of mass destruction. Saudi Arabia is a signatory of the Non-Proliferation Treaty, and Saudi Arabia and the PRC have provided US officials with assurances that the missiles will remain conventional. The Saudi government has issued a written statement that, "nuclear and chemical warheads would not be obtained or used with the missiles." US experts believe that Saudi Arabia has kept its word, although the Saudis have refused a US request to inspect the missile sites in Saudi Arabia.[299]

Saudi Arabia bought the CSS-2 for a number of reasons. Its relations with the US over arms sales had reached a low point when the purchase was made, and Saudi Arabia felt the purchase would be a major demonstration of its independence. Equally, Saudi Arabia felt threatened by the fact that Iran, Iraq, and Yemen had long-range surface-to-surface missiles and it did not. Saudi Arabia was particularly interested in acquiring systems that could hit Tehran, while being deployed outside the range of Iranian surface-to-surface missiles.

There are good reasons to question the military value of such missiles, however, as long as they are only equipped with conventional warheads.[300] The CSS-2s deployed in the PRC are all nuclear-armed missiles. Each can carry one to three megaton warheads. They have a maximum range of about 2,200 miles (3,500 kilometers), an inertial guidance system, and a single-stage, refrigerated liquid fuel rocket motor. The version of the CSS-2 that the PRC has sold to Saudi Arabia is very different. It is heavily modified and has a special large conventional warhead, which weighs up to 3,500 to 4,000 pounds. This added warhead weight cuts the maximum range of the missile to anywhere from 1,550 nautical miles (2,400 kilometers) to 1,950 nautical miles (3,100 kilometers).

A conventional warhead of this size is more effective than the warhead on a Scud, but is scarcely a weapon of mass destruction, or even an effective conventional weapon. Assuming an optimal ratio of HE to total weight, the warhead of the CSS-2 could destroy buildings out to a radius of 200–250 feet, seriously damage buildings out to a radius of 300–350 feet, and kill or injure people with projectiles to distances of up to 1,000 feet.[301] This is the damage equivalent of three to four 2,000 pound bombs, or about the same destructive power as a single sortie by a modern strike fighter.

The CSS-2 has other limitations. It is an obsolete missile that was first designed in 1971. While an improved version has been deployed, most experts still estimate that the missile has a CEP of nearly two to four kilometers, and lacks the accuracy to hit anything other than large area targets like cities or industrial facilities. Even with the improved warhead, each missile would still only have the effective lethality of a single 2,000 pound bomb. It requires large amounts of technical support and ground equipment, and takes hours to make ready for firing.[302]

The Saudi purchase of the CSS-2 thus raises serious issues on several grounds:

- A very costly weapons system is being procured in very small numbers with relatively low lethality.
- As now configured, the missile system may do more to provoke attack or escalation than to deter attack or provide retaliatory capability. This point became clear to the Saudis during the Gulf War. King Fahd rejected advice to retaliate against Iraqi strikes because he felt that strikes that simply killed civilians would have a provocative, rather than a deterrent effect;
- On the other hand, Saudi acquisition of chemical or nuclear warheads would radically improve the value of the system as a deterrent or retaliatory weapon.

At best, the CSS-2 acts as a low-level deterrent and a symbol of Saudi Arabia's willingness to retaliate against Iraqi and Iranian strikes. At worst, the missiles are a potential excuse for Iranian or Iraqi missile strikes, and their use could trigger a process of retaliation against which Saudi Arabia would have little real defense capability. Israel, which initially showed concern about the system, no longer seems to see it as any kind of direct threat. Israel has the capability to launch air strikes against the Saudi missile sites, but is unlikely to consider preemptive strikes unless radical changes take place in Saudi Arabia's political posture or regime.

Finally, the CSS-2 presents a potential problem for arms control. Long-term Saudi motives will remain uncertain to its neighbors despite Saudi pledges, foreign intelligence reports, and any inspection agreements. Such concerns have already led to fears that Saudi investments in imaging satellites might be used for intelligence and targeting purposes.[303]

The CSS-2 gives other countries an added incentive and excuse to join the missile arms race, acquire weapons of mass destruction, or preempt in a conflict. The Saudi purchase of the CSS-2 is an understandable reaction to such problems as Israeli nuclear capabilities, the search for prestige, the Iran-Iraq missile war, and a desire to assert Saudi independence from the US, but it may ultimately do Saudi Arabia more harm than good.[304]

14

Saudi Arabia, the Gulf, and the West

It is tempting to see Saudi security largely in terms of Saudi military development and external threats. As is the case with all of the Southern Gulf states, however, such a focus is too narrow to deal with the problems Saudi Arabia faces and the real issues in Gulf security. Saudi Arabia's highest single priority is not dealing with external threats, but dealing with the problems of development and internal stability.

Reform and the Saudi Government

Saudi Arabia is only as strong as the loyalty of its people, and this loyalty is ultimately dependent on Saudi Arabia's ability to fund its "social contract." Although Saudi Arabia must maintain many of the social services it provides for its citizens, it must also move towards a pattern of development that sharply reduces its dependence on foreign labor and which offers its rapidly growing population new jobs and real career opportunities. While Saudi Arabia must remain sensitive to its Islamic character and ensure that Islamic extremism cannot challenge the legitimacy of the Saudi Government, it must also moves towards a broader participation by its people in the government. Saudi Arabia must adopt fiscal reforms and replace an unaffordable welfare state with a new mix of social services and a much larger and more competitive private sector.

Saudi Arabia must evolve if it is to preserve its internal stability. It must continue to expand steadily the role of the Majlis, and find ways of allowing peaceful debate of social and economic issues and secularism versus Islam. It must allow popular debate and increasing popular control of its national resources. It must come to grips with the issue of defining a rule of law that applies to all its citizens, to the royal family as well as ordinary citizens. It must provide for a uniform commercial code and fully competitive privatization, while resolving the inevitable tensions and conflicts between religious and secular law.

As has been discussed earlier, this requires the following reforms:

- The leadership of the royal family needs to set clear limits to the future benefits members of the royal family receive from the state and to phase out special privileges and commissions. It needs to transfer all revenues from oil and gas to the state budget, and to ensure that princes obey the rule of law and are not seen as "corrupt" or abusing the powers of the state. The royal family already has the wealth to do this, and it does not take much vision to see that the Saudi monarchy cannot give 15,000 princes the same rights and privileges it once gave several thousand.
- The Majlis as Shura needs to be steadily expanded in power, and in regional and sectarian representation, to provide an evolution towards a more representative form of government. The Majlis has made a good beginning, but it needs younger members, members that are moderate critics of the royal family, and some Shi'ites that are permitted to speak for this ethnic group. It needs to play a more direct role in reviewing the Saudi budget, and its debates need to be more open and reported in the media. It may be some years before Saudi Arabia is ready for an elected Majlis or National Assembly, but the Saudi government needs to be more open and some body other than the royal family needs to be seen as playing a major role in decision-making. The present closed, over-centralized process of government breeds extremist opposition.
- The Saudi royal family and government needs to face the fact that Saudi oil wealth is limited and that Saudi Arabia faces a potential demographic crisis. Strong leadership is needed to persuade the Wahhabi ulema that voluntary population control is needed and Saudi families that they should limit their number of children. There needs to be a firm understanding that even the best economic development plan cannot maintain the present standard of real per capita wealth in Saudi Arabia without a sharper decline in the birth rate and that population growth is a major factor affecting political stability.
- The Saudi royal family and government, as well as all educated Saudis, need to start asking existential questions about the future of Saudi society and the role of young Saudis in that society. Even today, most educated Saudi women face a dead end at the end of their education and most Saudi young men graduate into purposeless jobs that offer little real future or productive value to the economy. The impact of Saudi demographics on Saudi society and the Saudi job market is disguised by the fact that half of the population is still under 18 and living with an extended family. With the next half decade, however, something like 20% of the present native popula-

tion will leave home and will have no where to go. Only radical efforts to stimulate the private sector and remove foreign labor can begin to deal with this problem.

- At the same time, these same demographic pressures illustrate why the government cannot succeed in dealing with Islamic extremism by a combination of accommodating the most fundamental and regressive Wahhabi practices while forcibly repressing Islamic extremists that actively criticize the government. These policies are dragging Saudi Arabia back into a past that cannot be viable in the future and which makes the problems young Saudis face in finding rewarding careers and a valid place in society even more difficult. The Saudi royal family and government need to face the problem of social alienation and religion much more directly, and push for slow but steady reform. They need to face the fact that the present cost of such efforts at change is likely to be much lower than waiting and relying on the present policy.
- It is unrealistic and impractical for Saudi Arabia to attempt to adopt Western standards of human rights, and the West needs to be careful not to be trapped into supporting the efforts of Islamic extremists who claim to advocate human rights and democracy as a way of attacking the Saudi regime. At the same time, Saudi Arabia does need to give Saudi Shi'ites a special religious status and proper economic rights, emphasize the protections of the individual already granted under Saudi law, and sharply rein in the growing abuses of the religious police. The government must reestablish public faith in the Saudi legal process and the rule of law.

The Saudi "Social Contract"

Saudi Arabia must redefine its "social contract." It must begin to tax directly at least its wealthier citizens, eliminate most subsidies and convert to market prices, diversify its economy, make a full commitment to privatization and adopt much more stringent restrictions on foreign labor in order to put far more native citizens to work. Saudi Arabia must ensure that oil wealth is shared throughout its society. At the same time, it must move beyond a petroleum and service-based economy, and a subsidized welfare state. This is not simply a matter of dealing with declining oil revenues per capita. It is a matter of creating a work ethic and economy that employs young Saudis, giving them a real career and share in the future of the nation, and steadily reducing Saudi Arabia's dependence on foreign labor.

As has been discussed earlier in this analysis, Saudi Arabia must take strong measures in the following key areas:

- Force radical reductions in the number of foreign workers, with priority for reductions in servants and in trades that allow the most rapid conversion to native labor. Eliminate economic disincentives for employers hiring native labor, and creating disincentives for hiring foreign labor. Saudi Arabia's young and well-educated population needs to replace its foreign workers as quickly as possible, and it will only develop a work ethic and suitable skills once it is thrust into the labor market.
- Limit population growth.
- Reduce those aspects of state subsidies and welfare that distort the economy and discourage the native population from seeking jobs. It must steadily reduce dependence on welfare, and replace subsidies with jobs. Water, electricity, motor gasoline, basic foods, and many services need to be priced at market levels and subsidies to citizens need to be replaced with jobs and economic opportunities.
- Restructure the educational system to focus on job training and competitiveness. Create strong, new incentives for faculty and students to focus on job-related education, sharply down-size other forms of educational funding and activity, and eliminate high-overhead educational activities without economic benefits.
- Reform the structure of the national budget to reduce the amount of money going directly to royal accounts, and ensure that most of the nation's revenues and foreign reserves are integrated into the national budget and into the planning process. Clearly separate royal and national income and investment holdings.
- Place limits on the transfer of state funds to princes and members of the royal family outside the actual ruling family, and transfers of unearned income to members of other leading families.
- Ensure that all income from enterprises with state financing is reflected in the national budget and is integrated into the national economic development and planning program.
- Freeze and then reduce the number of civil servants, and restructure and down-size the civil service to focus on productive areas of activity with a much smaller pool of manpower. Cut back sharply on state employees by the year 2000.
- Establish market criteria for all major state and state-supported investments, requiring detailed and independent risk assessment and projections of comparative return on investment, with a substantial penalty for state versus privately funded projects and ventures. Down-size the scale of programs to reduce investment and cash flow costs and the risk of cost-escalation.
- Carry out much more rapid and extensive privatization to increase the efficiency of Saudi Arabian investments in downstream and

upstream operations, create real jobs and career opportunities for native Saudi Arabians, and to open investment opportunities to a much wider range of investors. Privatization must be managed in ways that ensure all Saudi Arabians have an opportunity to share in the privatization process and not conducted in a manner that benefits only a small, elite group of investors and discourages popular confidence and willingness to invest in Saudi Arabia.

- Stop subsidizing Saudi Arabian firms and businesses in ways which prevent economic growth and development, and which deprive the government of revenue. Present policies strongly favor Saudi Arabian citizens and Saudi Arabian-owned companies. Income taxes are only levied on foreign corporations and foreign interests in Saudi Arabian corporations, at rates that may range as high as 55 percent of net income. Individuals are not subject to income taxes, eliminating a key source of revenue, as well as a means of ensuring the more equitable distribution of income. Saudi Arabia needs to tax its citizens and companies and ensure that wealthier Saudi Arabian's make a proper contribution to social services and defense.

- Allow foreign investment on more competitive terms. Saudi Arabia currently allows only limited foreign investment in certain sectors of the economy, in minority partnerships, and on terms compatible with continued Saudi Arabian control of all basic economic activities. Some sectors of the economy—including oil, banking, insurance and real estate—have been virtually closed to foreign investment. Foreigners (with the exception of nationals from some GCC states) are not permitted to trade in Saudi Arabia, except through the medium of Saudi firms. Protection should not extend to the point where it eliminates efficiency and competitiveness, and restricts economic expansion. Saudi Arabia needs to act decisively on proposals such as allowing foreign equity participation in the banking sector and in the upstream oil sector.

- Create new incentives to invest in local industries and business and disincentives for the expatriation of capital.

- Avoid offset requirements that simply create disguised unemployment or non-competitive ventures that act as a further state-sponsored distortion of the economy.

- Tax earnings and sales with progressive taxes that reduce or eliminate budget deficits, encourage local investment, and create strong disincentives for the expatriation of capital, including all foreign holdings of capital and property by members of elite and ruling families.

- Shift goods to market prices. Remove distortions in the economy and underpricing of water, oil, and gas.

• Establish a firm rule of law for all property, contract, permitting, and business activity and reduce state bureaucratic and permitting barriers to private investment.

• Place national security spending on the same basis as other state spending. Integrate it fully into the national budget, including investment and equipment purchases. Replace the present emphasis on judging purchases on the basis of initial procurement costs and technical features with a full assessment of life cycle cost— including training, maintenance, and facilities—and with specific procedures for evaluating the value of standardization and interoperability with existing national equipment and facilities, those of other Gulf states, and those of the US and other power projection forces.

• Saudi Arabia must redefine its support of Islam to preserve its traditional religious character without tolerating either domestic Islamic extremists or the funding of extremist movements overseas. Improved job opportunities and economic management can help deal with many social issues, and a peaceful debate over the evolution of Islam in Saudi Arabia is critical to peaceful social change. The government, however, cannot confuse a right to peaceful debate with a tolerance of violence or violent rhetoric, and it must be more careful to distinguish between the support of legitimate peaceful Islamic causes outside Saudi Arabia from the support of terrorism and violence.

Saudi Arabia must come firmly to grips with the need to reform the social impact of its economy. The key economic challenge Saudi Arabia faces is not its current balance of payments or budget deficit, but to create a form of capitalism that suits Saudi social custom, which is run and staffed by Saudis, and which steadily expands the productive sector beyond oil and gas exports and large-scale downstream operations.

There seems to be little doubt that some leading members of the Saudi royal family and many Saudi technocrats understand these priorities. At the same time, it is not always clear they appreciate their urgency or the scale of the problems involved. As is the case in other Southern Gulf states, it is often easier to talk about budget reform, reducing foreign labor, privatization, and social change than it is to implement such change.

At the same time, the West needs to show more sensitivity to the critical importance of Saudi internal stability. On the one hand, some in the West make impossible demands, for instance, that Saudi Arabia adopt Western legal, political, and social customs at a time when the Saudi government must pay close attention to the challenge of Islamic extremism and demonstrate its continuing commitment to Islamic fundamentalism. On the other hand, Western governments are far too prone to pressure Saudi Arabia into making massive new purchases of arms, and seeking unrealistic reimbursements for defending Western strategic interests. They also ask the Saudi government for aid in areas which do not correspond to vital Saudi strategic interests. It is the West, much more than the Saudi government, that must learn to live with the fact that Saudi economic development and internal stability are the foundation upon which every other aspect of Saudi Arabia's strategic position must be built.

Saudi Military Development

Saudi Arabia has accomplished a great deal in the face of many obstacles. It has succeeded in using its wealth to create military forces that were able to fight effectively against first-line Iraqi forces in the Gulf War, and which are now strong enough to deal with many low-intensity contingencies, and limit the amount of US reinforcements needed in mid-intensity contingencies. Saudi Arabia is by far the strongest and most modern military force in the Southern Gulf, and the only force large enough to provide the support, training, C^4I/BM, and other specialized capabilities necessary to sustain modern land-air combat and provide the infrastructure for effective regional cooperation.

At the same time, Saudi Arabia remains vulnerable to Iran and Iraq. It can only achieve security against Iran and Iraq through cooperative defense both with its Southern Gulf neighbors and with the West. It will not have the manpower its needs to fully man even modest expansion plans for another decade. It will take five to ten years before Saudi Arabia can fully absorb its current major equipment orders and deploy this equipment in combat effective forces.

Even then, it will only be able to secure itself against an all-out Iraqi attack with active American support. The Gulf War has left Iraq a revanchist state, with 60% of its army intact and the capability to overrun Kuwait's military forces in a matter of days regardless of Kuwait's present force improvement plans.

Saudi Arabia is within five to seven minutes flying time from Iran, from the earliest point of detection by an AWACS to over-flying key Saudi targets on the Gulf coast. Missile attacks would offer even less warning and present more problems for defense. While Iran cannot bring the bulk of its land power to bear without major increases in amphibious lift, it can bring naval and air pressure to bear on tanker and air traffic through the Gulf, and threaten Saudi Arabia in other ways.

Saudi Cooperation with Other Southern Gulf States

Saudi Arabia faces equally serious challenges because of the lack of any clear plan for military cooperation between the Kingdom, other moderate Gulf states, and its Gulf neighbors. Some widely discussed options simply are not practical. The failure of the Damascus Declaration to produce any Egyptian nor Syrian forces in the Gulf involves more than debates over politics and money. Neither Egypt or Syria are organized to project effective combat forces. They lack most of the technological advantages of US forces, and they are not equipped and trained to provide the Saudi Air Force and Saudi Army with the mix of interoperable capabilities they need. Although they are Arab and Muslim, they also bring all the political liabilities to bear of being states with separate interests and with strategic objectives which often differ from those of Saudi Arabia.

Similarly, the Gulf Cooperation Council has made progress in many political areas, but little progress in military areas. Its failure to agree on effective plans for cooperation, interoperability, and integration have left the military role of the GCC a largely symbolic one. Rhetoric is not a substitute for reality, and the GCC will only play a major role in regional security once it can develop integrated air defenses, integrated mine warfare and maritime surveillance capabilities, an ability to deal with Iranian surface and ASW forces, rapid reaction forces that can actually fight, and the ability to defend Kuwait and Eastern Saudi Arabia against land attack.

In spite of massive spending since the Gulf War, the southern Gulf has made far too little progress in far too many areas which are critical priorities for cooperative defense. Saudi Arabia needs to look beyond its own military modernization program and take tangible steps to expand Gulf cooperation. Even if this is not possible on a GCC-wide basis, Saudi Arabia must work with Bahrain and Kuwait in:

- Creating an effective planning system for collective defense, and truly standardized and/or interoperable forces.
- Integrating its C^{4}I and sensor nets for air and naval combat, including BVR and night warfare.
- Focusing on deploying its forces to support the joint land defense of the Kuwaiti/Northwestern Saudi borders and reinforcing other Gulf states like Oman in the event of any Iranian amphibious or airborne action.
- Creating joint air defense and air attack capabilities.
- Creating joint air and naval strike forces.
- Establishing effective cross reinforcement and tactical mobility capabilities.

- Preparing fully for outside or over-the-horizon reinforcement by the US and other Western powers.
- Setting up joint training, support, and infrastructure facilities.
- Creating common advanced training systems that develop a brigade and wing-level capability for combined arms and joint warfare, and which can support realistic field training exercises of the kind practiced by US and Israeli forces.
- Improving its capability to provide urban and urban area security and to fight unconventional warfare and low-intensity combat.

Saudi Arabia does not need massive new arms purchases in the near to mid-term, but it does need to consolidate its modernization programs to reduce its number of different suppliers and major weapons types and focus on procuring interoperable and/or standardized equipment to provide the capability to perform the following missions:

- Heavy armor, artillery, attack helicopters, and mobile air defense equipment for defense of the upper Gulf.
- Interoperability and standardization with US power projection forces.
- Interoperable offensive air capability with stand-off, all-weather precision weapons and anti-armor/anti-ship capability.
- Interoperable air defense equipment, including heavy surface-to-air missiles, BVR/AWX fighters, AEW & surveillance capability, ARM & ECM capability. (Growth to ATBM and cruise missile defense capability)
- Maritime surveillance systems, and equipment for defense against maritime surveillance, and unconventional warfare.
- Mine detection and clearing systems.
- Improved urban, area, and border security equipment for unconventional warfare and low-intensity conflict.
- Advanced training aids.
- Support and sustainment equipment.

In the process, Saudi Arabia needs to recognize that it cannot afford the risk of military procurement efforts that emphasize politics and high technology "glitter" over military effectiveness and sustainability. It also needs to recognize that its effectiveness is heavily dependent on interoperability with US and Kuwaiti forces. The issue for Saudi Arabian military procurements is not one of buying the best possible equipment on paper, but rather reaching the maximum possible standardization with the power projection capabilities of US land and air forces, and procuring the training, munitions, and support facilities to deal with the threat from Iraq and Iraq. Saudi Arabia must take every possible step to eliminate the waste of funds on:

- Unique equipment types and one-of-a-kind modifications.
- "Glitter factor" weapons; "developmental" equipment and technology.
- Arms buys made from Europe for political purposes where there is no credible prospect that the seller country can project major land and air forces.
- Non-interoperable weapons and systems.
- Submarines and ASW systems.
- Major surface warfare ships.
- Major equipment for divided or "dual" forces.
- New types of equipment which increase the maintenance, sustainability, and training problem, or layer new types over old.
- New types of equipment which strain the financial and manpower resources of Saudi Arabia, and overload military units that are already experiencing absorption and conversion problems in using the equipment they possess or have on order.

Saudi Arabia is the only GCC state that can serve as the central focus of such activity. At least for the next decade, there is no other Southern Gulf state that will be able to use heavy armored forces, modern air control and warning systems, maritime forces and surveillance systems, mine sweeping forces, integrated air defense and anti-tactical ballistic missile defenses, heliborne assault and other rapid reaction forces, and C^4I/BM systems in ways that can provide an effective deterrent and defense against large scale Iranian and Iraqi attacks.

Saudi Arabia and Western Power Projection

Saudi Arabia has long played a critical role in supporting Western power projection, when this has been necessary to meet threats from nations like Iran and Iraq. Although Saudi Arabia does not have a formal status of forces agreement with the US, it has long maintained close military ties. The US first leased port and air base facilities in Dhahran, Saudi Arabia in 1943. It renewed these leases on April 22, 1957 and maintained them until April 2, 1962—when they were canceled both for political reasons and because the US Strategic Air Command ceased to forward deploy the B-47. Saudi Arabia renewed its US Military Training Mission Agreement with the US in June, 1992.[305]

During the late 1970s and 1980s, Saudi Arabia responded to the growing threat posed by a radical Iran by increasing the size of its air bases and port facilities which would aid in US power projection to Saudi Arabia. The US also created massive stockpiles of munitions and equipment, and support facilities, that could be used by US forces deploying to Saudi

Arabia. Saudi Arabia purchased $16 billion worth of US military construction services during this period, and supervised military construction worth billions of dollars more.[306]

The US and Saudi Arabia cooperated closely in setting up combined air and naval defenses against Iran, beginning in 1983, when Iraq came under serious military pressure from Iran. The two countries conducted joint exercises, and cooperated in establishing the "Fahd Line," which created an Air Defense Identification Zone and forward air defense system off the Saudi coast. The US and Saudi Arabia have jointly operated E-3A AWACS units in Saudi Arabia ever since. The US and Saudi Arabia also cooperated closely during the tanker war of 1987–1988.

Saudi Arabia took the lead in organizing the Arab world's effort to force Iraq to leave Kuwait in 1990, and worked closely with the US in first developing effective defenses against further Iraqi aggression and then liberating Kuwait. Saudi Arabia supported the US in deploying massive land and air forces to Saudi Arabia during the Gulf War, and jointly commanded UN Coalition forces with the US during Desert Storm. Saudi Arabia also provided the US with $12.809 billion in direct aid during the Gulf War, and $4.045 billion in goods and services, for a total of $16.854 billion.[307]

Since the Gulf War, Saudi Arabia has recognized that the US is the only power that can provide Saudi Arabia with the kind of land and air reinforcements that can fight "24-hour-a-day" intensive combat, launch highly maneuverable armored counter-offensives, strike deep and repeatedly with long-range precision air attacks, check and deter missile and air attacks with weapons of mass destruction, and provide "force multipliers" like satellite intelligence and targeting, advanced electronic warfare capabilities, and sophisticated battle management and C^4I systems.

As a result, Saudi Arabia has expanded its security arrangements with the US. The US and Saudi Arabia have expanded the USMTM agreement to increase US access to Saudi air and seaports, including Jubail, and have improved the capabilities of the joint AWACS force. The US deploys a wing of aircraft in southern Saudi Arabia, including F-117 and U-2 aircraft, and the Saudi Air Force has supported the enforcement of the "no fly" zone in Southern Iraq.[308]

Saudi Arabia allows the USAF to regularly rotate combat units in and out of Saudi airbases, and the US Military Mission now has 69 military, four civilian, and nine local personnel. Saudi Arabia has increased stocks of selected spares and electronics to support US forces in deploying— including enough parts and supplies to support 15 USAF tactical fighter equivalents—and has increased the number of joint exercises with US forces.[309] It is standardizing key aspects of its C^4I system to make them interoperable with US C^4I systems, including theater missile defense arrangements for Saudi Arabia's Patriot missiles. Saudi Arabia has ordered $1.6 billion worth of US military construction services since the Gulf War—$610.8 million of which has been delivered.[310]

Saudi Arabia has long been one of the largest single customers for US military exports—and Saudi purchases have both increased interoperability and sustainability with US forces, and have reduced the unit cost of equipment purchased by US forces. Between FY1950 and FY1990, Saudi Arabia purchased $35,876.0 million worth of US Foreign Military Sales (FMS), and has taken delivery on $23,799.4 million worth.[311] Since the Gulf War, it has purchased $24,835.5 million worth of US Foreign Military Sales (FMS), and taken delivery on $8,818 million worth.[312] These purchases include US M-1 tanks, M-2/M-3 armored vehicles, and US artillery and related support systems. Such purchases increase Saudi interoperability with US forces and Saudi capability to support the rapid deployment of heavy US ground forces to Saudi Arabia.

Problems in Saudi Security
Cooperation with the West

Saudi cooperation with the West, however, is not always easy or without its risks. Britain and France are now the only European states with significant power projection capabilities into the Gulf, and both are steadily cutting their potential pool of power projection forces. Britain and France lack strategic lift, and the ability to project large sustainable forces. It would take Britain at least two months to project a single heavy armored division that could actually be sustained in intense combat, and it is unclear that France could deploy more than a brigade.

There are also uncertainties in US and Saudi cooperation. Saudi Arabia reached a tentative agreement for common training with US forces in September, 1991, but Saudi Arabia rejected US proposals to preposition two division sets of ground combat equipment in Saudi Arabia— although the US could have left such equipment there when its forces completed their withdrawal from the Gulf at the end of 1991.[313]

This rejection was partly a result of Saudi concern with the opposition from Islamic fundamentalists and partly a result of an unrealistic Saudi sensitivity to the nuances of sovereignty. At the same time, the US was slow to understand the Saudi emphasis on informal cooperation and low-profile activities. Saudi internal and external stability has long depended on keeping strategic cooperation as quiet as possible, while the US has been insistent on formal and public arrangements.

The US insistence on formal arrangements may have hurt both the US and Saudi Arabia after the Gulf War. According to some reports, Saudi Arabia offered to allow US Army prepositioning of major armor, artillery, and other equipment in Saudi warehouses at Saudi cost and under joint US-Saudi Guard. The US insisted on a formal status of forces agreement, flying the US flag, total US control of the facility, and large numbers of US personnel. It also presented the US plan complete with long computer lists of additional equipment. Saudi officials have privately indicated that Saudi Arabia then rejected the US plan because of the way in which it was presented, and because the US insistence on an overt basing facility openly violated the royal family's pledge to the Islamic clergy not to grant bases or formally base non-Muslim forces in the Kingdom. The US plan would almost certainly have resulted in a crisis with hard-line Islamic fundamentalists.

These problems have not blocked many other forms of cooperation between Saudi and US forces. Saudi Arabia has agreed to expand the 15-year old Military Training Mission Treaty it signed in 1977. It reached an agreement for joint US and Saudi land force training in 1991, and exercises have been held regularly since that time. Saudi Arabia also cooperated closely with the US when the US had to rush forces to Kuwait in October, 1994.[314] After the Saudi rejection of the original US plan for prepositioning of equipment, the US proposed arrangements under the MTM treaty calling for the storage of up to 200 M-1A2s and 200 M-2s in the Kingdom, plus spare parts and enough Air Force equipment to support five to six fighter wings. This would have been only one-third of the amount of pre-positioned equipment that the US originally proposed.[315] Nevertheless, Saudi Arabia again rejected even this level of land force prepositioning in November, 1994, and the Saudi refusal to allow the US to preposition full unit equipment sets on Saudi soil has placed serious limits on the ability of the US to provide heavy ground forces as a counterbalance to Iran and Iraq.[316]

In August, 1992—when the US, UK, and France established a "no fly zone" over Iraq—Saudi Arabia not only allowed US aircraft to operate, but also provided refueling tankers, combat air defense patrols, and support from Saudi AWACS. This support was critical to the US, Britain, and France since it allowed them to establish the "no fly zone" over Iraq with less than 150 aircraft. They would have had to provide roughly 100 more aircraft without Saudi support. Since that time, Saudi Arabia has permitted the US to station combat aircraft in-country continuously, including U-2 intelligence aircraft and F-117 strike fighters. Such cooperation is vital to maintaining the interoperability of the Saudi and US air forces, as is continued cooperation in training, exercises, acquiring stockpiles of munitions and supplies, designing repair and maintenance facilities, improving C^4I/BM systems, and a host of other factors.[317]

The US has also reacted to these problems in Saudi-US cooperation by reshaping its strategy and force plans to rely more on informal cooperation, and different forms of prepositioning. These plans are reflected in the results of the Bottom Up Review of US defense plans for FY1995–FY1999 that Secretary of Defense Les Aspin announced on September 1, 1993. US planners would still have liked to preposition the equipment for two heavy divisions in Saudi Arabia and Kuwait, and in locations that allowed the US to airlift in troops and deploy forward rapidly to defend the Kuwaiti-Iraqi and Saudi-Iraqi borders. The US concluded, however, that Saudi sensitivities to a large-scale US land presence—even in the form of centers with prepositioned equipment—would force the US to rely on more limited prepositioning in other countries, and on the periodic deployment of US forces in exercises and other training activity.[318]

As a result, the US has emphasized cooperation with Saudi Arabia in maintaining a limited presence of US air units, in improving Saudi C^4I/battle management capabilities, in making Saudi air and land forces interoperable with US forces, and in improving Saudi basing and infrastructure to support both Saudi and US forces in defending Kuwait and meeting other defensive needs in the Gulf.

The US is dealing with the problem of land-force prepositioning by maintaining a seven ship maritime prepositioning ship squadron at Diego Garcia. It is seeking to raise the level of prepositioned US Army equipment in or near the Gulf to a level of three heavy armored brigades by prepositioning equipment on land for one brigade in Kuwait, and an additional brigade set in Qatar. The US is also prepositioning one "swing" brigade set at sea that would normally be deployed afloat near the Gulf, but which could go to Asia or elsewhere in the world. This prepositioning could allow at least one heavy division in place to halt an Iraqi invasion within 14 to 21 days.

The Need for a Stable Saudi and Western Strategic Partnership

The West presents other strategic and military problems for Saudi Arabia. The West still sometimes fails to provide Saudi Arabia with the right arms transfers, training, and support effort. Relations with the US are still troubled by domestic political debates over the impact of such arms transfers on the security of Israel. European suppliers often profiteer, rather than ensure suitable packages of training and support.

The US, in particular, has also shown far too little sensitivity to Saudi Arabia's economic problems and internal needs. It has constantly pressed for additional funds to pay for US deployments to the Gulf, or for Saudi Arabia to furnish other forms of aid. The US has sometimes attempted to overcharge Saudi Arabia for US deployments into the region—including an absurd effort to seek reimbursement for the "depreciation" resulting from the deployment of a US carrier battle group to the Gulf, in response to Iraq's October, 1994 deployment of troops to the Iraqi border. The US has also failed to adjust its burden-sharing policies to the reality that Saudi resources are now finite and Saudi Arabia must give priority to the needs of its own people.

The West must be careful in pressing for military sales, or aid, in ways which do not meet vital Saudi security needs and which do not take into account Saudi Arabia's domestic economic situation and social needs. It must also distinguish between the hopes and desires of Western educated Gulf professionals and reality. In the case of Saudi Arabia, there are instances of corruption and the abuse of civil law within the royal family. However, the conduct of the Saudi professional and middle class—particularly the Hejazi who are often critics of the royal family—is scarcely better. The same is equally true of the clergy, in part because of the archaic methods of religious funding and taxation still used throughout much of the Islamic world. Demanding change is very different from having the practical ability to achieve real progress.

The West also needs to show caution in pressing Saudi Arabia and the other Southern Gulf states to move towards Western-style democracy, legal systems, and secular approaches to social change. The Saudi royal family, like every royal family in the Southern Gulf, can and should do more to move towards representative institutions, improve civil rights, and engender a more stable rule of law. The West needs to understand, however, that the Saudi royal family and most Gulf royal families can only make such changes as fast as their societies can accept them. In Saudi Arabia, for example, there is already a major fundamentalist reaction to the existing rate of change. Accelerating the pace of change, or any kind of elections, would lead to conservative reaction, rather than actual progress.

Saudi Arabia prefers to use private and informal methods in modernizing, in supporting the Arab-Israeli peace process, and in limiting the influence of Arab and Islamic radicals; the West and Israel prefer formal and visible arrangements. Israel has often made the mistake of treating Saudi Arabia and other moderate and conservative Arab states as enemies, and insisting on formal arrangements as signs of progress. It is important for both the West and Israel to understand that Saudi Arabia must preserve its Islamic character, avoid provoking Arabic radicals, and minimize the risk of confrontation with Iran, Iraq, and Syria. Informal success is always preferable to formal failure, but this is a lesson that the US and Israel have found very difficult to learn.

While these internal problems will not prevent Saudi Arabia from slowly improving its military capabilities, they do mean that any major progress in collective or cooperative defense efforts will be slow and rely on changes in Western attitudes as well as changes in Saudi attitudes.

Much will depend on US ability to implement the force improvement plans called for as part of the Bottom Up Review, to preposition equipment and munitions on Saudi soil, and on Saudi willingness to buy equipment that US forces could use in an emergency. Much will also depend on Saudi and Kuwaiti willingness to ensure that US land forces can deploy to the northern Gulf in time to defend either country against an invasion by Iraq. No nation likes to admit its dependence on another, but the success of Saudi military forces ultimately depends on the effectiveness of US power projection capabilities. Saudi Arabia will remain as dependent on the West for security as the West is dependent on Saudi Arabia for oil.

Sources and Methods

This volume is part of a series of volumes on each of the Gulf states which has been developed by the Center for Strategic and International Studies as part of a dynamic net assessment of the Middle East. This project has had the sponsorship of each of the Southern Gulf states as well as US sponsors of the CSIS, and each text has been widely distributed for comment to experts and officials in each Southern Gulf country, to US experts and officials, to several international agencies and institutions, and various private experts.

Sources

The author has drawn heavily on the inputs of such reviewers throughout the text. It was agreed with each reviewer, however, that no individual or agency should be attributed at any point in the text except by specific request, and that all data used be attributed to sources that are openly available to the public. The reader should be aware of this in reviewing the footnotes. Only open sources are normally referred to in the text, although the data contained in the analysis has often been extensively modified to reflect expert comment.

There are other aspects of the sources used of which the reader should be aware. It was possible to visit each Southern Gulf states at various times during the preparation of this book and to talk to local officials experts. Some provided detailed comments on the text. Interviews also took place with experts in the United States, United Kingdom, France, Switzerland and Germany. Portions of the manuscript were circulated for informal review by European officials and diplomats in some cases. Once again, no details regarding such visits or comments are referenced in the text.

Data from open sources are deliberately drawn from a wide range of sources. Virtually all of these sources are at least in partial conflict. There is no consensus over demographic data, budget data, military expenditures and arms transfers, force numbers, unit designations, or weapons types.

While the use of computer data bases allowed some cross-correlation and checking of such sources, the reporting on factors like force strengths, unit types and identities and tactics often could not be reconciled. Citing multiple sources for each case is not possible and involves many detailed judgments by the author in reconciling different reports and data.

The Internet and several on-line services were also used extensively. Since such data bases are dynamic, and change or are deleted over time, there is no clear way to footnote much of this material. Recent press sources are generally cited, but are often only part of the material consulted.

Methods

A broad effort has been made to standardize the analysis of each country, but it became clear early in the project that adopting a standard format did not suit the differences that emerged between countries. The emphasis throughout this phase of the CSIS net assessment has been on analyzing the detailed trends within individual states and this aspect of the analysis has been given priority over country-to-country consistency.

In many cases, the author adjusted the figures and data use in the analysis on a "best guess" basis, drawing on some thirty years of experience in the field. In some other cases, the original data provided by a given source were used without adjustment to ensure comparability, even though this leads to some conflicts in dates, place names, force strengths, etc. within the material presented—particularly between summary tables surveying a number of countries and the best estimates for a specific country in the text. In such cases, it seemed best to provide contradictory estimates to give the reader some idea of the range of uncertainty involved.

Extensive use is made of graphics to allow the reader to easily interpret complex statistical tables and see long-term trends. The graphic program used was deliberately standardized, and kept relatively simple, to allow the material portrayed to be as comparable as possible. Such graphics have the drawback, however, that they often disguise differences in scale and exaggerate or minimize key trends. The reader should carefully examine the scale used in the left-hand axis of each graphs.

Most of the value judgments regarding military effectiveness are made on the basis of American military experience and standards. Although the author has lived in the Middle East, and worked as a US advisor to several Middle Eastern governments, he feels that any attempt to create some Middle Eastern standard of reference is likely to be far more arbitrary than basing such judgments on his own military background.

Mapping and location names presented a major problem. The author used US Army and US Air Force detailed maps, commercial maps, and in some cases commercial satellite photos. In many cases, however, the place names and terrain descriptions used in the combat reporting by both sides, and by independent observers, presented major contradictions that could not be resolved from available maps. No standardization emerged as to the spelling of place names. Sharp differences emerged in the geographic data published by various governments, and in the conflicting methods of transliterating Arabic and Farsi place names into English

The same problem applied in reconciling the names of organizations and individuals—particularly those being transliterated from Arabic and Farsi. It again became painfully obvious that no progress is being made in reconciling the conflicting methods of transliterating such names into English. A limited effort has been made to standardize the spellings used in this text, but many different spellings are tied to the relational data bases used in preparing the analysis and the preservation of the original spelling is necessary to identify the source and tie it to the transcript of related interviews.

Notes

Chapter One

1. The military manpower, force strength, and equipment estimates in this section are made by the author using a wide range of sources, including computerized data bases, interviews, and press clipping services. Most are impossible to reference in ways of use to the reader. The force strength statistics are generally taken from interviews, and from the sources reference for each paragraph. They also draw heavily on his *The Gulf and the Search for Strategic Stability* (Boulder, Westview, 1984) *The Gulf and the West* (Boulder, Westview, 1988), and *After the Storm, The Changing Military Balance in the Middle East* (Boulder, Westview, 1993).

Extensive use has also been made of the annual editions of the International Institute for Strategic Studies *Military Balance* (IISS, London); *Military Technology, World Defense Almanac*; and the Jaffee Center for Strategic Studies, *The Military Balance in the Middle East* (JCSS, Tel Aviv). Material has also been drawn from computer print outs from NEXIS, the United States Naval Institute data base, and from the DMS/FI Market Intelligence Reports data base.

Weapons data are taken from many sources, including computerized material available in NEXIS, and various editions of *Jane's Fighting Ships* (Jane's Publishing); *Jane's Naval Weapons Systems* (Jane's Publishing); *Jane's Armor and Artillery* (Jane's Publishing); *Jane's Infantry Weapons* (Jane's Publishing); *Jane's Military Vehicles and Logistics* (Jane's Publishing); *Jane's Land-Base Air Defense* (Jane's Publishing); *Jane's All the World's Aircraft* (Jane's Publishing); *Jane's Battlefield Surveillance Systems,* (Jane's Publishing); *Jane's Radar and Electronic Warfare Systems* (Jane's Publishing), *Jane's C3I Systems* (Jane's Publishing); *Jane's Air-Launched Weapons Systems* (Jane's Publishing); *Jane's Defense Appointments & Procurement Handbook (Middle East Edition)* (Jane's Publishing); *Tanks of the World* (Bernard and Grafe); *Weyer's Warships* (Bernard and Grafe); and *Warplanes of the World* (Bernard and Grafe).

Other military background, effectiveness, strength, organizational, and history data are taken from Anthony H. Cordesman, *Weapons of Mass Destruction in the Middle East, London,* Brassey's/RUSI, 1991; Anthony H. Cordesman and Abraham Wagner, *The Lessons of Modern War, Volume II,* Boulder, Westview, 1989; the relevant country or war sections of Herbert K. Tillema, *International Conflict Since 1945,* Boulder, Westview, 1991; Department of Defense, *Conduct of the Persian Gulf War; Final Report to Congress,* Washington, Department of Defense, April, 1992; Department of Defense and Department of State, *Congressional Presentation for Security Assistance Programs, Fiscal Year 1995,* Washington, Department of State,

1992; various annual editions of John Laffin's *The World in Conflict* or *War Annual*, London, Brassey's, and John Keegan, *World Armies*, London, Macmillan, 1983.

2. CIA, *World Factbook, 1995,* "Saudi Arabia."

3. CIA, *World Factbook, 1995,* "Saudi Arabia."

4. ACDA, *World Military Expenditures and Arms Transfers, 1993–1994,* pp. 80 and 128.

Chapter Two

5. Rosemary Hollis, *Gulf Security: No Consensus,* London, RUSI, 1993; .

6. Interview with Prince Khalid bin Sultan., March, 1991.

7. Interview with senior Saudi official, November, 1993.

8. Cohen, Dr. Eliot A, Director, *Gulf War Air Power Survey, Volume V,* Washington, US Air Force/Government Printing Office, 1993, pp. 232 and 279–287. Note that these data are not consistent form table to table.

9. As of mid-1995. CIA, *World Factbook, 1995,* "Saudi Arabia" and "Yemen."

10. *Middle East Economic Digest,* June 30, 1995, p. 9; *Saudi Arabia,* May, 1995, p. 7; Washington Times, June 7, 1995, p. A-17.

11. World Bank, *World Population Projections, 1994–1995,* Washington, World Bank, 1995, pp. 512–513; World Bank, *Trends in Developing Countries,* Washington, World Bank, 1995, pp. 558–561.

12. Reuters, July 10, 1995, 0552.

13. For maps of the disputed claims, and a controversial but detailed history of the dispute, see J. B. Kelly, *Arabia, the Gulf, and the West,* New York, Basic Books, 1980, pp. 56–57, and pp. 65–76.

14. J. B. Kelly, *Arabia, the Gulf, and the West,* New York, Basic Books, 1980, pp. 187–188; Helen Chapin Metz, *Persian Gulf States,* Washington, Department of the Army, DA Pam 550–185, January, 1993, pp. 191–194.

15. *Washington Post,* October 1, 1993, p. A-19; October 2, 1992, p. A-41; *Philadelphia Inquirer,* October 3, 1992, p. D-7; *Washington Times,* October 2, 1992, p. A-9.

16. J. B. Kelly, *Arabia, the Gulf, and the West,* New York, Basic Books, 1980, pp. 56–57; Helen Chapin Metz, *Persian Gulf States,* Washington, Department of the Army, DA Pam 550–185, January, 1993, pp. 191–194.

17. *Wall Street Journal,* March 21, 1996, p. A-1; *The Estimate,* January 19, 1996, March 1, 1996.

18. *Wall Street Journal,* March 21, 1996, p. A-1; *The Estimate,* January 19, 1996, March 1, 1996.

19. *Jane's Defense Weekly,* July 29, 1995, p. 15.

20. Based on interviews during 1991–1995. For a different description of Egypt's performance during the Gulf War, see Anthony H. Cordesman, *The Gulf War, Lessons of Modern War, Volume IV,* Boulder, Westview, 1996.

Chapter Three

21. Robert Cullen, "Uneasy Lies the Head That Wears a Crown," *Nuclear Energy,* Third Quarter 1995, p. 24.

22. *The Estimate*, January 5, 1996, p. 11.

23. Cullen, p. 24.

24. *The Estimate*, January 5, 1996, p. 11.

25. *Baltimore Sun*, January 4, 1996, P. 2A.

26. *New York Times*, January 2, 1996, p. A-3.

27. *New York Times*, January 2, 1996, p. A-3; *Washington Post*, January 2, 1996, p. A-20; *Washington Times*, January 3, 1996, p. A-10; Executive News Service, February 22, 1996, 1858; For typical press report on possible problems within the royal family see the *Economist*, March 18, 1995, pp. 21–27, and James Bruce, "Fundamentalist unrest threatens stability in the Gulf," *Washington Times*, April 9, 1995, p. A-9.

28. *Washington Times*, January 3, 1996, p. A-10.

29. *New York Times*, January 2, 1996, p. A-3; *The Estimate*, January 5, 1996, p. 11; *Washington Times*, January 3, 1996, p. A-10.

30. Estimates range from 2,000 to 7,000 princes. The higher figure represents many sons with little or no influence who are descended from collateral branches of the family. The 2,000 figure is a rough estimate of the number who have any real influence. The main power is concentrated in first and second generation sons descended directly from Abdul Aziz.

31. This dismissal was partly the result of the fact that Khalid had used US Green Berets during the build-up for Desert Storm to help reorganize Saudi forces, and remove some of their bureaucratic rigidities. This caused considerable resentment, and made Khalid's promotion more difficult, although it significantly improved Saudi performance during the Gulf War. *New York Times*, October 15, 1991, p. 1; *Washington Post*, March 15, 1992, p. A-35.

32. Saudi Arabia feels the Koran is the constitution under Islamic law. The Basic Laws, however, perform much the same function as constitutional guarantees in the West.

33. *New York Times*, August 6, 1991, p. A-5, November 18, 1991, p. A-3, December 31, 1991, p. A-1, March 30, 1992, p. A-6; *Washington Post*, December 31, 1991, p. A-10, March 2, 1992, p. A-1, March 6, 1992, p. A-16, September 18, 1992, p. A-31; *Boston Globe*, September 18, 1992, p. 6; *Chicago Tribune*, September 18, 1992, p. I-4; *Philadelphia Inquirer*, September 18, 1992, p. B-22; *Newsweek*, March 16, 1992, p. 45.

34. *Washington Post*, August 22, 1993, p. A-24; *Washington Times*, August 22, 1993, p. A-9; US State Department, *Country Report on Human Rights Practices for 1994*, Washington, GPO, February, 1995, pp. 1165–1173.

35. *Saudi Arabia*, Volume 12, Number 2, February, 1995, pp. 1–2.

36. Reuters, August 2, 1995, 1133; *Middle East Economic Digest*, April 5, 1996, pp. 28–30.

37. Reuters, August 2, 1995, 1133, 1421, August 3, 1995, 0800, August 4, 1995, 1013; *Los Angeles Times*, August 3, 1995; p. A-8; *New York Times*, August 3, 1998, p. A-8; *Wall Street Journal*, p. A-5, B-5; ASI-AFP-IR99 08-02 0588; RTR0494 OVER 50 August 2, 1995, 1936; *The Estimate*, July 21-August 3, 1995, pp. 2–4.

38. Reuters, August 2, 1995, 1133, 1421, August 3, 1995, 0800, August 4, 1995, 1013; *Los Angeles Times*, August 3, 1995; p. A-8; *New York Times*, August 3, 1998, p.

A-8; *Wall Street Journal*, p. A-5, B-5; ASI-AFP-IR99 08-02 0588; RTR0494 OVER 50 August 2, 1995, 1936; *The Estimate*, July 21-August 3, 1995, pp. 2–4; *Middle East Economic Digest*, August 18, 1995, pp. 2–3.

39. Reuters, July 7, 1995, 1513.

40. CIA, *World Factbook, 1995*, "Saudi Arabia." Further statistical and analytic background is taken from material provided by the World Bank, including "Will Arab Workers Prosper or Be Left Out in the Twenty-First Century?", August, 1995; "Forging a Partnership for Environmental Action," December, 1994; and "A Population Perspective on Development: The Middle East and North Africa," August, 1994.

41. CIA, *World Factbook, 1995*, "Saudi Arabia."

42. World Bank, *World Population Projections, 1994–1995*, Washington, World Bank, 1994; *Middle East Economic Digest*, July 28, 1995, p. 11; *CIA World Factbook, 1995*, "Iran."

43. *Saudi Commerce and Economic Review*, No. 22, February, 1996, p. 6.

44. World Bank, "Will Arab Workers Prosper or Be Left Out in the Twenty-First Century?", August, 1995, p. 8.

45. World Bank, *World Population Projections, 1994–1995*, Washington, World Bank, 1994; *Middle East Economic Digest*, July 28, 1995, p. 11; *CIA World Factbook, 1995*, "Iran".

46. ACDA, *World Military Expenditures and Arms Transfers, 1993–1994*, Table I.

47. CIA, *World Factbook, 1995*, "Saudi Arabia."

48. For more background, see Milton Viorst, "The Storm and the Citadel," *Foreign Affairs*, Jan/Feb 1996, pp. 98–99; F. Gregory Gause, *Oil Monarchies: Domestic and Security Challenges in the Arab Gulf States*, New York, Council on Foreign Relations, 1994; Augustus R. Norton, "The Future of Civil Society in the Middle East," *Middle East Journal*, Spring, 1993; Mary Tetrault, "Gulf Winds," *Current History*, January 1996; and Michael Collins Dunn, "Is the Sky Falling?" *Middle East Policy*, Vol. III, No. 4, 1995.

49. *New York Times*, December 22, 1992, p. A-10.

50. *New York Times*, May 1, 1993, p. A-4; US State Department, *Country Report on Human Rights Practices for 1994*, Washington, GPO, February, 1995, pp. 1165–1173, and Internet version for 1996, downloaded April 5, 1996.

51. *Los Angeles Times*, November 14, 1995, p. A-6.

52. *Los Angeles Times*, November 14, 1995, p. A-6; US State Department, *Country Report on Human Rights Practices for 1994*, Washington, GPO, February, 1995, pp. 1165–1173 and Internet version for 1996, downloaded April 5, 1996.

53. For example, see the report on Mas'ari in the *Independent*, May 23, 1995.

54. *Los Angeles Times*, November 14, 1995, p. A-6; *Washington Post*, November 14, 1995, p. A-1.

55. US State Department, *Country Report on Human Rights Practices for 1994*, Washington, GPO, February, 1995, pp. 1165–1173 and Internet version for 1996, downloaded April 5, 1996.

56. US State Department, *Country Report on Human Rights Practices for 1994*, Washington, GPO, February, 1995, pp. 1165–1173 and Internet version for 1996, downloaded April 5, 1996.

57. *Washington Post*, April 19, 1996, p. A-31.

58. US State Department, *Country Report on Human Rights Practices for 1994*, Washington, GPO, February, 1995, pp. 1165–1173 and Internet version for 1996, downloaded April 5, 1996.

59. *Los Angeles Times*, November 15, 1995, p. A-7; *Washington Times*, November 15, 1995, p. B-11.

60. *Boston Globe*, November 15, 1995, p. 2; *Jane's Defense Weekly*, November 25, 1995, p. 5; *Jane's Intelligence Review Pointer*, January 1996, p. 6; *New York Times*, January 11, 199, p. A-8; *New York Times*, November 15, 1995, p. A-7; *Washington Post*, November 14, 1995, p. A-15.

61. *Washington Times*, November 16, 1995, p. A-13.

62. *Los Angeles Times*, November 14, 1995, p. A-1.

63. *Wall Street Journal*, December 26, 1995, p. A-7.

64. *Philadelphia Inquirer*, November 16, 1995, p. A-11.

65. *Washington Post*, April 23, 1996, p. A-13; *Chicago Tribune*, November 15, 1995, p. I-3; *Jane's Defense Weekly*, November 25, 1995, p. 23; *New York Times*, January 11, 1996, p. A-8; *Washington Post*, February 5, 1996, p. A-22; *Los Angeles Times*, April 23, 1996, p. A-2; *Boston Globe*, April 23, 1996, p. 2.

66. *Washington Post*, December 10, 1995, p. A-28.

67. Reuters Ltd., January 31, 1996.

68. *Washington Post*, November 15, 1995, p. A-26; *Washington Post*, November 14, 1995, p. A-15.

69. *Boston Globe*, May 17, 1996, p. 16.

70. The author has encountered many of these attitudes during his visits to Saudi Arabia. For typical US reporting see the *Baltimore Sun*, July 28, 1991, p. 11-A; *Security Intelligence*, February 10, 1992, p. 8; *New York Times*, January 30, 1992, p. 3 and March 1, 1992, p. 8; *Amnesty International Report 1994*, NY, Amnesty International 1994, pp. 254–256; US State Department, *Country Report on Human Rights Practices for 1994*, Washington, GPO, February, 1995, pp. 1165–1173.

71. The reader should be aware that this often leads to exaggerated reports of tension and corruption. Anyone who has lived in Saudi Arabia becomes aware that royal family rumors, and rumors of internal conflicts, are almost a national sport. The Hejazi are masters of this sport, although sometimes surpassed by whatever businessman who has just suffered in a deal with one of the princes. It is far harder for a Westerner to understand the pressures building up within the Islamic fundamentalists, but the movement does affect a significant number of Saudi youths, and often has intense support at the university level. Cassettes are circulated nationally, and many very well educated Saudis, as well as many traditionalists, support fundamentalism.

72. Figures referring to 60%–70% Shi'ite do not seem to be correct. See US State Department, *Country Report on Human Rights Practices for 1994*, Washington, GPO, February, 1995, pp. 1165–1173.

73. *Christian Science Monitor*, March 16, 1992, p. 19; Dilip Hero, "Saudi Reforms: Too Little and 32 Years Late," *The Nation*, April 13, 1992, pp. 486–487; *Newsweek*, March 16, 1992, p. 45; *New York Times*, December 31, 1991, p. A-1, January 1, 1992, p. 3, February 25, 1992, p. A-6, March 2, 1992, p. A-1, March 9, 1992, pp. A1 and

A7, March 30, 1992, p. A-6; Fred Halliday, "Facelift for a tribal dictatorship, "*Guardian Weekly,* March 15, 1992; *Manchester Guardian Weekly,* March 8, 1992, p. 10; *Economist,* March 7, 1992, pp. 42–43; *Washington Post,* December 31, 1992, p. A-10, March 6, 1992, p. A16; *Financial Times,* March 3, 1992, p. 4; *Boston Globe,* September 18, 1992, p. 6.

Chapter Four

74. Economist Intelligence Unit, *Saudi Arabia—Country Profile,* 1st Quarter, 1995.

75. *Saudi Commerce and Economic Review,* No. 22, February 1996, pp. 10–19.

76. *Wall Street Journal,* June 4, 1996, p. A-14.

77. World Bank, "Forging a Partnership for Environmental Action," Washington, December, 1994, p. 24.

78. *Middle East Economic Digest,* January 12, 1996, p. 15.

79. CIA, *World Factbook, 1995,* "Saudi Arabia.

80. *Saudi Commerce and Economic Review,* No. 22, February, 1996, pp. 10–19.

81. Congressional Quarterly, *The Middle East, 7th Edition,* Washington, Congressional Quarterly, 1990, p. 117.

82. Reuters, August 8, 1994, 1013; *Middle East Economic Digest,* August 18, 1995, p. 3.

83. *Middle East Economic Digest,* "Special Report: Saudi Arabia", March 10, 1995, pp. 28–30, and April 5, 1996, pp. 35–49; *Saudi Arabia,* Monthly Newsletter from the Royal Embassy of Saudi Arabia, Washington, DC, February, 1996, p. 3; and interviews with US experts.

84. *Saudi Commerce and Economic Review,* No. 22, February, 1996, pp. 10–19, and *Middle East Economic Digest,* "Special Report: Saudi Arabia", April 5, 1996, pp. 35–49.

85. *Saudi Commerce and Economic Review,* No. 22, February, 1996, pp. 10–1919, and *Middle East Economic Digest,* "Special Report: Saudi Arabia", April 5, 1996, pp. 35–49

86. *Saudi Commerce and Economic Review,* No. 22, February, 1996, pp. 10–1919, and *Middle East Economic Digest,* "Special Report: Saudi Arabia", April 5, 1996, pp. 35–49

87. IMF; *Middle East Economic Digest,* April 5, 1996, p. 43.

88. An effort to impose taxes of up to 30% on foreigners was withdrawn shortly after it was proposed. Nearly two-thirds of the bonds were bought by the Saudi Arabian government. *Wall Street Journal,* December 31, 1987, p. 4; January 5, 1988, p. 21, January 6, 1988, p. 12, January 7, 1988, p. 16, January 12, 1988, p. 2; *Washington Post,* December 31, 1987, p. E-3, January 12, 1988, p. C-3; *Economist,* January 16–22, 1988, p. 59; *New York Times,* January 6, 1988, p. A-1; *Chicago Tribune,* January 27, 1988, p. 3–7.

89. *New York Times,* August 22, 1993; *Washington Post,* August 29, 1993, p. C-2.

90. *Jane's Defense Weekly,* December 5, 1992, p. 5; *Business Week,* February 15, 1993, p. 50.

91. *Middle East Economic Digest,* January 17, 1992, pp. 4–5, March 20, 1992, pp. 10–16.

92. *Jane's Defense Weekly*, December 5, 1992, p. 5; *Business Week*, February 15, 1993, p. 50.

93. IMF Article 4 Report, 1994 and 1995; *Middle East Economic Digest*, "Special Report: Saudi Arabia," March 10, 1995, pp. 28–30 and April 5, 1996, pp. 30–43; Reuters, August 7, 1995, 0552, 1420; Executive News Service, July 31, 1995, 0905; *Middle East Economic Digest*, August 18, 1995, p. 3; *Middle East Economic Digest*, January 12, 1996, pp. 15–16, and calculations by the author.

94. *New York Times*, June 19, 1995, p. D-2; IMF Article 4 Report, 1994 and *Middle East Economic Digest*, "Special Report: Saudi Arabia," March 10, 1995, pp. 28–30; Reuters, August 7, 1995, 0552, 1420; Executive News Service, July 31, 1995, 0905; *Middle East Economic Digest*, January 12, 1996, pp. 15–16; *Middle East Economic Digest*, November 3, 1995, p. 38.

95. IMF Article 4 Report, 1995, and *Middle East Economic Digest*, April 5, 1996, pp. 30–43.

96. IMF Article 4 Report, 1994 and 1995; *Middle East Economic Digest*, "Special Report: Saudi Arabia," March 10, 1995, pp. 28–30 and April 5, 1996, pp. 30–43; Reuters, August 7, 1995, 0552, 1420; Executive News Service, July 31, 1995, 0905; *Middle East Economic Digest*, August 18, 1995, p. 3; *Middle East Economic Digest*, January 12, 1996, pp. 15–16.

97. *Middle East Economic Digest*, January 12, 1996, pp. 15–16, and calculations by the author.

98. *Middle East Economic Digest*, "Special Report: Saudi Arabia," March 10, 1995, pp. 28–30; *Middle East Economic Digest*, November 3, 1995, p. 37.

99. *Middle East Economic Digest*, "Special Report: Saudi Arabia," March 10, 1995, pp. 28–30.

100. *Neu Zurcher Zeitung*, April 15, 1995; Executive News Service, August 7, 1995, 0552, August 31, 1995, 0942; *Economist*, May 27, 1995;

101. *Middle East Economic Digest*, "Special Report: Saudi Arabia," March 10, 1995, pp. 28–30; *Middle East Economic Digest*, November 3, 1995, p. 37.

102. *Middle East Economic Digest*, April 5, 1996, p. 48.

103. *The Financial Times*, January 30, 1996, p. 6.

104. *Middle East Economic Digest*, April 26, 1996, p. 27.

105. *Middle East Economic Digest*, April 26, 1996, p. 27.

106. *Washington Post*, June 6, 1995, p. D-2; *Washington Times*, June 6, 1995, p. B-6; Executive News Service, August 7, 1995, 0552, August 31, 1995, 0942, *Wall Street Journal*, September 22, 1995, p. B-4.

107. *Los Angeles Times*, January 28, 1992, p. C-1; working papers from the Royal Institute of International Affairs (RIAA) conference on Saudi society, economy, and security, October 4–5, 1993.

108. *Los Angeles Times*, January 28, 1992, p. C-1; working papers from the Royal Institute of International Affairs (RIAA) conference on Saudi society, economy, and security, October 4–5, 1993.

109. *Middle East Economic Digest*, March 1, 1996, p. 3.

110. *Middle East Economic Digest*, January 17, 1992, pp. 4–5, March 20, 1992, pp. 10–16.

111. Data are taken from working papers distributed during the Royal Institute of International Affairs conference on Saudi Arabia in October 4–5, 1993.

112. D. F. Hepburn, Bahrain Petroleum Company, CENTCOM SWA Symposium, May 17, 1994.

113. CIA, *World Factbook, 1995*, "Saudi Arabia." Further statistical and analytic background is taken from material provided by the World Bank, including "Will Arab Workers Prosper or Be Left Out in the Twenty-First Century?", August, 1995; "Forging a Partnership for Environmental Action," December, 1994; and "A Population Perspective on Development: The Middle East and North Africa," August, 1994.

114. *Middle East Economic Digest*, April 21, 1995, pp. 32–33.

115. IEA, *Middle East Oil and Gas*, Paris, OECD/IEA, 1995, p. 200.

116. *Middle East Economic Digest*, April 21, 1995, pp. 32–33; *Middle East Economic Digest, Special Report: Saudi Arabia*, March 10, 1995, pp. 28–30.

117. DOE/EIA On-line Internet data basis, analysis section, country section. Accessed July 25, 1995.

118. DOE/EIA On-line Internet data basis, analysis section, country section. Accessed July 25, 1995.

119. RTR0475 3 OVR 504, August 2, 1995, 1936; *Washington Times*, August 5, 1995, p. B-7; DOE/EIA On-line Internet data basis, analysis section, country section. Accessed July 25, 1995; *Wall Street Journal*, "Saudi Arabia," September 22, 1995.

120. *Wall Street Journal*, "Saudi Arabia," September 22, 1995; *Middle East Economic Digest*, August 18, 1995, pp. 2–16; Executive News Service, August 7, 1995, 1420, September 18, 1995, 1631.

121. *Saudi Arabia*, Volume 13, Number 2, February, 1996, p. 3.

122. Executive News Service, October 11, 1995, 1631; UPI, October 11, 1995, 1631.

123. Executive News Service, July 20, 1995, 0306.

124. This estimate of the size of the total labor force may be low. The CIA estimates the Saudi labor force to be about 5.0–6.0 million, of which roughly 60% is still foreign. CIA, *World Factbook, 1994*, p. 345, and CIA, *World Factbook, 1995*, "Saudi Arabia." The percentages by ethnic group for total population are taken from the IISS, *Military Balance, 1994–1995*, p. 137. Further statistical and analytic background is taken from material provided by the World Bank, including "Will Arab Workers Prosper or Be Left Out in the Twenty-First Century?", August, 1995; "Forging a Partnership for Environmental Action," December, 1994; and "A Population Perspective on Development: The Middle East and North Africa," August, 1994. Also see Executive News Service, October 11, 1995, 1631; UPI, October 11, 1995, 1631.

125. *Middle East Economic Digest*, April 5, 1996, pp. 54–57.

126. CIA, *World Factbook, 1995*, "Saudi Arabia."

127. Executive News Service, September 18, 1995, 1631; *Wall Street Journal*, "Saudi Arabia," September 22, 1995.

128. Executive News Service, July 20, 1995, 0306.

129. Saudi Ministry of Information, October, 1995; Executive News Service, September 18, 1995, 1631; Wall Street Journal, "Saudi Arabia," September 22, 1995.

130. *Saudi Arabia*, Volume 13, Number 1, January, 1996, p. 3; *Middle East Economic Digest*, April 5, 1996, pp. 30–43.

131. Saudi Ministry of Information, October, 1995; Executive News Service, September 18, 1995, 1631; Wall Street Journal, "Saudi Arabia," September 22, 1995.

Chapter Five

132. Much of this text is adapted from DOE/Energy Information Agency (EIA), On-line Internet data base, analysis section, country analysis. Other sources include IEA, *Middle East Oil and Gas*, Paris, OECD/IEA, 1995, Annexes 1E and 2K; EIA, *Annual Energy Outlook, 1995*, DOE/EIA–0383(95), January 1995; EIA, International Energy Outlook, 1995, DOE/EIA–0484(95), June, 1995. Other data are taken from *Middle East Economic Digest*, "Special Report on Oil and Gas," September 22, 1995, pp. 20–22. The IEA estimated the Saudi share of world reserves as 25.7% in 1995.

133. *Oil and Gas Journal*, September 23, 1991, p. 62; *Middle East Economic Digest*, "Special Report on Oil and Gas," September 22, 1995, pp. 20–22.

134. *Middle East Economic Digest*, "Special Report on Oil and Gas," September 22, 1995, pp. 20–22.

135. Energy Information Agency (EIA), *International Energy Outlook, 1994*, DOE/EIA 0484(94), July, 1994, pp. 14–26; EIA, *International Petroleum Status Report*, DOE/EIA 0520(94)1), November, 1994, pp. 6–7; IEA, *Middle East Oil and Gas*, Paris, OECD/IEA, 1995, Annexes 1E and 2K; International Petroleum Encyclopedia, 1993, Tulsa, PennWell Press, 1993, p. 280; *Middle East Economic Digest*, "Special Report on Oil and Gas," September 22, 1995, pp. 20–22. Estimates of reserves have become increasingly more political in recent years as each major producer in the Gulf has tried to exaggerate its reserves and relative importance.

136. IEA, *Middle East Oil and Gas*, Paris, OECD/IEA, 1995, Annex 1E; DOE/Energy Information Agency (EIA), On-line Internet data base, analysis section, country analysis.

137. IEA, *Middle East Oil and Gas*, Paris, OECD/IEA, 1995, Annex 1E; DOE/Energy Information Agency (EIA), On-line Internet data base, analysis section, country analysis.

138. *New York Times*, April 28, 1995, p. D-6.

139. IEA, *Middle East Oil and Gas*, Paris, OECD/IEA, 1995, Annex 1E; DOE/Energy Information Agency (EIA), On-line Internet data base, analysis section, country analysis.

140. IEA, *Middle East Oil and Gas*, Paris, OECD/IEA, 1995, Annex 1E.

141. *Middle East Economic Digest*, "Special Report on Oil and Gas," September 22, 1995, pp. 20–22; IEA, *Middle East Oil and Gas*, Paris, OECD/IEA, 1995, Annexes 1E and 2K.

142. IEA, *Middle East Oil and Gas*, Paris, OECD/IEA, 1995, Annex 1E; DOE/Energy Information Agency (EIA), On-line Internet data base, analysis section, country analysis.

143. IEA, *Middle East Oil and Gas*, Paris, OECD/IEA, 1995.

144. *Middle East Economic Digest*, August 18, 1995, p. 3.

145. *Saudi Arabia*, Volume 13, Number 1, January, 1996, p. 5.

146. *Washington Post*, May 14, 1996, p. D-1; *New York Times*, May 14, 1996, p. D-12.

147. Energy Information Agency (EIA), *International Energy Outlook, 1994*, DOE/EIA 0484(94), July, 1994, pp. 14–26; IEA, *Middle East Oil and Gas*, Paris, OECD/IEA, 1995, Annexes 1E and 2K; EIA, *International Petroleum Status Report*, DOE/EIA 0520(94)1), November, 1994, pp. 6–7; International Petroleum Encyclopedia, 1993, Tulsa, PennWell Press, 1993, p. 280; *Middle East Economic Digest*, "Special Report on Oil and Gas," September 22, 1995, pp. 20–22. Estimates of reserves have become increasingly more political in recent years as each major producer in the Gulf has tried to exaggerate its reserves and relative importance.

148. Energy Information Agency (EIA), *International Energy Outlook, 1994*, DOE/EIA 0484(94), July, 1994, pp. 14–26; IEA, *Middle East Oil and Gas*, Paris, OECD/IEA, 1995, Annexes 1E and 2K; EIA, *International Petroleum Status Report*, DOE/EIA 0520(94)1), November, 1994, pp. 6–7; International Petroleum Encyclopedia, 1993, Tulsa, PennWell Press, 1993, p. 280; *Middle East Economic Digest*, "Special Report on Oil and Gas," September 22, 1995, pp. 20–22. Estimates of reserves have become increasingly more political in recent years as each major producer in the Gulf has tried to exaggerate its reserves and relative importance.

149. EIA, *International Energy Outlook, 1995*, p. 37; IEA, *Middle East Oil and Gas*, Paris, OECD/IEA, 1995, Annexes 1E and 2K.

150. IEA, *Middle East Oil and Gas*, Paris, OECD/IEA, 1995, p. 307.

151. IEA, *Middle East Oil and Gas*, Paris, OECD/IEA, 1995, Annex 1E; DOE/Energy Information Agency (EIA), On-line Internet data base, analysis section, country analysis.

152. IEA, *Middle East Oil and Gas*, Paris, OECD/IEA, 1995, Annex 1E; DOE/Energy Information Agency (EIA), On-line Internet data base, analysis section, country analysis.

153. EIA, *International Energy Outlook, 1995*, p. 29; IEA, *Middle East Oil and Gas*, Paris, OECD/IEA, 1995, Annexes 1E and 2K.

Chapter Six

154. IISS, *Military Balance, 1994–1995*, p. 137; *New York Times*, December 16, 1992, p. A-8.

155. CIA, *World Factbook, 1995*, "Saudi Arabia."

156. IISS, *Military Balance, 1994–1995*, p. 137; CIA, *World Factbook, 1995*, "Saudi Arabia."

157. Unless otherwise specified, the military data quoted here are taken from the relevant country sections of various annual editions of the IISS, *Military Bal-*

ance; CIA, *The World Factbook*; and Ze'ev Eytan, *The Middle East Military Balance*, Jaffee Center for Strategic Studies, Tel Aviv University, Tel Aviv.)

158. These Pakistani forces left the Kingdom in 1988 and 1989.

159. *Jane's Defense Weekly*, May 22, 1996, p. 4.

160. Saudi government officials again raised the possibility of instituting a draft in late 1994. See Reuters, 11–23–94 00:39 AET.

161. *Jane's Defense Weekly*, May 15, 1985; *New York Times*, April 28, 1985.

162. The data available to the author were so much in conflict that it proved impossible to provide even a useful range.

163. Saudi Arabia shifted its fiscal year to a calendar year in 1988. The data provided on the Saudi defense and security budget in Rials and dollars for FY1986 to 1993 was provided by the Saudi Embassy in Washington in October, 1993.

164. These figures do not include Saudi military aid to other Arab states, which seems to have peaked in FY1985, when a combination of aid to Iraq and Syria may have driven foreign aid expenditures to over $5 billion. Data are based on excerpts of the Saudi national budgets, and reporting by the IISS. CIA, ACDA, SIPRI, and other estimates often differ significantly. The reader should also be aware that many major arms transactions in all Middle East countries are handled privately by their defense ministers, often on a multi-year basis. Many of these transactions are not reported to or through the central bank. Saudi Arabia, like other oil exporting states, complicates this situation further by using oil barter arrangements, offset arrangements, and constantly renegotiating major arms deals while deliveries are in progress. The data published in the IISS *Military Balance, 1987–1988*, indicate that the total manpower fit for service could be about 50–70% of the CIA estimate. (See p. 110).

165. *Defense News*, January 18, 1988, p. 4.

166. Based on estimates by the International Institute for Strategic Studies.

167. *Middle East Economic Digest*, January 17, 1992, pp. 4–5.

168. The reader should be aware that there is little historical consistency in ACDA or CIA estimates of Saudi defense spending and estimates are constantly revised by billions of dollars for relatively long periods of time. While ACDA provides an estimate of spending in constant dollars, an examination of the conversion method quickly reveals that it is little more than a guesstimate. See Arms Control and Disarmament Agency (ACDA), *World Military Expenditures and Arms Transfers, 1989*, Washington, GPO, 1990, Table I, Arms Control and Disarmament Agency (ACDA), *World Military Expenditures and Arms Transfers, 1991–1992*, Washington, GPO, 1994, Table I;), *World Military Expenditures and Arms Transfers, 1993–1994*, Washington, GPO, 1995, Table I; ACDA printout dated May 14, 1996; and Saudi Arabia section in the CIA, *World Factbook, 1991* and *1992*.

169. The FY1988 budget was planned to have a $10 billion deficit, with $8 billion in foreign borrowing. It involved the first foreign borrowing in 25 years and the first increase in taxes in eight years—all on foreign businesses. The actual budget reached a $15–17 billion deficit by the year's end, with some $10 billion in financing. *Economist*, January 16, 1988, p. 59; *Defense News*, January 18, 1988, p. 4.

170. Calculations made by the author using various tables provided by the Saudi Embassy in Washington in October, 1993, and April, 1995.

171. *Defense News*, November 20–26, 1995, p. 27.

172. Richard F. Grimmett, *Conventional Arms Transfers to the Third World, 1985–1992*, Washington, Congressional Research Service, CRS–93–656F, July 19, 1993, p. 59 and 69.

173. Arms Control and Disarmament Agency (ACDA), *World Military Expenditures and Arms Transfers, 1989*, Washington, GPO, 1990, Table II; ACDA printout dated May 14, 1996.

174. Richard F. Grimmett in *Conventional Arms Transfers to Developing Nations, 1987–1994*, Congressional Research Service 95–862F, August 4, 1994, pp. 56–57 and 68.

175. Arms Control and Disarmament Agency (ACDA), *World Military Expenditures and Arms Transfers, 1985*, Washington, GPO, 1985, pp. 133–134; ACDA printout dated May 14, 1996.

176. Arms Control and Disarmament Agency (ACDA), *World Military Expenditures and Arms Transfers, 1989*, Washington, GPO, 1990, pp. 117–118 ACDA printout dated May 14, 1996.

177. ACDA changed its way of reporting arms sales by source in 1992. Arms Control and Disarmament Agency (ACDA), *World Military Expenditures and Arms Transfers, 1990*, Table III, Washington, GPO, 1992; ACDA printout dated May 14, 1996.

178. ACDA changed its way of reporting arms sales by source in 1992. Arms Control and Disarmament Agency (ACDA), *World Military Expenditures and Arms Transfers, 1990*, Table III, Washington, GPO, 1992; Arms Control and Disarmament Agency (ACDA), *World Military Expenditures and Arms Transfers, 1991–1992*, Table III, Washington, GPO, 1994; and Arms Control and Disarmament Agency (ACDA), *World Military Expenditures and Arms Transfers, 1993–19940*, Table III, Washington, GPO, 1995; ACDA printout dated May 14, 1996.

179. See "High Costs of the Persian Gulf War," Arms Control and Disarmament Agency (ACDA), *World Military Expenditures and Arms Transfers, 1987*, Washington, GPO, 1988, pp. 21–23; ACDA printout dated May 14, 1996; and Richard F. Grimmett, *Trends in Conventional Arms Transfers to the Third World by Major Supplier, 1982–1989*, Congressional Research Service, Library of Congress, Washington, 90–298F, June 19, 1990.

180. Richard F. Grimmett in *Conventional Arms Transfers to Developing Nations, 1987–1994*, Congressional Research Service 95–862F, August 4, 1994, pp. 56–57 and 68.

181. Richard F. Grimmett in *Conventional Arms Transfers to Developing Nations, 1987–1994*, Congressional Research Service 95–862F, August 4, 1994, pp. 56–57 and 68.

182. Arms Control and Disarmament Agency (ACDA), *World Military Expenditures and Arms Transfers, 1994–1995*, Washington, GPO, 1996, Table III.

183. Arms Control and Disarmament Agency (ACDA), *World Military Expenditures and Arms Transfers, 1994–1995*, Washington, GPO, 1996, Table III.

184. US Defense Security Assistance Agency (DSAA), "Foreign Military Sales, Foreign Military Construction Sales and Military Assistance Facts as of September 30, 1994," Department of Defense, Washington, 1995.

185. *New York Times*, August 22, 1993.

186. *New York Times*, August 22, 1993.

187. Richard F. Grimmett, "Saudi Arabia: Restructuring Arms Payments to the US," Washington, Congressional Research Service, 94-356F, April 25, 1994; *New York Times*, January 3, 1994, p. A-3, January 18, 1994, p. A-8; Department of Defense, "Saudi Stretch Out," February 1, 1994, *Wall Street Journal*, January 31, 1994, p. A2; Reuters, April 5, 1994; *Defense News*, January 10, 1994, p. 1, May 30, 1994, p. 1; *Aviation Week*, February 7, 1994, p. 22; *Inside the Navy*, January 3, 1994, p. 3; *Christian Science Monitor*, December 20, 1993, p. C-1.

Chapter Seven

188. Unless otherwise specified, the military data quoted here are taken from the relevant country sections of various annual editions of the IISS, *Military Balance*; CIA, *The World Factbook*,; and Ze'ev Eytan, *The Middle East Military Balance*, Jaffee Center for Strategic Studies, Tel Aviv University, Tel Aviv.), the author's publications and other sources mentioned at the start of the section on Saudi Arabia, and Dr. Andrew Rathmell, "Saudi Arabia's Military Build-up—An Extravagant Error," *Jane's Intelligence Review*, November, 1994, pp. 500–504.

189. Interview with senior Saudi official, November, 1993.

190. An airborne ranger battalion is deployed at Tabuk.

191. Major General Dennis Malcor was sent to Saudi Arabia to survey its military requirements after the Gulf War. *Washington Post*, March 15, 1992, p. A-35; *New York Times*, October 15, 1991, p. A-1; *Jane's Defense Weekly*, December 14, 1991, p. 1175.

192. Richard F. Grimmett, "Arms Sales to Saudi Arabia," Congressional Research Service, IB91007, August 28, 1991, p. 4.

193. *Inside the Army*, April 6, 1992, p. 1; *Inside the Pentagon*, April 9, 1992, p. 2.

194. Department of Defense, "Sale of Abrams Tanks to Saudi Arabia," Background Information, 1 November, 1989.

195. Department of Defense fax, July 18, 1990; *Defense Week*, March 12, 1990, p. 3.

196. Executive News Service, September 23, 1995, 0557.

197. *Defense News*, November 13, 1989, p. 3, March 12, 1990, p. 3; *Washington Post*, October 12, 1989, p. A-9; October 16, 1989, p. A-17; Department of Defense Background Paper, November 1, 1989; *Insight*, September 25, 1989, p. 34; *Philadelphia Inquirer*, September 30, 1989, p. 5-A; *New York Times*, September 28, 1989, p. A-1.

198. *Louisville Courier Journal*, November 6, 1992, p. B-3; *Defense News*, June 21, 1993, p. 14; *Jane's Defense Weekly*, February 20, 1993, p. 8.

199. *Jane's Defense Weekly*, February 26, 1994, p. 4.

200. *Jane's Defense Weekly*, February 6, 1988, p. 191, March 7, 1992, July 25, 1992, p. 18, August 15, 1992, p. 5; Richard F. Grimmett, "Arms Sales to Saudi Arabia," Congressional Research Service, IB91007, August 28, 1991, p. 4; *Defense Daily*, February 14, 1992, p. 251; *Defense News*, March 30, 1992, p. 6.

201. *Jane's Defense Weekly*, February 6, 1988, p. 191, March 7, 1992; *Defense Daily*, February 14, 1992, p. 251; *Defense News*, March 30, 1992, p. 6.

202. *Defense News*, March 30, 1992, p. 6; *Defense Daily*, February 14, 1992, p. 251; *Jane's Defense Weekly*, February 6, 1988, p. 191, March 7, 1992; *Inside the Army*, April 6, 1992, p. 1; *Inside the Pentagon*, April 9, 1992, p. 2.

203. *Jane's Defense Weekly*, February 6, 1988, p. 191, March 7, 1992; *Defense Daily*, February 14, 1992, p. 251; *Defense News*, March 30, 1992, p. 6; Executive News Service, August 11, 1995, 0625.

204. *Jane's Defense Weekly*, April 17, 1996, p. 10.

205. *Jane's Defense Weekly*, May 1, 1996, p. 36.

206. *Defense News*, January 8–14, 1996, p. 20. *Jane's Defense Weekly*, January 17, 1996, p. 15, April 17, 1996, p. 36; *Middle East Economic Digest*, January 19, 1996, p. 7.

207. *Jane's Defense Weekly*, November 4, 1995, p. 8.

208. *Defense News*, March 30, 1992, p. 6; *Defense Daily*, February 14, 1992, p. 251; *Jane's Defense Weekly*, February 6, 1988, p. 191, March 7, 1992; *Inside the Army*, April 6, 1992, p. 1; *Inside the Pentagon*, April 9, 1992, p. 2.

209. IISS, Military Balance, DMS computer data base, interviews in Saudi Arabia in February, 1991, discussions with Saudi experts in December, 1990, and *Defense News*, February 22, 1988, p. 3. These figures are based largely on Saudi data obtained in March, 1991 and February, 1993, and differ significantly from IISS and most Western data bases.

210. The first 200 M-2s were produced at a rate of 2 in FY1989, 98 in FY1990, and 100 in FY1991. *Jane's Defense Weekly*, September 9, 1989, p. 452; *Wall Street Journal*, June 2, 1988, p. 56; *Aviation Week*, June 17, 1991, p. 129.

211. *Defense News*, June 6, 1994.

212. DMS computer data base, interviews in Saudi Arabia in February, 1991, discussions with Saudi experts in December, 1990, and *Defense News*, February 22, 1988, p. 3.

213. Richard F. Grimmett, "Arms Sales to Saudi Arabia," Congressional Research Service, IB91007, August 28, 1991, p. 4.

214. *Aviation Week*, June 17, 1991, p. 129; Richard F. Grimmett, "Arms Sales to Saudi Arabia," Congressional Research Service, IB91007, August 28, 1991, p. 4; IISS and JCSS military balances; DMS computer data base, interviews in Saudi Arabia in February, 1991, discussions with Saudi experts in December, 1990, and *Defense News*, February 22, 1988, p. 3.

215. *Jane's Defense Weekly*, March 11, 1989, p. 393.

216. Richard F. Grimmett, "Arms Sales to Saudi Arabia," Congressional Research Service, IB91007, August 28, 1991, p. 4.

217. Richard F. Grimmett, "Arms Sales to Saudi Arabia," Congressional Research Service, IB91007, August 28, 1991, p. 4; *Jane's Defense Weekly*, December 17, 1988, p. 1546, June 25, 1989, p. 1296.

218. *Aviation Week*, April 2, 1990, p. 44; *Jane's Defense Weekly*, November 16, 1991, p. 927; *Wall Street Journal*, October 7, 1991, p. 16.

219. *Jane's Defense Weekly*, December 14, 1991, p. 1175, June 13, 1992, p. 1013. Richard F. Grimmett, "Arms Sales to Saudi Arabia," Congressional Research Service, IB91007, August 28, 1991, p. 4.

220. *Jane's Defense Weekly*, July 22, 1989, p. 105; IISS, *Military Balance, 1992–1993*, pp. 120–121; *Military Technology, World Defense Almanac, 1992–1993*, Vol. XVII, Issue 1-1993, ISSN-0722-3226. pp. 157–159.

221. *Journal of Electronic Defense,* February, 1994, p. 17.

222. Department of Defense Notice Pursuant to Section 62(A) of the Arms Export Control Act, Transmittal No. 9-93, July 19, 1993.

Chapter Eight

223. Unless otherwise specified, the military data quoted here are taken from the relevant country sections of various annual editions of the IISS, *Military Balance*; CIA, *The World Factbook*; and Ze'ev Eytan, *The Middle East Military Balance*, Jaffee Center for Strategic Studies, Tel Aviv University, Tel Aviv.), the author's publications and other sources mentioned at the start of the section on Saudi Arabia, and Dr. Andrew Rathmell, "Saudi Arabia's Military Build-up—An Extravagant Error," *Jane's Intelligence Review,* November, 1994, pp. 500–504.

224. IISS, *Military Balance, 1992–1993,* pp. 120–121; *Military Technology, World Defense Almanac, 1992–1993,* Vol. XVII, Issue 1–1993, ISSN-0722-3226. pp. 157–159.

225. *Jane's Defense Weekly,* March 7, 1992, p. 388; *Jane's Defense Weekly,* January 24, 1996, p. 18; *Military Technology, World Defense Almanac, 1992–1993,* Vol. XVII, Issue 1-1993, ISSN-0722-3226. pp. 157–159.

226. Author's estimate based on interviews in Saudi Arabia; "Saudi National Guard Fact Sheet," DSAA I-01514, June 5, 1990; FMC data; DMS computer print outs; and the IISS and JCSS military balances.

227. *Military Technology, World Defense Almanac, 1992–1993,* Vol. XVII, Issue 1–1993, ISSN-0722-3226. pp. 157–159. Some reports indicate long-range plans to buy 1,200 to 2,100 Piranhas.

228. For an interesting Israeli view of the role of the National Guard in the mid-1980s, see Mordechai Abir, "Saudi Security and Military Endeavor," *The Jerusalem Quarterly,* No. 33, Fall 1984, pp. 79–94.

229. *Chicago Tribune,* November 14, 1995, p. I-1; *Washington Post,* November 14, 1995, p. A-15.

230. *Baltimore Sun,* November 14, 1995, p. 1A; *Chicago Tribune,* November 14, 1995, p. I-1; *Washington Times,* May, 4, 1995, p. B-9.

231. *Armed Forces Journal,* May 1994, p. 39.

Chapter Nine

232. Unless otherwise specified, the military data quoted here are taken from the relevant country sections of various annual editions of *Jane's Fighting Ships,* the IISS, *Military Balance;* CIA, *The World Factbook;* and Ze'ev Eytan, *The Middle East Military Balance,* Jaffee Center for Strategic Studies, Tel Aviv University, Tel Aviv.), the author's publications and other sources mentioned at the start of the section on Saudi Arabia, and Dr. Andrew Rathmell, "Saudi Arabia's Military Build-up—An Extravagant Error," *Jane's Intelligence Review,* November, 1994, pp. 500–504.

233. Based on *Jane's Fighting Ships, 1994–1995,* London, Jane's, 1994, p. 610; IISS, *Military Balance, 1994–1995,* pp. 120–121; *Military Technology, World Defense Almanac, 1992–1993,* Vol. XVII, Issue 1-1993, ISSN-0722-3226. pp. 157–159.

234. Based on *Jane's Fighting Ships, 1994–1995*, London, Jane's, 1994, p. 610; IISS, *Military Balance, 1994–1995*, pp. 120–121; *Military Technology, World Defense Almanac, 1992–1993*, Vol. XVII, Issue 1-1993, ISSN-0722-3226. pp. 157–159.

235. Historical sources for the analysis of the Saudi Navy include James Bruce and Paul Bear, "Latest Arab Force Levels Operating in the Gulf, *Jane's Defense Weekly*, December 12, 1987, pp. 1360–1361; and various editions of the "Middle Eastern, North African, and South Asian Navies," sections of the March issue of *Proceedings*.

236. Historical sources for the analysis of the Saudi Navy include James Bruce and Paul Bear, "Latest Arab Force Levels Operating in the Gulf," *Jane's Defense Weekly*, December 12, 1987, pp. 1360–1361; and various editions of the "Middle Eastern, North African, and South Asian Navies," sections of the March issue of *Proceedings*.

237. These include 20 AS-365N Dauphin helicopters with AS-15TT air-to-surface missiles, and 4 search and rescue versions of the same helicopter.

238. They are Tacoma-class ASUWs, with 2X4 Harpoon launchers, and 2X3 ASTT (Mark 46 light weight torpedo launchers).

239. *Jane's Fighting Ships, 1994–1995*, London, Jane's 1994, p. 610.

240. These are French F-2000 class vessels with 4 X 533 mm and 2 X 406 mm ASTT torpedo launchers, one Dauphin helicopter, one 100 mm gun, and 8 Otomat 2 missile launchers.

241. *Jane's Fighting Ships, 1994–1995*, London, Jane's, 1994, p. 610.

242. *Jane's Fighting Ships, 1994–1995*, London, Jane's, 1994, p. 610.

243. Richard F. Grimmett, "Arms Sales to Saudi Arabia," Congressional Research Service, IB91007, August 28, 1991, p. 4.

244. Executive News Service, July 25, 1995, 1749.

245. The new contract had a total value of $3.6 billion; 35% is to be offset. *Jane's Defense Weekly*, October 8, 1994, p. 1; November 22, 1993, p. 18, December 3, 1994, p. 4; *Defense News*, February 7, 1994, p. 36; *Financial Times*, January 10, 1994, p. 4; *Middle East Economic Digest*, September 15, 1995, pp. 13–14.

246. *Jane's Defense Weekly*, October 8, 1994, p. 1; November 22, 1993, p. 18, December 3, 1994, p. 4; *Defense News*, February 7, 1994, p. 36; *Financial Times*, January 10, 1994, p. 4; *Middle East Economic Digest*, September 15, 1995, pp. 13–14.

247. *Jane's Defense Weekly*, December 17, 1988, p. 1546, June 25, 1989, p. 1296, October 8, 1994, p. 1, November 22, 1993, p. 18, December 3, 1994, p. 4; *Defense News*, February 7, 1994, p. 36; *London Financial Times*, June 13, 1989, p. B-5; *Wall Street Journal*, June 7, 1988, p. 31; *International Defense Review*, 7/1989, p. 884.

248. The Sandown class ships have glass reinforced plastic hulls, Type 2903 Variable Depth Sonar, remote control mine disposal systems, and Plessey NAUTIS-M command, control, and navigation systems. *Defense News*, March 20, 1989, p. 24, April 24, 1989, p. 28; *Jane's Defense Weekly*, October 26, 1991, p. 770, and February 20, 1993, p. 15.

249. *Military Technology, World Defense Almanac, 1992–1993*, Vol. XVII, Issue 1-1993, ISSN-0722-3226. pp. 157–159.

250. *Jane's Defense Weekly*, July 16, 1987, p. 58.

251. *Jane's Defense Weekly*, December 12, 1987, pp. 1360–1361.

252. *Washington Times*, May 27, 1995, p. A-11.

Chapter Ten

253. Unless otherwise specified, the military data quoted here are taken from the relevant country sections of various annual editions of the IISS, *Military Balance*; CIA, *The World Factbook*; and Ze'ev Eytan, *The Middle East Military Balance*, Jaffee Center for Strategic Studies, Tel Aviv University, Tel Aviv.), the author's publications and other sources mentioned at the start of the section on Saudi Arabia, and Dr. Andrew Rathmell, "Saudi Arabia's Military Build-up—An Extravagant Error," *Jane's Intelligence Review*, November, 1994, pp. 500–504.

254. Cohen, Dr. Eliot A, Director, *Gulf War Air Power Survey, Volume V*, Washington, US Air Force/Government Printing Office, 1993, pp. 232 and 279–287. Note that these data are not consistent form table to table.

255. Cohen, Dr. Eliot A, Director, *Gulf War Air Power Survey, Volume V*, Washington, US Air Force/Government Printing Office, 1993, pp. 316–317, 335, 340, 343, 641, 653–654.

256. *Washington Post*, July 30, 1991, p. A-12; Richard F. Grimmett, "Arms Sales to Saudi Arabia," Congressional Research Service, IB91007, August 28, 1991, p. 4.

257. Fax from Department of Defense, OSD/LA, January 11, 1987; *Baltimore Sun*, September 26, 1989, p. E-9; *Jane's Defense Weekly*, October 7, 1989, p. 744.

258. *Middle East Economic Digest*, January 19, 1996, pp. 7.

259. *Jane's Defense Weekly*, February 13, 1993, p. 41; *Middle East Economic Digest*, January 19, 1996, p. 7.

260. *Jane's Defense Weekly*, February 13, 1993, p. 41.

261. *Jane's Defense Weekly*, July 9, 1988, p. 23, July 16, 1988, p. 59, July 23, 1988, p. 111 and 122–123, March 28, 1992, pp. 533–535; *Newsweek*, July 25, 198, p. 47; *New York Times*, July 11, 1988, p. 1 and July 12, p. 3.

262. *Jane's Defense Weekly*, July 9, 1988, p. 23, July 16, 1988, p. 59, and July 23, 1988, p. 111 and 122–123, June 15, 1991, p. 998, October 26, 1991, p. 770, March 28, 1992, pp. 533–535; *Newsweek*, July 25, 198, p. 47; *New York Times*, July 11, 1988, p. 1 and July 12, p. 3.

263. See the author's *The Gulf and the Search for Strategic Stability*, pp. 122–126.

264. *Defense News*, January 8–14, 1996, pp. 1, 20.

265. *Middle East Economic Digest*, January 19, 1996, p. 7; *Wall Street Journal*, January 5, 1996, p. A6.

266. Richard F. Grimmett, "Arms Sales to Saudi Arabia," Congressional Research Service, IB91007, August 28, 1991, p. 3; Defense News, September 7, 1992, p. 7.

267. *Aviation Week*, September 21, 1992, p. 26; *New York Times*, September 12, 1992, p. A-1, September 15, 1992, p. A-1; Defense News, January 30, 1994, p. 32, June 62, 1994, p. 30. February 13, 1995, p. 21.

268. Comparisons based on data provided by McDonnell Douglas; *Aviation Week*, September 21, 1992, p. 26; *New York Times*, September 12, 1992, p. A-1, Sep-

tember 15, 1992, p. A-1; *Business Week*, March 16, 1992, p. 37; *Defense Daily*, January 28, 1992, p. 133; *London Financial Times*, November 6, 1991, p. 1, January 21, 1992, p. 28; *Washington Post*, November 6, 1991, p. C-1, January 24, 1992, p. 7, September 3, 1992, p. A-39; *Jane's Defense Weekly*, October 26, 1991, p. 770, January 25, 1992, p. 102; *Guardian*, November 7, 1991, p. 11; *Wall Street Journal*, November 6, 1991, p. 3; *Aerospace Daily*, October 28, 1991, p. 152, November 8, 1991, p. 221, November 14, 1991, p. 247; *Defense News*, February 24, 1991, p. 3, December 23, 1991, p. 1. The one issue that was not decided was the engine for the XP. The F-15E is powered by the Pratt and Whitney F-100-229 engine, but can be powered by the GE F-110. The two companies competed for the sale of the 168 engines for the XP, and it was later announced that Pratt and Whitney had won.

269. There are unconfirmed reports that air force officers loyal to the Shah ensured that the F-14s were not fully operational.

270. *Aviation Week*, September 21, 1992, p. 26; *New York Times*, September 12, 1992, p. A-1, September 15, 1992, p. A-1; *Washington Post*, September 27, 1992, p. A-16; *National Journal*, September 26, 1992, P. 2199; *St. Louis Post Dispatch*, April 10, 1999, P. 3-C; *Washington Post*, October 17, 1992, p. A-17; *Defense News*, September 14, 1992, pp. 1,50; March 29, 1993, p. 2.

271. *Defense News*, January 24, 1994, p. 32; January 23, 1995, p. 1, February 13, 1995, p. 22; *Jane's Defense Weekly*, September 30, 1995, p. 19.

272. *Jane's Defense Weekly*, February 6, 1993, p. 6, February 13, 1993, pp. 38–42; *New York Times*, January 30, 1993, p. 3; *Defense News*, October 12, 1992, p. 3; *Manchester Guardian*, October 25 ,1992, p. 9; *Financial Times*, November 18, 1992, p. 10; *Financial Times*, January 29, 1993, p. 1.

273. *Financial Times*, January 29, 1993, p. 1; Armed Forces Journal, November, 1994, p. 41.

274. The deal would be in addition to the $3.5 billion Al Yamamah I sale and bring total related sales to around $10 billion. *Jane's Defense Weekly*, April 11, 1992, p. 597; *Flight International*, April 21, 1992, p. 21; *Defense News*, August 31, 1992, p. 40.

275. *Signal*, August, 1991, p. 116; *Aviation Week*, December 5, 1988, p. 23; *Aerospace Daily*, October 28, 1991, p. 152.

276. *Defense News*, January 24, 1994, p. 32; January 23, 1995, p. 1, February 13, 1995, p. 22; *Jane's Defense Weekly*, September 30, 1995, p. 19.

277. *Baltimore Sun*, June 6, 199C, p. 20C.

278. Richard F. Grimmett, "Arms Sales to Saudi Arabia," Congressional Research Service, IB91007, August 28, 1991, p. 3; Defense News, September 7, 1992, p. 7.

Chapter Eleven

279. Unless otherwise specified, the military data quoted here are taken from the relevant country sections of various annual editions of the IISS, *Military Balance*; CIA, *The World Factbook*; and Ze'ev Eytan, *The Middle East Military Balance*, Jaffee Center for Strategic Studies, Tel Aviv University, Tel Aviv), the author's publications and other sources mentioned at the start of the section on Saudi Ara-

bia, and Dr. Andrew Rathmell, "Saudi Arabia's Military Build-up—An Extravagant Error," *Jane's Intelligence Review*, November, 1994, pp. 500–504.

280. For typical reporting see IISS, *Military Balance, 1992–1993*, pp. 120–121; *Military Technology, World Defense Almanac, 1992–1993*, Vol. XVII, Issue 1–1993, ISSN-0722-3226. pp. 157–159. The Hawks are MIM-23Bs.

281. IISS, *Military Balance, 1992–1993*, p. 121.

282. DSAA, June, 1996; Richard F. Grimmett, "Arms Sales to Saudi Arabia," Congressional Research Service, IB91007, August 28, 1991, p. 3; *Defense News*, September 23, 1991, pp. 1 and 36, March 1, 1993, p. 17; *Washington Post*, November 12, 1991, p. C-1, *New York Times*, November 9, 1991, p. 3; *Jane's Defense Weekly*, October 19, 191, p. 699; *Washington Times*, October 24, 1991, p. A-4; *Defense Daily*, November 8, 1991, p. 223, November 11, 1991, p. A-14; *Wall Street Journal*, December 24, 1992, p. 2.

283. Raytheon background brief, February 1992; *Defense News*, September 23, 1991, pp. 1 and 36, March 1, 1993, p. 17; *Aviation Week*, January 4, 1993, p. 25; *New York Times*, February 17, 1993, p. D-4; Washington Post, December 24, 1992, p. A-8.

284. *Jane's Radar: National and International Air Defense, 1994–1995*, pp. 24–25; *Jane's Air Defense Systems, 1994–1995*, pp. 805–806; *Jane's Command Information Systems, 1994–1995*, pp. 47 and 127.

285. *Flight International*, July 23, 1991, p. 18; *Jane's Defense Weekly*, July 15, 1989, p. 57.

286. *Flight International*, July 23, 1991, p. 18; *Jane's Defense Weekly*, July 15, 1989, p. 57.

287. *Jane's Defense Weekly*, July 15, 1989, p. 57, January 19, 1991, July 20, 1991, p. 97; *London Financial Times*, July 5, 1991, p. 5; *Flight International*, July 23, 1991, p. 18.

288. *Jane's Defense Weekly*, January 19, 1991, July 20, 1991, p. 97; *London Financial Times*, July 5, 1991, p. 5; *Flight International*, July 23, 1991, p. 18.

289. The Saudi Air Defense Corps renewed its contract for technical assistance support from Raytheon for its IHawk surface-to-air missiles in May, 1986. This contract has been running since 1976, and was renewed for three years at a cost of $518 million. *Jane's Defense Weekly*, June 7, 1986, p. 1019.

Chapter Twelve

290. See *Jane's Fighting Ships*, IISS, *Military Balance, 1992–1993*, pp. 120–121; *Military Technology, World Defense Almanac, 1992–1993*, Vol. XVII, Issue 1-1993, ISSN-0722-3226. pp. 157–159.

291. *Defense News*, November 11, 1991, p. 36; *Washington Technology*, September 24, 1992, p. 1.

292. US State Department, *Country Report on Human Rights Practices for 1994*, Washington, GPO, February, 1995, pp. 1165–1173.

293. US State Department, *Country Report on Human Rights Practices for 1994*, Washington, GPO, February, 1995, pp. 1165–1173.

294. US State Department, *Country Report on Human Rights Practices for 1994*, Washington, GPO, February, 1995, pp. 1165–1173.

295. *New York Times,* April 22, 1995, p. A-5; *Los Angeles Times,* April 21, 1995, pp. A-9, A-26; *USA Today,* April 26, 1995, p. 11A; *Washington Post,* April 22, 1995, p. A-24; *Washington Times,* April 22, 1995, p. A-8, April 24, 1995, p. A-11, May 3, 1995, p. A-12.

Chapter Thirteen

296. *Defense News,* April 8, 1991, p. 1; *Defense and Foreign Affairs Weekly,* November 28, 1988, p. 1; *Washington Post,* September 20, 1988, p. A-8; *Jane's Defense Weekly,* October 1, 1988, pp. 744–755.

297. *Jane's Defense Weekly,* October 1, 1988, pp. 744–755.

298. *Jane's Defense Weekly,* October 1, 1990, pp. 744–746.

299. *Washington Times,* October 4, 1988, p. A-2; *Christian Science Monitor,* October 8, 1988, p. 2.

300. Shuey, Lenhart, Snyder, Donnelley, Mielke, and Moteff, *Missile Proliferation: Survey of Emerging Missile Forces,* Washington, DC, Congressional Research Service, Report 88-642F, February 9, 1989, pp. 64–65.

301. The warhead could also be enhanced with submunitions, a proximity fuse to detonate before impact to give an optimum burst pattern and widen the area covered by shrapnel, and a time delay fuse to allow the warhead to fully penetrate a building before exploding. Shuey, Lenhart, Snyder, Donnelley, Mielke, and Moteff, *Missile Proliferation: Survey of Emerging Missile Forces,* Washington, DC, Congressional Research Service, Report 88-642F, February 9, 1989, pp. 23–24.

302. US experts have never monitored a test of the conventional version of the missile. CEP stands for circular error probable, and is an indication of a missile's accuracy. The figure represents the radius of a circle in which half the warheads are expected to fall. It should be noted, however, that the theoretical figures apply only to missiles that operate perfectly up to the point which the missile has left the launcher and at least is first booster and guidance system are operating perfectly. Operational CEPs can only be "guesstimated," but will be much lower. Missiles generally do not have fail-safe warheads. A substantial number will have partial failures and deliver their warhead far from their intended targets. *Jane's Defense Weekly,* October 1, 1990, pp. 744–746; Fred Donovan, "Mideast Missile Flexing," *Arms Control Today,* May, 1990, p. 31; Shuey, Lenhart, Snyder, Donnelley, Mielke, and Moteff, *Missile Proliferation: Survey of Emerging Missile Forces,* Washington, DC, Congressional Research Service, Report 88-642F, February 9, 1989.

303. *Defense News,* October 17, 1994; Letter to Honorable Rondal H. Brown, October 6, 1994 by 63 US senators.

304. *Wall Street Journal,* April 4, 1988, p. 13; *Arms Control Today, May, 1988,* p. 24; *New York Times,* April 26, 1988, p. A-10; *Los Angeles Times,* May 4, 1988, p. I-7; *Washington Times,* May 4, 1988, p. 8; *Washington Post,* March, 1988, p. 1.

Chapter Fourteen

305. Gulshan Dietl, *Through Two Wars and Beyond: A Study of the Gulf Cooperation Council,* New Delhi, Lancers Books, 1991, p. 140.

306. Defense Security Assistance Agency (DSAA), Foreign Military Sales, *Foreign Military Construction Sales, and Military Assistance Facts As of September 30, 1993*, Washington, DC; FMS Control and Reports Division, Comptroller, DSAA, 1994, pp. 10–11.

307. Stephen Dagget and Gary J. Pagliano, "Persian Gulf War: US Costs and Allied Financial Contributions," Congressional Research Service IB91019, September, 21, 1992, pp. 11–13.

308. *Jane's Intelligence Review*, November 1, 1994, p. 500.

309. Dale Bruner, "US Military and Security Relations with the Southern Gulf States," Washington, NSSP, Georgetown University, May 8, 1995.

310. Defense Security Assistance Agency (DSAA), Foreign Military Sales, *Foreign Military Construction Sales, and Military Assistance Facts As of September 30, 1993*, Washington, DC, pp. 10–11; US Department of State, *Congressional Presentation: Foreign Operations Fiscal Year 1996*, p. 499.

311. Defense Security Assistance Agency (DSAA), Foreign Military Sales, *Foreign Military Construction Sales, and Military Assistance Facts As of September 30, 1993*, Washington, DC; FMS Control and Reports Division, Comptroller, DSAA, 1994, pp. 2–3, 16–17. Covers FY1991-FY1993.

312. Defense Security Assistance Agency (DSAA), Foreign Military Sales, *Foreign Military Construction Sales, and Military Assistance Facts As of September 30, 1993*, Washington, DC; FMS Control and Reports Division, Comptroller, DSAA, 1994, pp. 2–3, 16–17.

313. At one point, the US seems to have considered a plan to preposition enough equipment for an entire Corps of three divisions and 150,000 men. *New York Times*, October 15, 1992, p. A-1.

314. *Washington Times*, November 7, 1994, p. A-16; *Defense News*, December 19, 1994, p. 3.

315. *Jane's Defense Weekly*, September 14, 1991, p. 452, November 2, 1991, p. 793, January 25, 1992, p. 107, April 4, 1992, p. 549; *New York Times*, October 13, 1991, p. A-1; *Los Angeles Times*, August 5, 1991, p. 4; October 22, 1991, A-3; *Washington Post*, October 20, 1991, p. 1; March 17, 1992, p. 35, May 31, 1992, p. A-10; *Washington Times*, November 7, 1994, p. A-16; *Defense News*, December 19, 1994, p. 3.

316. *Philadelphia Inquirer*, November 5, 1994, p. 4; *New York Times*, November 4, 1994, March 13, 1995, p. A-7; Federal News Service, November 14, 1994.

317. It should be noted that the US already had 300 combat aircraft in Saudi Arabia and 150 on two carriers, and that Saudi Arabia objected to additional deployments, not to cooperation with the US New York Times, September 25, 1991, p. A-14, September 27, 1991, p. A-1, September 30 ,1991, p. A-5.

318. Ibid.

About the Book and Author

Since the Gulf War, Saudi Arabia's tenuous security situation has been altered by an ongoing U.S. presence. This volume provides detailed analysis of the state of the Saudi economy and military forces, its growing internal security problems and the stability of its regime, and its reliability as an energy exporter.

Anthony H. Cordesman has served in senior positions in the office for the secretary of defense, NATO, and the U.S. Senate. He is currently a senior fellow and Co-Director of the Middle East Program at the Center for Strategic and International Studies, an adjunct professor of national security studies at Georgetown University, and a special consultant on military affairs for ABC News. He lives in Washington, D.C.